T0277314

Summer
of '63

Revie's Plan for
Leeds United

Summer of '63

Gary Edwards

Foreword by
Ralph Ineson

First published by Pitch Publishing, 2022

Pitch Publishing
9 Donnington Park,
85 Birdham Road,
Chichester,
West Sussex,
PO20 7AJ
www.pitchpublishing.co.uk
info@pitchpublishing.co.uk

ISBN 978 1 80150 183 5

Typesetting and origination by Pitch Publishing
Printed and bound in Great Britain by TJ Books, Padstow

Contents

With heartfelt thanks to
Don Revie OBE

In 1961, when I was 14 years old, almost every club in Britain wanted to sign me. Our street was always full of cars with representatives of dozens of different clubs. An employee from Old Trafford left a briefcase on behalf of the club – it contained £5,000 to secure my services and set my family up for a very long time. That amount of money could have bought every house in the street. Leeds United could not come anywhere near that amount, but instead Don Revie spoke to my parents offering a payment structure and assurance of my future wellbeing. My mother and father were greatly impressed by his vision for a struggling, virtually unknown Second Division English club. But with my parents' blessing, I had no hesitation in joining Leeds United.

Peter Lorimer

To Wub.

She's well known for her patience when I'm writing, with papers and notes strewn everywhere. But she was severely tested this time by more notes and bits of paper than ever before. Post-it notes were everywhere including those stuck to our dog, Blue. Thanks Wub, as always.

Acknowledgements

THE PITCH Publishing team have once again been fantastic: Jane Camillin, Duncan Olner, Alex Daley, Graham Hales, Gareth Davis and Dean Rockett.

The following people have been invaluable to this book: the late legends of Elland Road: Peter Lorimer, Jack Charlton and Norman Hunter; Victoria Wooldridge; Duncan Revie; Eddie Gray; Rod Johnson. The Johnson family: Margaret, Simon and Lisa. Johnny Giles; David Harvey; Gary Kelly. Special thanks to Kim Revie and Dave Cocker. Mike O'Grady; Nigel Davey; Yvonne Johanesson; Ralph Ineson; Tony Levison; Peter 'Stix' Lockwood; Robert Endeacott; Phil Shaw; Mark 'Skippy' Ledgard; Chris Horsfield; Neil Jeffries; Tony Winstanley; 'Sid' Johnson; Jim Keoghan; Dave Tomlinson; Tony Hill (RIP); Dr Raymond Ashton; Keith Johnson; Philip 'The Minstrel' Dobreen; Julia Sprake; Christopher Evans; Clive Miers; Bob Liddle; Kippax historians Edwin Charlston and Edgar Pickles; Steve Cooke; Royden Wood; Vicky Powell (Roy's daughter-in-law); Jim Lister.

Finally, massive thanks to all the Leeds fans as well as opposition fans who shared their great memories from the 1960s. There are far too many to mention individually, but they provide an absolute pivotal and unique part of this book, and I'm very grateful to all of you.

Foreword

GARY'S BOOKS are always a great read, and insight from a fan who has literally seen it all. Leeds fans are well accustomed to 'ups and downs'. At the point of writing this, we're all getting our breath back after avoiding a 'down' at Brentford, so here's a look at one of the most significant 'ups' in the club's history, promotion in 1963/64. My generation just missed the 'Glory Years' under Don Revie and grew up hearing and reading about that great side. Gary's book gives us a glimpse of how that team was built. Through his unwavering commitment and support of the club, he's got together a group of people to contribute to a great football book from a fan, a million miles away from the dry, ghost-written player memoirs that football writing often is. Enjoy the story of where it all started.

Ralph Ineson
Actor, narrator and Leeds United fan

1

Coffins and Kippax

ON THE morning of 4 September 1961, I had held the hand of Ma so tightly, she told me many years later that she was surprised it didn't draw blood. We were walking up Well Lane in our village of Kippax for my first day at school. Well Lane is a very steep hill of maybe a quarter of a mile and near to the top there were a couple of old houses, one of which always drew me to it. At the side of the house were two or three wooden stable-type doors and inside would be an old man making coffins. For years I could never pass without looking in over the lower half of the door.

At the very top of the lane on the main road there is a pub called the White Swan and just a small way up to the left stood Kippax Mixed Infant School, built in 1868. I have vague recollections of walking through the gate, still glued to Ma, across the playground and into a foreboding building to register for my first day. I hated the smell in the place and even years later when I worked as a decorator in many schools, that smell would always evoke memories of that very first day.

History tells me that two days before I started school, Leeds United had been beaten by Rotherham United 3-1 at Elland Road, around six or seven miles from Kippax.

A couple of hours into my first day at school, Ma was making the beds upstairs when I walked into the house. 'What are you doing home?' she said. 'What's wrong?'

I told her that I had run away with my friends Steven Hill and Kathleen Richardson. All three of us were then sat at the table and given beans on toast before being marched back up Well Lane. Ma told me all of this years later and unbelievably it was she who received a scalding from the teacher. When she told the teacher that she had fed us because we had missed dinner time, she was told, coldly, 'You shouldn't have done that, not getting fed would have been their punishment.' The smell of school dinners to this day turns my stomach.

Also starting school that day was John Revis. 'I remember almost freezing to death in the outdoor toilets and us all having to defrost our bottles of milk on the old iron radiators,' said John. 'On my first day I was sat between "Banger" and Terry Dent.'

Banger, aka Barry Higgins, and Terry are two great lads but they quickly emerged as the school's 'hard boys'. Back then, of course, school beatings were commonplace and some teachers were feared more than others, one of whom was PE teacher Mr Gill, a stout, bearded man who people still talk about all these years later.

John says, 'Barry Gill regularly whacked pupils with an old plimsoll amongst other things, but he had a specially toughened plimsoll for using on Barry Higgins and Terry Dent as the ordinary one seemed to have no effect on them.'

Years later, John went on to marry Susan, the sister of my mate Steven Hill. Susan also attended this school and recalls, 'The dining room had a massive open fireplace, sometimes roaring away and other times producing a massive black cloud of smoke choking everyone after fresh coal had been poured on it. Happy days! Somehow I can't see the health and safety regulations these days allowing that.' John has remained a Leeds United fan despite moving to Berkshire many years ago.

Both Barry and Terry went on to be brilliant rugby league players, Barry spending many years at Castleford Tigers. His key role at the club was to be sent on from the subs' bench to 'rough up' the opposing team if things weren't exactly going to plan.

On my first day at 'Big School' in 1967, I ended up in a fight with Terry. I wasn't totally unhappy when teachers broke us up.

Incidentally, it was at the very bottom of Well Lane where some years later I stole my first kiss. I can still remember who it was with, but, unfortunately, I can still also remember the overwhelming whiff of baked beans as we both puckered up. I assumed that the new light of my life had just had her tea shortly before coming to meet me.

The White Swan, which was built in 1915, became the home of a Leeds United supporters' club in 1927, serving fans around the area. One such member of this supporters' club was the man I had seen building coffins, Stan Humphreys, who worked for Albert Varley's undertakers.

On the third day of my school 'career', Leeds were beaten again, 2-0 at Norwich City. Playing at right-half for Leeds on the night of 6 September 1961 was Don Revie. But Revie was predominately an inside-right, having played previously for Leicester City, Hull City, Manchester City and then Sunderland, leaving for £12,000 to eventually arrive at Elland Road. It was at Manchester City where he developed the famous 'Revie Plan' – using deep-lying centre-forward tactics which had been originally formulated by the dominant Hungarian national team of the 1950s. The plan was pivotal in Manchester City winning the 1956 FA Cup with Revie as captain.

Revie had made his Leeds debut in a 3-2 win at home to Newcastle United on 29 November 1958 (I was two years old by then), at inside-left. A crowd of 24,000 arrived at Elland Road where Jackie Overfield, a beauty from Chris Crowe and an own goal saw United over the line, although Revie's debut was somewhat low-key. But Revie's innovation skills and foresight had already attracted the attention of many observers.

Sam Bolton had been the chairman at Leeds United since 1948 and was a fascinating character. Born and bred in Hunslet, Leeds, he played at half-back for Rothwell White Rose FC at John O'Gaunts. He supported Leeds City and then United. He served in the Coldstream Guards and the Royal Flying Corps during World War I and was also the mayor of Leeds in the mid-1960s. He became a director at Leeds United in 1945 and perhaps his most inspiring achievement was introducing Harry Reynolds to the board ten years later.

A tough Yorkshireman from Holbeck, Reynolds, born from working-class parents, rose literally through the ranks of working at every conceivable job ranging from a bakery to a fireman, to sweeping the platforms of railway stations.

Talking of which, Graham Cooke was born in Kippax and now lives in Ottawa, Canada, 'My dad, Henry, was a member of the White Swan Leeds fans in the 1930s, and he even went to away games. He once met Mr Reynolds at Kippax railway station in the early 1960s. He was in Kippax on business, there was a factory near to the church and I think he was going there. My dad just saw him by chance at the station where he was working as an odd job man, and he recognised him straight away. My dad said he looked like a sergeant major and had shiny shoes. He could never remember what they talked about. "We talked about Leeds United," he would say.'

By the end of the 1950s Reynolds had ventured into the steel business, progressing quite rapidly into becoming a millionaire which was certainly to Leeds United's advantage. He was without doubt a major factor in Don Revie becoming Leeds manager and at such a pivotal time.

Reynolds, speaking in 1967, said, 'Don had no football managerial experience at all, but of course, he had a wealth of football experience and above all, he had football knowledge – in abundance.'

Reynolds had been on the board and succeeded Sam Bolton as chairman in 1961.

One image of my infant school is still carved into my memory. Periodically, a large, mysterious, murky grey caravanette-type vehicle used to appear in the playground and would park up in the far corner. It would remain there for a couple of days. It was in fact a dentist; I hated the sight of it, and John Revis reminds me that the dentist was called Atkinson – 'Butcher Atkinson'. The experience inside that caravan, with pliers, drills and maybe a hacksaw, prevented me going to a dentist after I'd left school for many years.

Meanwhile, I was oblivious of much more important activities going on at Elland Road.

In March 1961 Don Revie had walked into chairman Reynolds's office beneath the West Stand to ask for some advice. Don had seen that Bournemouth were seeking a manager. At the time, he was 34 and still operating as player-manager at Leeds but saw this vacancy on the south coast as an opportunity to become a full-time boss.

Reynolds said, 'Don saw the position at Bournemouth, who had been in the Third Division ever since their formation in 1923, as his way into football management. Bournemouth were looking for a new manager and the directors at Bournemouth asked their senior players for recommendations. The most senior player was the Irish international goalkeeper Tommy Godwin who had been at Leicester City as a boy with Don Revie and been very impressed. Revie had a season and a half left in him as a player, so I gave him my permission to apply. But when I was writing his reference, it occurred to me that with all these recommendations, we could do with him ourselves. So I tore up the letter.'

Bournemouth's right-half Bill McGarry was eventually given the managerial role at Dean Court.

But it was this approach from Bournemouth that changed the course of history for Leeds United. Reynolds weighed up Revie as a player – and then decided to handpick him for the managerial chair, a real hot seat, in every sense of the word. Not that Leeds were bad bosses as it were, who fired every manager after a few months, but it was simply that things had run right down in terms of players, results and money. So any new manager would have a pile of problems to face.

Reynolds had come in with every intention of being a real working chairman. Of course his money was there to bolster any offers made for new players. And there was never any doubt that the new manager, untried as he was, would be given a fair crack of the whip to prove he could do the job. Revie was given a breathing space in which to find his managerial feet; he would be given time to decide upon his plans, and the cash with which to carry them out. Results would then decide whether he had succeeded or failed. It would be upon those results that Reynolds would judge his manager, but only after a fair length of testing time for Revie's policy. That's how chairman and manager worked in those days – closely and in harmony. Reynolds was certainly prepared to back his manager – and time would prove that he had handpicked a winner.

On the day of Revie's Leeds debut, in goal was Royden (Roy) Wood. I was introduced to Roy by a friend of mine, Gordon Sheppard from Kippax, around 2014. We were in a pub called the Picture House in Castleford, four miles from Kippax, availing ourselves quite happily with the 'pound a pint' on offer. Roy, around 6ft 4in tall, had a great presence about him and was a really decent bloke.

He had joined Leeds in 1952. 'I made my debut early in the 1953/54 season,' said Roy. 'It was against Derby County. We won 2-1. Leeds manager Major Frank Buckley had seen me playing for Clitheroe on a stormy, wet night and he asked me to sign for Leeds United. I couldn't believe it.'

Revie had arrived at Leeds with quite an admirable reputation. 'We were all a bit in awe of Don when he came to the club,' Roy remembered. 'He'd been at Leicester City, Hull City, Man City and Sunderland. He'd been Footballer of the Year and won the FA Cup with Man City. I remember him being a thinker, deep in thought a lot of the time, but he often looked unhappy, other players noticed it too.'

Jack Charlton had arrived at Elland Road in 1950 and made his debut in the last game of the season previous to Roy Wood's debut, but didn't break into the first team until a few years later. John Charles also played in the same side as Roy. 'Charles was one of the greatest players that there will ever be,' said Roy, 'but I often had to give him a bollocking when he'd make the odd defensive error.'

In the 1956 FA Cup Leeds played Cardiff City in the third round at Elland Road. Roy was in goal, Charles played at centre-half and Charlton was at centre-forward. 'We lost 2-1,' Roy laughed. 'And John dropped a couple of clangers, which I had a word with him about and the following season we drew Cardiff again in the same round, at home.'

Raich Carter had taken over as manager back in 1953 and for this second cup game against the Welsh side he switched Charles and Charlton, but Leeds again lost 2-1. Unbelievably, in the 1958 third round Leeds drew Cardiff yet again at Elland Road. And amazingly they lost that one too – 2-1.

But Charlton struggled in his early years and it would be a while on before he made any sort of impact. That also applied to the club as a whole.

2

From a King to a Jack

JACK CHARLTON had joined Leeds United as a 15-year-old in 1950 after he had been spotted by a club scout playing for Ashington YMCA at left-back. He was considering his career options after leaving Hurst Park Modern School in Ashington, and standing at 6ft 2in he fancied becoming a policeman. He applied to be a police cadet, but in the meantime as a fallback he had embarked on a six-month apprenticeship at the colliery where his dad worked. He was still waiting to hear back from the police when Leeds United knocked on the family door inviting him to a trial. Dad Bob wasn't really that interested in football; away from the grime of the pit he preferred to spend his time going to whippet race meetings, fishing and clay pigeon shooting, of which he was an expert. He liked nothing better than having a pint with mates at the Ashington Working Men's Club. Of course he recognised the special football talent of his two sons, but mum Cissie was definitely the driving force behind the ambitions of Jack and Bobby.

Both parents travelled with Jack to Leeds, with Cissie doing all the talking.

The trial match itself was played on a Saturday in an appalling blizzard, but almost freezing to death paid off in the end as Jack was offered terms by Major Frank Buckley. The three Charltons then returned home to the north-east with the good news, but after grabbing some clothes Jack returned to Leeds the following morning to move into digs provided for by the club. Meanwhile, the Monday morning post to the Charlton household delivered a letter from Morpeth police informing young Jack that he had been accepted into the police force. But Jack decided he liked Leeds United, even though he wasn't totally convinced that the club liked him, 'When I joined Leeds, I felt they were getting someone who would turn out to be a good player, but as time went on, my mood began to change.'

Charlton had made his Leeds debut at home to Doncaster Rovers on the final day of the 1952/53 season, but didn't play a single game during the following campaign. Then in 1954/55 he played one game, a 3-2 home defeat by Lincoln City.

Cecil Wright was in the Elland Road crowd of 22,000 that day, 'A friend of mine, Jimmy Hurst, was a Leeds fan from Doncaster and was friends with Leeds player Peter Vickers, who also lived in Doncaster. I was stood with Jimmy on the Kop and he said that Vickers had told him about this "long gangly bastard" who was playing centre-half, for Leeds.'

'He looks really clumsy, but there is something about him, he could turn out to be a good player,' said Vickers at the time.

During the game, 'gangly' Charlton hoofed the ball upfield and it fell straight in the path of Vickers, who instinctively hit it first time and it flew past the head of the Lincoln keeper into the net for Leeds' second goal.

Charlton's next game was almost 13 months later, on 24 September 1955 – a 4-1 win against Rotherham – and he kept his place for the remainder of the season.

A couple of games after the Lincoln defeat, Leeds had given the centre-half position to John Charles, who had been their standout player for several seasons, alternating between centre-half to centre-forward with the greatest of ease.

There was a teacher at Kippax Mixed Infant School, who I can vaguely remember. I think his name was Mr Robb. He was a Leeds fan; the first one I had ever known in fact. I would have been about eight, perhaps nine. He would talk to us at PE and games lessons about Leeds United. I had absolutely no idea where Elland Road was and he would talk all the time about this man, this player, called John Charles. And I had absolutely no idea who he was either.

Charles had arrived at Elland Road (he also had no idea where it was) in 1949. He had been spotted as a teenager by Leeds' South Wales scout Jack Pickard in Cwmbwrla, Swansea. Pickard then visited John's parents at 19 Alice Street for permission to take John to Leeds for a trial. John's mum immediately said he couldn't go as he didn't have a passport! But John's dad knew of Major Frank Buckley, the Leeds manager, and was suitably impressed. So John took the long train journey to West Yorkshire really not knowing what to expect. He was accompanied on the train by two other young trialists, Harry Griffiths and Bobby Hennings – neither of whom were taken on by Second Division Leeds and both returned to Wales and played for Swansea Town. Griffiths went on to become a Welsh international.

Major Buckley signed 17-year-old John, who made his debut in a goalless draw at Blackburn Rovers on 23 April 1949, slotting seamlessly into the heart of United's defence. Charles had turned out for United in a friendly at Queen of the South four days earlier, on Easter Tuesday. Playing up front for the Scottish top-flight side that day was Scotland international Billy Houliston, a tough centre-forward who had run England ragged at Wembley a week earlier in a 3-1 victory. After a 0-0 draw, in which Charles's astute tactical skill and sheer presence had already attracted admirers, Houliston was said to have told reporters, 'John Charles is the best centre-half I have ever met.'

Charles went on to establish himself as the centre-half, but it would be nine games into his Leeds career before he finished in a winning side, a 1-0 victory at Sheffield United almost five months later. That aside, he became an absolute phenomenon.

He operated at either centre-half or centre-forward. He scored goals from defence but it was certainly at centre-forward that he was at his most prolific.

When asked in 1996 by journalist Ken Jones about which position he preferred, without hesitation Charles replied, 'Centre-forward, no question. A defender can kick five shots off the line but goalscorers get the glory.' When Major Buckley did play Charles at centre-forward, the Welshman quickly became renowned for his bullet headers and rocket-like shots, known to have knocked many a defender unconscious. It has often been rumoured that Charles once hit a shot so hard that it rebounded off the visitors' goalpost and landed in Leeds' own half.

Barry Foster, chief football reporter at the *Yorkshire Post*, even thought he had witnessed this incident himself, but wasn't sure in the midst of time that it actually did happen. That was until it was confirmed to him that it most certainly did, by another sports journalist at the *Post*, Jack Gillings.

Charles's goalscoring ability knew no bounds; he made 39 appearances in 1953/54 and scored 42 goals, setting a club record that still stands today and leading the entire Football League that season.

By now, Charles had been a Welsh international for over four years and Major Buckley had left the club, but was rightly proud in bringing the player to Leeds, calling him 'the most brilliant association footballer in the game today and one of the most outstanding in my 50 years in football'. Buckley added, 'Charles is the best in the world and I'm very proud of him.'

Raich Carter took over but Charles, eager to play in the First Division, subsequently left the directors in a state of shock by requesting a transfer. The board immediately held an emergency meeting which lasted for three hours. The outcome came as a huge relief to United fans when chairman Sam Bolton announced that the request had been turned down, saying, 'Why would we sell a brilliant player like John Charles? It is our intention to get into the First Division and we cannot do that by selling our best player.'

Many teams had expressed an interest in buying Charles, with the Cardiff City chairman Trevor Morris driving to Leeds and sitting outside the boardroom for the duration of the meeting after declaring that his club would basically pay any price for the star.

John Walker was only a young lad at the time, 'We lived just around the corner from John Charles in Middleton and we got to know what time he would be leaving his house for a home game. He would sometimes get a bus, but if we were lucky, he would walk to Elland Road in those days. We followed him up Middleton Park Avenue and turned left at the main road heading towards the ground. There would be six or seven of us all walking behind him (Pied Piper springs to mind) and then when we got to the top of the hill we would turn back to go home as John continued down the hill towards Dewsbury Road, followed by the next group of young fans.

'I never saw Charles play during his first time at Leeds, but I got his autograph more times than I can remember! He once signed my shirt, a light-coloured cotton one, he signed it with a biro and when I got home my mother went mental. She ragged it off me and threw it into our old washer and then told me to go to bed – it was about 11 in the morning!'

Pat Connor used to travel on our coach to away games in the 1980s and always brought a jar of gherkins on board with him. As he chomped away he would rattle off stories about Charles, 'I wasn't allowed to go to watch Leeds when I was younger, but would sometimes skip school and go down to Elland Road and watch him training, that way my dad didn't know I'd been. Charles hit a football harder than I've ever seen in my life and there was a little bloke in overalls playing hell with Charles all the time, 'cos when the ball hit the fence it would bend all the mesh, or buckle the frame, a lot of the time the ball went straight through the fence and into the car park below. I never got to see Charles play in the early years, but I was there when he returned to Leeds.'

Meanwhile, 1954/55 got under way and Sam Bolton, after defiantly holding on to Charles, reinforced his claim that the club would be trying hard for promotion with a heroic push, finishing fourth at the end of that season. United were just one point behind Rotherham United, who finished on 54, the same as Birmingham City and Luton Town who were promoted with Rotherham missing out only on goal average.

The following season saw Charles get his wish as United were promoted behind champions Sheffield Wednesday. It was the stage that the 6ft 2in 'Gentle Giant' was longing for and the first game back in the First Division saw United demolish Everton 5-1 in front of a 31,000 Elland Road crowd, Charles notching a bullet header to add to one by Jack Overfield and a superb hat-trick by Harold Brook.

The following Thursday, United travelled to Charlton Athletic where Charles grabbed a brace to beat their hosts 2-1. Leeds stayed in London for their game at Tottenham Hotspur on the Saturday but were brought down to earth with a crushing 5-1 defeat. They then steadied the ship by beating Charlton again, this time 4-0 at Elland Road. United were more than holding their own in the top flight but a few days after a fine 2-1 win at Wolves (Charles scoring two) and with Leeds lying in second place, tragedy struck at Elland Road.

In the very small hours of Tuesday, 18 September 1956, the sky above Elland Road turned from pitch black to bright orange – the West Stand was on fire. Several fire crews tackled the blaze and several hours later the blaze was out, but it had claimed the West Stand. Early dawn revealed a charred wreckage still smouldering, with the odd flicker of a flame and the stench of smoke everywhere. The West Stand had stood there since 1906 and now it was gone, along with a full range of equipment and, perhaps even more importantly, vital and significant club records. The consequences would be too dire for the fans to contemplate.

Leeds' fixture four days later was at home to Aston Villa, but that looked in serious doubt. All the kit and boots had been destroyed by the fire along with footballs, nets and flags. Raich Carter, however, ordered 40 pairs of boots and new kit. He even told the players to start wearing their new boots immediately and to never take them off, including at night, so that they were bedded in for Saturday's match. Sam Bolton declared, 'The game against Aston Villa will go ahead as planned.'

On matchday, residents across from the ground offered their homes as makeshift dressing rooms for both sets of players and officials – but the club opted to use the dressing rooms of the Whitehall Printers Sports Ground which was situated on the junction of Elland Road and Lowfields Road.

Leeds beat Villa, thanks inevitably to a Charles strike, but failed to win any of their next five games. But crucial victories before the West Stand fire had ensured that, despite an indifferent season, they managed to finish in eighth position. The final two months of the season saw 12 goals from Charles, including a brace in the final game, at home to Sunderland – a 3-1 victory that would be Charles's last appearance for Leeds.

After just one term in the First Division Leeds had lost their crown jewel. The fire had severely crippled United's finances and despite substantial assistance from the Lord Mayor of Leeds by way of a public appeal, the building of a new stand was estimated at £100,000 but cost £30,000 more; the sale of Charles was inevitable. United had previously fought off all comers for their prize asset, but this latest bid came from the continent.

Juventus were a struggling Italian side, scrapping frantically to avoid relegation. Their president Umberto Agnelli was the son of the owner of the Fiat motor company. He had recently seen Charles turn out for Wales against Ireland and was suitably impressed – he was under pressure to turn things around in Turin and saw the signing of Charles as his saviour. But word spread quickly across the continent that Leeds were willing to listen to offers for their prize asset. Inter Milan, Real Madrid and Lazio were among the top clubs to register interest. Leeds were adamant that they would not sell Charles to another club in England, but were open to offers from clubs in Europe. Agnelli said, 'We need Charles badly and we are determined to get him,' and with that he and a few delegates flew to Leeds to meet with chairman Sam Bolton and other directors at the Queens Hotel in Leeds.

Ian Whitely, now 86, was a concierge at the hotel at the time, ' My dad, Norman, was a massive Leeds fan and it was common knowledge that Charles would be leaving Leeds United and people from Juventus were in Leeds. I nearly fainted when Charles walked through the main entrance surrounded by eight or nine suited men with briefcases, and a few photographers. I didn't have time or the opportunity to let my dad know, but I was even more disappointed that I didn't get to enter the room where the meeting took place. It was on the third floor, room 200 – something – just to take in tea or coffee would have been something to tell my dad. Some of the small delegation including Charles went up in the lift, and for some reason the rest climbed the stairs.'

The deal was actually thrashed out in room 233, with the complicated personal terms being carried out in room 222 once a transfer fee had been agreed upon. By now the press had converged in large numbers downstairs in the foyer.

After an hour of hard bargaining on both sides, an agreement was made between Leeds and Juventus, and with Charles's agreement, a deal was struck. The fee was £65,000, a record for a British player. Charles received £10,000 on top of a salary of £70 a month, plus a bonus of £25 for an away win and £15 for a home win. He was also given his own choice of a Turin apartment, a Fiat car for two years and a two-year contract. Not bad for a lad who cost United a tenner in January 1949.

After a thorough medical, paying particular attention to Charles's knees after two cartilage operations, Juventus's doctor, Professor Amilcare Basatti, declared, 'John Charles is the fittest man I know playing football. I have never seen a better human machine in a lifetime of medicine.'

I never saw John Charles play, but his supreme skills and sportsmanship were legendary. I have seen footage of him at a game at Highbury where he was bearing down on yet another goal, when an Arsenal defender went down injured. Charles, without a second thought, immediately put the ball out of play.

Before departing for Turin, and although contracts had been signed, Charles was allowed to play his final game in front of an Elland Road crowd of 29,328 on Monday, 22 April 1957, the last day of the season. Visitors Sunderland were captained by a certain Don Revie, and Roy Wood was once again in the Leeds goal for a 3-1 victory for the hosts. Over a pint in the Picture House, Roy once told me that this game had probably been his best for the club. The *Yorkshire Post* agreed with him, 'But for the sound goalkeeping of Wood, Sunderland would have scored more than the goal left-winger Colin Grainger gave them between Charles's first and second. Wood made four saves of outstanding merit. Revie was Sunderland's best player.'

After the game, as the fans disappeared into the night, Charles was whisked into a waiting car behind the West Stand by Juventus scout Gigi Peronace. Some supporters waved the car off as it drove through the gates, turning left on to Elland Road and heading for the train station. After an overnight train to London, Charles and the rest of the waiting party flew off to Turin.

3

A Stirling Effort

IN THE aftermath of John Charles's departure, the team unsurprisingly struggled the following season and manager Raich Carter was disappointed when, thinking he would receive substantial funds from the transfer, he was given just £12,000 to buy Airdrie's Hugh Baird in June 1957. The board then informed Carter that they would not be renewing his five-year contract. Carter argued, with some justification it has to be said, that he had taken Leeds from mid-table in the Second Division to fourth place, followed by promotion to the First Division, and a creditable eighth position the following season.

Carter could not hide his bitter disappointment, saying, 'We finished 17th this season, after the directors had sold Charles, the greatest player in the world, and given me far less than half his transfer fee to spend on replacing him. This last season could never be more than a holding season once a player like Charles had gone.'

Leeds finished just six points better off than bottom-placed Sheffield Wednesday and in the close season, Bill Lambton, the club's trainer, was appointed acting manager, then full-time boss, but he had little experience. In fairness, however, Lambton revived the development policy that Major Frank Buckley had instigated a few years previous and this would be so beneficial to his successors. After Irish international Wilbur Cush quit the captaincy, Lambton had no hesitation in offering it to his marquee signing, Don Revie. United slightly improved the following season, 1958/59, finishing 15th, but Lambton resigned saying, 'I have considered this course of action for some time owing to interference from directors in my training methods.'

It was those training methods, incidentally, that caused Grenville Hair and Jack Overfield to demand transfers as players revolted against Lambton.

Yorkshireman Jack Taylor was recruited from Queens Park Rangers to replace Lambton. But the situation on the field was far from good.

In 1960, Colin Grainger, who had scored for Sunderland in John Charles's final game, became a Leeds player, making his debut at Liverpool in August. Being from Wakefield, a move back to his native Yorkshire was ideal for him. But at Elland Road it was a young Scot who caught his attention: 17-year-old Billy Bremner.

Grainger said, 'I watched him in training and it was obvious that he was going to be a very good player. He was so mature, he fought for every ball and despite being small, stood head and shoulders above anyone else on the park.'

Bremner had shown that same promise throughout his school years, at St Mary's Primary School in his hometown of Raploch in the district of Stirling and later at St Modan's Secondary School. Several English clubs had shown an interest in young Bremner, including Sheffield Wednesday and Aston Villa, and he had trials at Arsenal and Chelsea, although both deemed him too small to become a professional footballer. It was in Scotland, however, where Billy yearned to play; he had watched both Rangers and Celtic as a boy, attending one when the other was away, never once becoming embroiled in the religious divide, and his dream seemed to have come true when his beloved Celtic invited Billy and his mate Tommy Henderson for a day's training at Parkhead. The two young players could not believe their luck.

In the meantime, however, Leeds United had arrived on the scene and Lambton and chairman Harry Reynolds had travelled north of the border to speak to them both. Billy, unsurprisingly, had never heard of the club and didn't have a clue where Leeds was. Strangely, though, the first team that Billy ever supported was English. I was in the audience at an event at the Parkside Inn in Pontefract when Billy was speaking on 19 October 1995.

'I had no idea where it was, but I fell in love with Exeter City, because of their name!' he said. 'I followed their results every week and even went to a game there, sometime in the 1960s.'

Lambton convinced Bremner and Henderson to travel to Leeds for a trial, with the full blessing of Billy's father, who had told his son in no uncertain terms that playing for Celtic or Rangers was out of the question, because he didn't want him caught up with any 'religious controversy' and 'sectarianism' – so they were going to England – and that was final.

Roy Wood was in goal when Bremner made his debut at Chelsea on 23 January 1960, 'I only played a couple of games with Billy before I retired. One was his debut; you could see even at that young age he was something special.

'We stayed in a London hotel the night before the Chelsea game and Don Revie arranged it so that he roomed with Billy. Almost immediately there was this father/son-like bond between them.'

Bremner had been unsure as to whether or not he would be playing – until Revie told him in the club car park back at Leeds. He would be on the right wing, with Revie at inside-right. This had come about as regular winger Chris Crowe was on national service and had to play for the army. Then Revie insisted that Bremner be in bed by 10pm and at seven the next morning Don asked Billy to accompany him on a long walk in order to settle any nerves that the youngster may have had.

These were the early signs of Revie's paternal instincts, which would become one of his many managerial hallmarks. As they walked and talked, Revie warned 17-year-old Bremner that the Chelsea players would certainly try every trick in the book to unsettle him with little remarks and the odd dig in the back, but to rise above it and to concentrate on his own game. Hours later the match kicked off at Stamford Bridge.

Very early on, Revie won the ball and immediately brought Bremner in for an early touch – it was plain sailing from there.

United travelled back to Leeds with both points after a 3-1 win. Revie, however, would keep a watchful eye on Bremner, knowing that he was finding it very difficult being away from his home in Scotland.

Roy Wood played once more with Billy after the Chelsea match, a 4-1 defeat at West Bromwich Albion. Wood retired after the next match, a 2-1 defeat at Newcastle United in mid-February.

Royden Wood had played over 200 games for Leeds, and in the mid-1950s he made 139 successive league appearances. One afternoon in the Picture House, Gordon Sheppard joked about Roy's name. 'Do you often get mistaken for Roy Wood of the group Wizzard?' he asked.

'Funny enough, no,' said Roy. 'But sometimes in the newspaper I was often called Ray Wood – when I had played well. Ray Wood was the goalkeeper at Old Trafford at the time. But when I had a poor game, I was called Roy Wood!'

A former classmate of mine from Kippax Infant School was Susan Eastwood, and a few years ago she gave me an old menu from a Leeds United Supporters Club event held at a restaurant called Polowny's, in the city centre. The date was Monday, 14 February 1955 and it is signed by all the team of that period, and as well as Wood, there are the names of Raich Carter, Grenville Hair, John Charles, Jimmy Dunn and many others.

'I used to love those supporters dos,' Roy remembers. 'Meeting the fans was always a highlight for me, although the food was sometimes a little too posh for my liking.'

Looking at the menu from that evening, I can see where Roy is coming from. The starter was melon frappe followed by consomme champignons or creme de volaille; the main was dindonneau roti farci au chipolata, petis pois au beurre or pommes gaufrettes et parmentier, followed by bomb glace auz fruits.

Despite coming from Merseyside, Roy soon made Yorkshire his home, living in the Bradford area. Simon Garforth runs his own removal company, Wades, and remembers him fondly, 'At the time I was working for George Pickersgill's removal company in Shipley, it was about 2004. We moved Roy Wood from Wrose in Bradford to the Rothwell area of Leeds. He was a big chap and thoroughly nice. He kindly gave me his old kit bag and signed it.'

I often drive through Castleford and pass the Picture House, which closed many years ago. I lost touch with Roy, but not once do I pass it and not think of my chats with the man – now into his 90s. What a nice bloke and a great character. I still have a little gift he once gave me: a £20 note with the Leeds United badge printed on it. It's a great joke item, although despite all our many conversations I never had Roy down as a major counterfeiter!

Recently I spoke to Vicky Powell, Roy's daughter-in-law, and told her how I enjoyed his company and stories over a pint or two in the pub in Castleford and I told her that I hadn't seen him for a while so I asked how he was getting on. Vicky said to me, 'He's doing good for a 91-year-old, although he's not too steady on his feet these days, so he's not out as much as he used to be. He's had a few falls, but he seems to roll well like the great goalkeeper he was.'

Meanwhile, the bond between Don Revie and Billy Bremner grew stronger as United battled against the drop into the Second Division. Following a dramatic 3-3 draw at Birmingham City on 9 March in which Revie got two goals and Bremner the other, they faced fellow strugglers Manchester City at Elland Road. In the City line-up that day was a young player whom Bremner would get to know well over the coming years. Denis Law made his debut in a fixture that ended 4-3 to Leeds, but not before both Bremner and Law had both scored their first goals for their respective clubs.

Both players would fiercely cross swords many times in cup and league games but would fight side by side for their beloved Scotland in that famous dark-blue jersey.

I was at Billy's funeral in 1997 and Denis was in floods of tears, distraught throughout.

Despite wins against Bolton Wanderers and Preston North End, both thanks to goals by Jack Charlton, Leeds entered the final three games with a real fight on their hands.

Sadly, consecutive defeats at Everton and Blackburn Rovers meant that a 1-0 home win against Nottingham Forest on the last day became irrelevant. United finished one point behind Forest and were relegated along with Luton Town.

Leeds fan Thomas Marchant was at that final game of the season, 'I went to all but two of the games at Elland Road that season. I lived on Winrose Drive in Belle Isle and used to go with my next-door neighbour Mick and three lads from nearby Middleton. We used to have a few pints in the Middleton Arms (known locally as the Miggy Arms) and then walk the mile or so down to Elland Road. I remember the atmosphere was subdued; because of previous results we would be relegated despite the result. We got to the top of Wesley Street and saw Grenville Hair, who wasn't playing that day but he was going to the game because he said that he wanted to be there. We liked that.'

The following October, after a home victory over Charlton Athletic, Thomas's next-door neighbour Mick was knocked down by a car and died at St James's Hospital, aged just 18 years old. Grenville Hair and Noel Peyton attended the funeral.

Jack Taylor simply couldn't motivate the team, and following relegation, and struggling in their subsequent Second Division campaign, he resigned on 13 March 1961 – just four days later, Don Revie was appointed as player-manager. Revie had by now, just as Wilbur Cush had done, relinquished the captaincy; displaying early signs of his famous superstitions, Revie claimed that he was 'an unlucky captain' and handed the armband to Fred Goodwin.

John Hurst was a Luton Town fan when they were relegated with Leeds in 1960, 'We lived just off the High

Street in Eggington, near Leighton Buzzard. We didn't live that far away from Bob Monkhouse, the great celebrity in the town. My dad, Reginald, first took me to see Town in 1958. I think it was my second ever game when I saw them play Leeds United at Kenilworth Road. We'd played at Leeds the week before, but I wasn't allowed to go with my dad and his mate, Edwin. My dad and his mate used to travel all over watching Luton and we used to laugh at them sometimes when they wore their straw boater hats and a big black and white rosette. They weren't a bit bothered and would also wear a blazer with a heavily embroidered club badge on the chest pocket. I went with my dad and Edwin, and a friend of mine called Raymond, to the 1959 FA Cup Final. I was 13. We lost 2-1, but that day at Wembley was probably the most exciting day that I have ever had. And my dad and Edwin were not the only ones wearing straw hats; they seemed to be everywhere!

'The following season we lost at home to Leeds with Don Revie scoring the only goal. My dad went to Elland Road to watch Town, but again I wasn't allowed to go as it was a family Christmas party for the children. I remember thinking that I'd much sooner have been at Leeds with my dad.'

Some people associate Luton Town with the popular comedian Eric Morecambe, who became their vice-president, but John says there's much more to the club, 'Luton Town has been our family's life. I am now 75 and just get to see the occasional game these days. My dad died seven years ago and was buried in his "lucky" Luton Town blazer with his trusty straw boater rested comfortably on his chest.'

Leeds met Luton again, at home on 8 March 1961, losing 2-1, but by the time the teams met in the reverse fixture on April Fool's Day, Revie was the player-manager. Leeds, incidentally, drew 1-1 courtesy of a Billy Bremner goal. Earlier that season Bremner had scored two goals in a 3-2 defeat at Norwich and then played in every game to its conclusion.

Jack Charlton had said after the departure of John Charles, 'I had to compete with the knowledge that "King" John Charles would be the automatic choice for Leeds ... at centre-forward or centre-half.'

Charlton freely admitted to wallowing in his own self-pity and felt a move away would be beneficial for both himself and the club, but there were no takers.

Then the sale of Charles occurred and would seemingly present Charlton with the ideal opportunity to properly establish himself at the centre of United's defence – and it did. He became the regular centre-half, even playing in his original position of left-back in a 2-0 home defeat to Luton Town, after which he was moved back to the middle. One would assume then that all would be happy in Charlton's world. But no. Charlton said, 'I was enjoying an extended run at centre-half, but I was never totally convinced that Leeds United looked on me as being the man they wanted.'

Revie had arrived at Elland Road in November 1958 and it is well documented how he and Charlton viscously locked horns on several occasions.

Charlton explained, 'Don Revie arrived at Elland Road as a player who had been around a bit. I won't say that Don Revie and I didn't hit it off, but we weren't exactly soulmates. As a player, in fact, Don didn't hesitate to speak his mind, and quite often I was on the receiving end of his opinions. When things started to go wrong, I used to let it show.

'Don Revie once glared at me and snarled, "It would be the best thing that could happen to you, if Leeds left you out, you've got a chip on your shoulder, and you're spoiling it for other players. You'd never do that for me." I was obsessed to the point that the only thing I wanted to do was get away from Leeds United and put in a transfer request.'

When Revie had become the manager, he had already realised the talent of Syd Owen and Les Cocker who had previously arrived from Luton Town as coach and trainer respectively. But it was Owen who next bore the brunt of Charlton's frustration.

One day Charlton walked into the office to collect his wage. It was there that he encountered Owen for the first time. Owen, of course, had heard that Charlton was somewhat unsettled and asked him, rather politely, what was wrong between him and the club. Charlton simply told Owen to 'shove off' or words to that effect.

Owen was a mild-mannered man, to a point, and he continued his conversation with Charlton, asking him to forget about a transfer – 'for a while'. But the self-proclaimed 'One-Man Awkward Squad' was in no mood to listen to Owen, or Cocker, who continued quietly working on the defender who would eventually become known, affectionately, as 'The Giraffe'.

Charlton was so incensed at Owen's 'interference' that he stormed into Revie's office and demanded that he 'got Syd Owen off my back, or there would be fisticuffs between us'. Revie told him to get out.

Early signs of Revie's man-management were beginning to spring up everywhere and on one occasion he called Charlton into his office to tell him that he didn't think he was the type of centre-half he wanted and he could have his transfer if he so wished. But he added, 'If you played the game right, and did the job that you're supposed to do, you would be playing for England.'

This shook Charlton to the core and it could well have been this moment that spurred him on to conform and in doing so enhance his career to such an extent that the big man never thought possible. He had been very critical of Owen's methods in training and rebelled at every turn, 'I felt he was always picking on me and pointing out the mistakes I was making. I really thought his ideas were crap.'

Much of this information was gleaned from countless 'Evening with Jack Charlton' events, at which I would scribble down on napkins, beer mats, till receipts, anything to hand really, but one statement that crops up on a regular basis was 'I was such a fuckin' idiot at times!'

Cocker once said, 'There was a team constantly working around Jack Charlton, moulding him into shape, but Jack always thought that everyone was out to get him. It was quite the opposite in fact. We saw the potential of "Big Jack" even if he didn't.'

This was emphasised when Charlton began feeling insecure about the impending return of John Charles in 1962. Charlton assumed that Charles would automatically walk back into the centre-half spot, leaving him 'out in the cold once more'.

Revie sensed Charlton's anxiety and moved quickly to reassure him. One morning Revie took Jack for a round of golf at Sand Moor Golf Club, close to the manager's home. It was while strolling around the course that day that Revie told Charlton that he was to be his centre-half and not John Charles. That was all Charlton needed to hear, 'Like a brick hitting me in the face, I realised the people around me were working in both mine and Leeds United's interest, and from then on, I never looked back.'

'The day that Syd Owen and Les Cocker arrived at Elland Road, I wasn't even training with the first team because of another dispute with the club.'

But eventually, after a few weeks under Owen and Cocker, Charlton admitted, 'My whole outlook began to change. I no longer felt I was wasting my time and these two coaches were obviously prepared to spend time with me, often 12-14 hours a day, improving my heading, passing, shooting, all of that. Between them, Les Cocker, Syd Owen, Don Revie and Maurice Lindley made me into an international player and also cajoled me into adopting the right frame of mind.'

Charlton was justified in finally recognising the vast experience of Owen. He too had been an established centre-half, for Luton, and played from 1947 to 1959, mostly as captain. He won three England caps and was Footballer of the Year in 1959. He toured with the Football Association in Australia, Rhodesia, West Indies and South Africa.

Luton fan John Hurst said, 'My dad's favourite player was easily Syd Owen, he even met him a few times. Dad was so proud, me too, when Syd led the Hatters out at Wembley for the 1959 FA Cup Final at Wembley. He was player-manager and captain by then.' A dispute over club policy a year later led to Owen resigning at Kenilworth Road and taking up a vacant position at Elland Road as coach. Revie was still a player, but he was very ambitious and was already seeing the club in the future. Owen was in the RAF and saw service in Palestine, Sicily, Italy, Austria and Egypt.

Cocker had become a coach at Luton in 1958 having previously played for Stockport County and Accrington Stanley, and was one of the first people in the country to hold an FA Coaching Certificate. In 1962 he was asked by England manager Walter Winterbottom to be a squad trainer for the national side. Previously a painter and decorator before becoming heavily involved in football, Cocker also saw service, with the Reconnaissance Regiment in France with the 53rd Division.

Revie's daughter, Kim, once told me that family meant everything to her dad, and we'll step into the Revie family a little later. Meanwhile, Don began building a family at Leeds United, as alongside Owen and Cocker he had Maurice Lindley as his trusty scout.

In 1957 Leeds had signed Gerry Francis, the club's first black player. Francis, a cobbler by trade, was spotted while playing for City and Suburban FC in Johannesburg. Manager Raich Carter invited him to England for a trial before subsequently signing him in the summer.

Francis had paid his own airfare to Yorkshire and became only the second black South African, after Steve Mokone, to play abroad professionally. Mokone, from Doornfontein, played for Pretoria Home Stars and when he was 18 he signed for Coventry City, making his debut in 1965. A few years later, Mokone served two prison terms in New York for violent assaults, although he claimed that the charges were fabricated.

Interestingly, between 1946 and 1959 a total of 52 South Africans played in the Football League – but only two, Francis and Mokone, were black. One of those white South Africans was John Hewie, who played for Scotland, where his father was born, at the 1958 World Cup finals in Sweden. During one game at Bury, an irate home fan shouted, 'Get back to South Africa, Hewie, you black bastard,' which was quite bizarre considering that Hewie is in fact white.

Roy Wood was Leeds' goalkeeper at the time, and remembers Gerry Francis arriving at Elland Road, 'He had a confident swagger about him, but not in a cocky sense. You got the impression that he could give as good as he got. I only played once with him, on his debut.' Francis made his debut against Birmingham City but didn't play again for almost two years. In his third Leeds appearance, he scored his first goal, against Everton in a 3-3 home draw.

Predictably, Francis suffered racial abuse after arriving in Yorkshire; as well as the taunts from some opponents and spectators, he wasn't sure whether he could share a bath or even socialise with his white team-mates. It was a culture shock for Francis to encounter the cold, rain, snow and mud, being raised on sun-baked pitches back home. But it was the racial abuse that was an ongoing thing. When he first got into the Leeds team, the captain, Eric Kerfoot, once heard an opponent call Francis a 'wog'. Kerfoot was fuming and tore into the offending player, telling him, 'His name is Gerry Francis, and that's all you need to call him!'

Francis recalled, 'The Leeds fans seemed to like me, even booing Chris Crowe when he got the right-wing position over me for a game.'

Raich Carter went above and beyond to make Francis feel at home, even inviting him to his house for tea. Francis, however, was somewhat uncomfortable with this, 'Coming from South Africa it didn't feel right for me to visit white people because I wasn't allowed to do this back home. Yet there was this great international footballer inviting me into his house. I felt awkward, but he brought me into his home to tell me what kind of player he thought I was and that I reminded him of himself in his younger playing days.

'At the end of the season all the players went "home"; some to Scotland or Ireland. I had nowhere to go because I didn't know anybody, so I was going to stay in Leeds. Raich asked what I was going to do. Thinking I would be bored, he suggested I help the groundstaff boys at Elland Road and also do a bit of training.

'There was this young lad who played centre-half in the reserves and juniors called Paddy Stanley, who went on to play for Halifax Town. His family were from Dublin, now living in north London at Boreham Wood. As he knew I had nobody to go to, he invited me to stay with him, his mum and dad and his sister, who had been a beauty queen in Ireland. They treated me so well and really made me feel at home.'

The image of 'tough, insular Yorkshire folk' did not always tie in with what Francis found, 'They were very hospitable on the whole and I really can't say anything bad about them.'

A few years ago, renowned journalist Phil Shaw interviewed Francis and kindly gave me permission to quote from that conversation.

Shaw said, 'I actually saw Francis score one of his goals! Lovely guy and great interviewee.'

In the interview, Francis reflected, 'When I first arrived in Yorkshire, one person in particular really looked after me: my landlady, Mrs Wiley. When I first arrived, I was in digs with her at Noster Hill in Beeston, not far from the ground.

'One morning I asked her where I could buy pens and paper so that I could write home. At the stores across the road [Beeston Road], she said, so I walked over and when I went in, there was a lady on her knees, scrubbing the floor. When I reached the counter and looked back I was amazed to see that she was white. I'd never seen a white woman doing that; at home only black people did that sort of thing. The woman looked at me as if to say, "Why the hell is he staring at me?" The shopkeeper said, "Young man, anything else I can get you?" She could see that I was looking. When I told Mrs Wiley, she had to sit me down and tell me calmly, "This is not South Africa. This is Yorkshire."'

Ernie Edmonds lived on Parkfield Avenue, across Beeston Road from Noster Hill, 'I had been a Leeds fan for about two years when Gerry Francis moved into lodgings on Noster Hill with some other Leeds players. My mate, Ken Irwin, lived on Noster Terrace and at the bottom of that street was a brick wall which when you looked over it you saw the best view of Elland Road anywhere. We would often be playing football in Ken's street and could see Gerry Francis looking over that wall and down at the ground. Sometimes when he was walking back up to his own street he would kick our football and have a laugh with us.'

Mrs Wiley was 'like a mother' to Francis, and later to Albert Johanneson after he also came from Germiston, near Johannesburg, to become Don Revie's first recommendation to his board of directors as player-manager early in 1961. Francis played three times with Johanneson – Albert on the left wing and Gerry on the right.

'Mrs Wiley treated us better than the white guys,' laughed Francis. 'If we came in and we were going to a party she would go out of her way to wash a shirt for us.

'That's why Billy [Bremner], who was in the same digs, moved out, he felt that she was favouring us and didn't do anything for the Scottish boys. Billy moved to a boarding house run by the mother of Tommy Leighton, another young player at Leeds.'

For a time, Francis had roomed with Bremner and his compatriot Tommy Henderson. They often fell asleep discussing their hopes, fears and experiences. Francis said, 'I first met them just after they had played for Scotland in a schoolboy international at Wembley. I didn't understand a bloody word they were saying! I couldn't make head nor tail of it. I asked Mrs Wiley what language they spoke in Scotland.

'When I learned English in South Africa we were taught to pronounce the words properly!'

Bremner, of course, would become Revie's talisman as Leeds began their relentless pursuit of honours. His burgeoning talent was instrumental in marginalising Francis, although both captain and manager were interested in learning about the football culture in South Africa's townships and how it might be applied to the English game.

In particular, Francis told them about the diminutive players who sat deep, like small centre-halves, and distributed the ball in the style of modern-day *liberos*, or playmakers. They were intrigued by the tales of a team called Naughty Boys from Sophiatown – an area where artists, musicians, writers and revolutionaries hung out, which was later destroyed by the apartheid regime – and their tiny, but hugely influential player called Toffee. Another team he told them about was George Goch, for whom Francis once played, and a four-foot-something schemer called Shakes.

Francis said, 'When Don Revie came, as a player, he invited me round for tea and picked my brains. When he became player-manager I thought he would do well because he was willing to listen. He really wanted to know about black teams in South Africa; he thought he might learn something useful. He wasn't interested in the white teams in Africa because they just copied the English style.

'Billy Bremner was obviously a great player but Leeds hadn't found a role for him then. I told Don how we used three little guys back home and he played Billy in that free role in a trial match. Even after I left Leeds I still trained with them, and Billy often asked me about the Naughty Boys.'

Shaw explained, 'After Leeds, Gerry lived in Tonbridge in Kent playing for the Kent part-timers, Tonbridge, now known as Tonbridge Angels.'

Francis continued, 'Eventually I decided I was going south. Myself and my lady who became my wife, Gloria, had been writing to each other as pen pals and sent one another photos. Out of the blue she said, "Oh, I'm coming over." It was just before the UK said they were not taking any more immigrants. The cut-off was a Wednesday and she arrived on the Tuesday. Three weeks later we were married and now we have two daughters and two grandchildren.'

It was while living in Tonbridge that Gerry Francis suffered his worst experience of racial abuse, 'I was playing for Tonbridge at Dover and you could hear everything at those small grounds. I'd run rings round their defence and when we were coming off at the end a fight broke out between our defender Gus Simmons and the lad who'd been marking me. It was a terrible punch-up.'

Francis is now living in Canada. Shaw said, 'In Canada, he and Gloria have long since retired and live near Toronto. Gerry tried to remain active, playing golf and joining in with a kids' soccer game now and again. I've kept in touch with his daughter Tracy who told me that her dad, sadly, is not as "switched on" as he once was.'

Francis said, 'Tommy Henderson now lives in South Africa and I met up with him on my last trip "home". I think about Jo'burg every day, but I don't know if there's anybody still alive that I played with. I have no regrets about my football career, though I do feel that I should still be living in England. I have very happy memories of Leeds and the people I met. I hope to make it back there one day to see some of my old team-mates but unfortunately the travelling is very expensive for us seniors. But I wish the club and the supporters well and hope to see them back up to where they belong – the top. They took a chance on a non-white player and I will always be grateful for that.'

But Billy Bremner was still unhappy and Revie knew that he had to pull out all the stops to prevent losing this raw talent, as he had studied this promising young Scot and saw great potential. He was determined to ensure that Bremner remained at Leeds, but the manager was certainly going to have his work cut out. In fact, just about the same time that I was running away from school and heading for home with my co-escapees, Steve Hill and Kathleen Richardson, Bremner was doing a similar thing and running back home to Scotland. His homesickness grew worse week by week, not helped by the fact that his long-time girlfriend, Vicky Dick, lived back in Scotland.

Wee Billy had a great childhood in Raploch and had many friends. He began his school days at St Mary's Primary School. While in 2018, visiting Raploch for a project to have a memorial in Raploch to honour Bremner, I, along with Chris Keene, Tony Winstanley and Bob Liddle, sat in on a meeting at the Raploch Community Centre and afterwards talked at length with a lady called Margaret Phillips. She was a close childhood friend of Billy's growing up on the rough Raploch estate. Billy and his friends would play football everyday, going swimming in the nearby River Forth, and cycling.

Margaret said, 'Among our friends were Alex Smith, Willliam McGuillam, Tony and Izzy Lafferty, John Hogg and a few others. We used to go to the school just down there' [she pointed along Drip Road, which still runs through Raploch, although these days it is partly a pedestrian thoroughfare flanked by new offices and apartments; the primary school they all went to is still there].

Continuing up Drip Road is a bar called Vinneys Bar and the proprietor knew Billy a few years later, and not far from the bar is Weir Street on which Billy grew up at number 35A, a three-room council house, sadly long since demolished.

'Izzy McDonald as she is now, was one of Billy's closest friends and also part of the family; Billy's grandma was Izzy's aunt. Izzy was an excellent footballer, and later played for Scotland. It was Izzy who gave Billy the nickname "Brock".'

The nickname developed from when the friends were playing football with other kids. They would split into different teams and each team had to pay a shilling with the winning team keeping the money. Billy would always say to Izzy, 'Are we going for broke?' With his accent, Izzy said it always sounded like 'Brock' and that became his nickname. Billy's team very rarely lost, and even at that young age it was obvious for all to see that he was an exceptional footballer.

Four years on from the beginning of our project, it has become a big concern. Plans are now well under way for a statue of Billy on a proposed site that we all agree is perfect. It is a grass mound with old steps around it that can easily be transformed to resemble the highly impressive Bremner Square that surrounds Billy's statue outside Elland Road. The site in Raploch has Stirling Castle as a backdrop. It is only a few hundred yards from where young Billy lived and just a few yards from where Alexander Bus Depot stood, where there were large green metal roll-shutter doors which Billy and his mate William would hammer their football against for target practice. William would wonder why nobody complained about the noise; then one day, someone did. This slightly older lad and Billy got embroiled in a wrestling match and this woman from a nearby garden shouted, 'Leave him alone, boys, he's only a boy!' To which Billy retorted, 'He's not a boy, missus, it's a man.' She then said, 'Well kick him then.'

It is satisfying to the four of us who began this project that Billy's memory is being restored, and that the young kids in the schools around the area, who sadly had never heard of Billy, are now busily involved with projects about their new hero. Around 20 organisations are now involved, including Raploch and Stirling councils, Stirling Albion, the Scottish FA and supporters' association, Hampden Park and the museum housed within it, Stirling University and many others. The aim is also to link the communities of Raploch and Temple Newsam in Leeds where Billy lived while at United.

Chris, myself, Tony, Bob, and now Heidi Haigh, a top, well-known Leeds fan who has joined our team, are delighted at the Sporting Heritage funds that are being granted for the project, and with Leeds being the European Capital of Culture in 2023 we are hoping the monies already accrued will continue to grow. Leeds United supporters are also to be invited to donate, including the club's massive overseas support, encompassing the huge, incredible fanbase in Scandinavia and across Ireland. A small part of the grants has been used to fund an innovative move to enjoy a two-hour walking tour around the area, pointing out places where Billy spent his youth. A small plaque stands beneath the Forth Bridge which says, 'Born in Raploch in 1942 Billy Bremner was rejected by Arsenal and Chelsea for being too small, he joined Leeds United in 1959. He captained United and won 54 Scottish Caps.'

Billy's early supporter was John Wynn, a Raploch newspaper seller who loved football but was careful to wear a football scarf that was double-sided so he could turn it to show the colours of the favoured team wherever he sold his papers. Pat McGuigan of Drip Road recalled how he used to coach young Billy. Many other Raploch boys followed Billy's lead and the Castleview Football Club thrives today as a result of his influence. The tour, expertly shown by guide

Karen Fraser, of Stirling University, takes you along a path in from the river and alongside a park.

Spanning the path at one point is a stone monument that reads, 'Billy Bremner spent his childhood swimming in the nearby River Forth and pestering for a game with the bigger lads at Shell Park. As a player for Leeds United he had the ability to win any game with one lightning strike of magic.'

Izzy Lafferty, a close friend of Billy, said that at his funeral, 'Many people came over to speak to me that day as if they had known me all their lives. Famous people like Jimmy Greaves, Bobby Charlton, and Ian St John. That was Billy for you, it was clear he just never stopped talking about Raploch.'

As we walked around the streets of the Raploch estate, it was easy to imagine a young Billy Bremner who had just run away from Leeds, arriving at the door of his home on Weir Street, and then hours later, Don Revie knocking on that very door, and gently and carefully escorting a troubled Billy into his car and then driving the couple of hundred miles back to Leeds. This scenario was played out on several occasions.

Further along the tour, Karen pointed out the very spot upon which the field stood where Billy famously acquired his nickname of 'Brock'. Although the estate in which Billy grew up has largely altered, there is something very emotional in retracing Billy's footsteps. Sadly, Izzy is in the early stages of dementia, although she can still recall a lot of things. Karen went to interview her at her home, but she said, 'The television was blaring out so loud with *Good Morning Britain* and *Loose Women* that it's difficult to pick everything up on my voice recorder!'

As Margaret Phillips told us of her memories that first evening in the community centre, she laughed when she said, 'Billy – that wee bastard got me smoking Woodbine cigarettes. He would share his ciggies with me and in turn I would get some and share them with him – we were both ten!' A few years ago, Margaret got her husband to drive her all the way to Elland Road just so that she could see Billy's statue.

Billy went to St Modan's Secondary School and it was there that he met Vicky, and just a few more years down the line they would become engaged. They quickly became inseparable – until he began his Leeds United career.

Of course, Revie knew that Bremner was chronically homesick. Not just for home, but for Vicky. He had gone down to Leeds with close friend Tommy Henderson and they had made a pact that if either one of them didn't make it in England then they would both return to Scotland together. While Billy was not a regular in the first team, he was gnawing away at the opportunity and was agonisingly close to a breakthrough. Henderson, on the other hand, who was also longing to return home, was released by the club.

Billy and Tommy were the closest that two friends could be and Billy felt bad when he kind of reneged on their pact. But with a few kind words from Henderson, they still parted as great pals. Henderson went on to play for Celtic and Hearts and was later signed by Leeds under Revie.

Revie, meanwhile, was still trying desperately to resolve Bremner's pining for a return home to Scotland. It was much worse than Revie had first thought. Homesickness was a real problem for young players of that era, and Leeds had more than their fair share. Young Norman Hunter was desperate to return home to the north-east after just a few months. He had been spotted playing for Chester-le-Street and joined the groundstaff in November 1960, but was unhappy being in digs and away from home. Signing professional terms six months later, however, settled him, and gradually he became one of Revie's disciples when he took over the managerial reins the same year.

Bremner, though, dealt his new boss an early blow by asking for a transfer. He was still unhappy being away from Scotland and, shortly after his request was made known, Hibernian came knocking at the door. This delighted Bremner, 'When I asked for a transfer soon after Don Revie became manager, it was not in any way anything to do with him personally. I just felt I could not wait for regular first-team football and I was also still a bit homesick. Hibs manager Walter Galbraith had put in a £25,000 bid for me and I was obviously happy with the idea of returning to Scotland and a career with the Edinburgh club.'

But Revie had seen Bremner's potential and was determined to hold on to his prospect. He disappointed Galbraith, and Bremner, by asking for £5,000 more than what Hibernian had offered. Don had seen the potential of this small, flame-haired dynamo he had in possession and was determined to keep him at Leeds.

Revie said, 'I needed to hold on to Billy, and I knew that Hibs couldn't afford £30,000.'

But Revie's concerns weren't over as Bremner displayed further urges to return home. In late September 1961, in his capacity as manager, Revie took it upon himself, without Bremner's knowledge, to travel alone to Scotland on a mission he hoped would end this saga once and for all. His destination was a factory in Stirling, the workplace of Vicky Dick. Revie used up her entire dinner hour trying to convince her that her long-time boyfriend was a vital piece of the huge jigsaw being put together at Leeds United, and claimed that they would become the best football team in Britain; a claim that even the incumbent Leeds players chuckled at.

But whatever Revie said to Vicky that day certainly worked wonders, and a few weeks later she had made plans to travel to West Yorkshire and set up home with Billy in Leeds.

Peter Teal was a Leeds fan at that time and recalls Billy and Vicky moving into their new home in the Temple Newsam area of Leeds, 'They were accommodated in a semi-detached house in Plantation Avenue, which was next door to my late aunt and uncle. My aunt liked to feel that they played some part in helping them both "settle down", so to speak, showing friendship, helping with household chores etc., although neither of them ever went to Elland Road.'

Shortly after 'settling in', Billy and Vicky were married on 14 November 1961, making Revie a very happy man indeed, for now. Meanwhile, Revie himself had also settled into life in Leeds and was relishing the challenge ahead.

4

The Don

EIGHT-YEAR-OLD DON Revie played football in the street behind his family home, 20 Bell Street in Middlesbrough. He was born Donald George Revie on 10 July 1927 and the 'football' he kicked against the wall was actually a bundle of rags. From a very early age he wanted to be a footballer. Bell Street was in the shadow of Ayresome Park and it was on the terraces there that he would cheer on Middlesbrough Football Club, where inside-forward Wilf 'Golden Boy' Mannion became his first hero.

Revie was a promising young player with Newport Boys' Club when he caught the attention of Bill Sanderson, manager of neighbours Middlesbrough Swifts. Sanderson would become an early influence on Revie's whole career, introducing him to dossiers on the opposition and insightful team talks and debriefs. The Swifts were, in effect, a nursery club for Leicester City, and it was this link between the two clubs that led to Revie joining Leicester, despite keen interest from Middlesbrough. This was in August 1944, and a week after arriving at Filbert Street, Revie made his professional debut in the wartime league.

After the war ended, and on the opening day of the 1946/47 season, Revie played his first Football League game, against Manchester City. But on 30 November, during a 1-1 home draw with Tottenham Hotspur, he broke his ankle, seriously threatening his playing career. Revie was absolutely distraught and became totally disillusioned. As he lay in his hospital bed feeling utterly sorry for himself, in walked the Leicester manager Johnny Duncan, and Revie asked straight away how bad the injury was. He was concerned that he would never play again. Duncan replied, 'Your ankle is broken in three places and the doctors say that you'll never kick a ball again.' Revie just closed his eyes and then Duncan said, 'They say it's a thousand to one against you ever playing again, Don.' Duncan then leant over Revie and looking him straight in the eyes said, 'What say we make you that one man in a thousand, son?'

Nineteen-year-old Revie, wiping a tear away, then said, 'I'll be that one man in a thousand if you say so, Boss.' It was then that Johnny Duncan became another huge influence on Revie as he set about convincing his young forward that he would return stronger than ever. Nineteen weeks later Revie played for Leicester's reserves, came through unscathed and continued with his career. He was eternally grateful to Duncan, of course, and the doctors and nurses. He later recalled, 'After the game I went straight into the Turks Head Hotel [owned by Johnny Duncan] and ordered a large whisky.' The barman, knowing that Revie wasn't really much of a drinker, looked astonished until Don told him, 'It's not for me. It's for the doctor.' Revie then took the drink over to the orthopaedic surgeon who had worked minor miracles on his ankle and gave him the drink, saying, 'This is for saving my career.' The doctor grinned and shook Revie's hand warmly.

Duncan won a Scottish cap, scoring against Wales in the 1926 Home Internationals. He had signed for Leicester City from Raith Rovers and on Christmas Day 1924 he scored a double hat-trick in a 7-0 win over Port Vale. He had signed for Leicester on the same day as his brother Tommy. Sadly, in 1939, Tommy died of a burst stomach ulcer and Johnny then became a surrogate father to Tommy's five children, one of whom was called Elsie Duncan.

Duncan continued as a father figure to a clearly troubled young Revie, offering him advice and confidence at every turn until he regained his fitness, and beyond, and Don became even more attached to the Duncans when he met Elsie while on a Scottish holiday in the summer of 1946. Elsie and her two sisters, Jenny and Agnes, had gone to live with Tommy's family in Lochgelly, Fife, and it was here that Don and Elsie met, and then married, three years later, October 1949, in Leicester. Her two brothers, David and John, had remained in Leicester with 'Uncle Jock'.

Now fully fit, Revie began feeling anxious to leave Leicester, even handing a transfer request to Duncan who reluctantly passed it to the board of directors. A few weeks later, high-flying Arsenal registered their interest. Revie travelled to Highbury, but always thought that Arsenal would be above his station and that he may struggle to establish himself in the first team there. Playing in the reserves wasn't something he could contemplate, so he turned down the move. The situation was similar when Manchester City invited him for talks, but after arriving at Maine Road with Elsie, Revie emerged from the talks saying, 'Somehow we did not seem to fit into the place.' He returned to Leicester to await more offers.

After a 2-1 victory at Boothferry Park in August 1949, Revie had walked into the Hull City dressing room to get the autograph of the legendary Raich Carter. After signing his book, Carter simply said, 'Nice game today, Don.'

Two months later Hull contacted Leicester with a view to signing Revie and on 11 November 1949, he travelled north with Leicester chairman Len Shipman and signed for Hull that night for £19,000. The following day, he turned out for his new club in a 2-1 home win over Coventry City. So it was with a heavy heart that Revie left Leicester, but he did so with the wise words of both Bill Sanderson and Johnny Duncan firmly planted in his head, which would become synonymous with how Revie's career panned out, both as a player and as a manager.

Revie made no secret that the reason he had signed for the Tigers was for the opportunity of playing alongside the great Raich Carter. Unfortunately things didn't work out as planned and after less than two years Revie left Hull, saying, 'I have nothing against the club, fans or players. They're a great bunch of lads. But I never really settled here.'

In October 1951, Manchester City paid £25,000 to finally take Revie to Maine Road. During a four-year period he was Footballer of the Year 1955, won the FA Cup in 1956 and was at the heart of the famous Revie Plan.

Based on the deep-lying centre-forward tactic used by the magnificent Hungarian team that thrashed England 6-3 on 25 November 1953, Manchester City reserve centre-forward Johnny Williamson developed a system on similar lines. It was a huge success for the reserves and was eventually adopted by the first team, using Revie in the deep-lying role. Although dubbed by the press as the Revie Plan, that name was something that embarrassed Revie and he never tired of making sure that the full credit went to Williamson, saying on more than one occasion, 'No matter what they say, Johnny, we both know where it came from.'

I recently asked Revie's daughter, Kim, who she considered to be her dad's best friend, and she said, without the slightest hesitation, 'Johnny Williamson, for sure. He and Dad played together at Manchester City and Johnny and his wife Lorraine were Mum and Dad's best friends throughout their whole lives.'

After a two-year stint at Sunderland, who had paid £22,000 for his services, Revie arrived at Leeds for the sum of £14,000, and by the time his playing career ended at Elland Road he had scored 108 goals in 501 career league and cup appearances, and had won six England caps, scoring four goals.

Of course, his playing career was highlighted by the Revie Plan – but it was a Revie Plan of a different kind that would soon be witnessed by success-starved United fans. Revie had first settled in Leeds as a player in 1958 with wife Elsie and four-year-old son Duncan, who had been born on the dark side of the Pennines while Don was playing for Manchester City. They moved into Southlands Avenue and Duncan quickly found a friend; the next-door neighbours' youngest member was a little blond kid who Duncan played football with. 'I can't remember his name as it was a long time ago, think it was Kevin,' said Duncan, 'but I do remember playing football in their back garden. Under the watchful eye of Dad of course.'

Leeds fan George Bilton lived on Harrogate Road in the 1960s and 1970s, 'I lived with my parents in a house right next to the Chained Bull pub and I would often see Don Revie pull up in the car park and go into the nearby newsagents. He would often nod as I sat on our garden wall with a friend of mine, Noel.' The Chained Bull was close to the outer ring road which orbits the city. On the opposite side of the ring road is the area where the Revie family set up home.

After Revie had taken over as manager in March 1961, his plan was still very early in the making. Syd Owen and Les

Cocker both arrived from Luton Town with good pedigree, but both were taken aback by the lack of discipline within the club. Jack Taylor had totally lost the respect of the players to the extent that many openly ignored anything he had to say. Owen had even hinted when he arrived at Elland Road that he had doubts over how long Revie could continue as a player, 'Great player, but his legs are gone.'

Taylor had some good young prospects in Paul Reaney, Paul Madeley and Norman Hunter, as well as reliable defender Willie Bell. Leeds had to avoid relegation to the Second Division to hold on to these players. Cocker and Owen had to coach these youngsters as well as wringing out all they could out of the 'seasoned' professionals. Taylor sometimes criticised their methods, claiming that they were pushing the players too hard in training, but Owen said, 'Taylor felt that our methods could do them physical damage, but Les and I both were of the opinion that a lot of hard work now, while they were still 17 or 18, would stand them in good stead for the future.'

Revie was coming to realise it was time to hang up his boots around the same time that goalkeeper Tommy Younger arrived at the club, in 1961. After slipping a disc while playing for Stoke City in 1959, Younger had been told that he should never play again. He was then invited to become the coach at Toronto City, Canada, where a specialist at the club got him playing again. Sir Stanley Matthews was in Canada with Younger and recommended him to Revie. However, the Leeds boss was initially doubtful, 'I knew Tommy's pedigree of course, he'd played for both Liverpool and Stoke and was a Scottish international and was very experienced; but he was in his 30s and he was known as a bad trainer, so therefore I was sceptical.'

Younger promised that he would give 100 per cent to the club and Revie agreed and signed him at the end of September 1961. Revie was only playing the odd game, his mind (and legs) seemingly elsewhere at the time. Younger, always outspoken, had already said that Revie should be at the helm, 'When I came to Leeds they were really struggling near the bottom of the table. I'd told Don that with the club in such a poor state that he couldn't possibly play and manage at the same time with any degree of success. But Don didn't agree with me.'

Then, on the way back home from a 2-1 defeat at Swansea on 21 October 1961, Revie was sat next to Younger on the coach. Younger said that Revie told him, 'You were right, Tommy, I'm trying to do far too much. I've played my last game for Leeds.' Although he did fill in for a few games after that, Revie made his final appearance in a 2-1 defeat at Huddersfield Town. He played at inside-right, and afterwards handed that shirt to Bobby Collins who made his debut the following week at home to Swansea.

Despite the criticisms aimed at Jack Taylor and Bill Lambton, Leeds did develop a youth policy that harvested young players such as Paul Reaney, Gary Sprake, Norman Hunter, Jimmy Greenhoff and others. It was something that Revie was determined to continue with, progressing it and taking it to the next level. As a Leeds player he had been taking a careful note and casting a watchful eye on who he thought could carry the club forward.

Duncan Revie once told me that sometimes you could almost see and hear the cogs whirring round in his dad's head, 'At our house in Southlands Avenue, we had a room at the back, and Dad would often sit at the table and I swear that you could hear his head clicking!' Don was so intense and he would write page after page of notes always seeming to be happy that he was there.

Billy Bremner said in the late 1960s, 'I became homesick during my early days at Elland Road, so too did Norman

Hunter. I so desperately wanted to leave and return to my native Scotland. And it took some very persuasive talking by Don Revie before I would agree to give it a "go" and allow myself a fair amount of time in which to settle down. I'm glad the boss talked me out of that mood of depression, just think what I would have missed!'

5

For the Love of Albert

IT WAS the Kippax Infant School Christmas party – fancy dress, maybe 1962, or '63 – my mate Andy Robinson, easily the best footballer I'd ever seen when we were kids growing up, had the best fancy dress I've ever seen to this day. I went as Yogi Bear. Sure-fire winner, I thought. My dear old Ma made me this fur (fake) outfit and a large Yogi Bear head was acquired by submitting about three million tops cut off from a Corn Flakes box. I was totally confident as I strolled in with a picnic basket – only to be upstaged by Andy dressed in the gleaming white Leeds United kit with the owl badge and fully 'blacked up' as Albert Johanneson. Imagine the uproar these days. It was genius. He wasn't mocking anybody, he was idolising his hero. And that's just what Albert was to us.

Albert Johanneson, a black South African, arrived in Leeds on the recommendation of a schoolteacher by the name of Barney Gaffney, initially on a three-month trial. There was no transfer fee and Leeds insisted that Johanneson part-fund his own transport from Johannesburg. It was Gaffney who funded Albert's trip. Manager Jack Taylor had a lengthy discussion with the player, a conversation which Albert later revealed he had found very intimidating. Syd

Owen had previously advised Albert to call the manager 'Boss', which he did after every sentence. Typical of life in early 1960s Britain, Taylor said to Johanneson, 'Albert, we have got another coloured lad here, Gerry Francis. He's black as well, so you are not on your own.'

In the match programme for the Huddersfield Town v Leeds United game on 21 January 1961, Francis was described as 'Francis G, right winger. Gerry, a coloured South African, is establishing himself in the front line. He scored two goals in last weekend's 3-0 win over Southampton. United have lost only one of the five matches in which he has been a marksman.'

Albert moved in to the same house as Francis, 13 Noster Hill in Beeston, close to Elland Road. It was a club house and was run by a lovely lady called Edna Wineley. She looked after the players as if they were her own kin.

Les Cocker had to get Albert used to playing in boots, because back in Johannesburg he had always played barefoot. At first, in boots, he appeared slow and clumsy until he got used to them. By the time Albert's trial came to an end, Don Revie had replaced Taylor as manager. If Albert had felt intimidated by Taylor, he was downright scared of Revie, 'He rarely spoke to me. He was very professional but seemed to me to be a bit aloof; he stood out from other players. And I wasn't sure I liked him.'

While he was still on trial, Albert witnessed racial harassment. He had travelled with the players to an FA Cup third-round tie against Sheffield Wednesday at Hillsborough on 7 January 1961. Albert said, 'I had travelled down to watch the match, I was with two office staff and another trialist sat in the back with me. No sooner had we arrived at the Hillsborough stadium, I was greeted with nasty comments from people going to the game; it was abuse about my colour and my country. They were referring to me as a "nigger boy" and asked if my colour washed off in the bath. I was embarrassed for the people in the car with me, but the one driving talked to me over his right shoulder and told me don't worry Albert, it's their problem not yours.

'I slinked down in the back to hide myself, but the abuse didn't stop even when we reached the officials' entrance. As the three people I was with entered the reception, I was stopped by a man on the door, saying that I wasn't welcome in there. The man, who I assumed to be a club official, still refused to let me in, and I knew I wasn't going to be allowed in any official part of the club. Then Billy Bremner came out, he'd heard about the commotion going on at the door and immediately demanded to know why I wasn't being allowed in. He went straight to the man who had refused me entry and told him that I was a Leeds United player and a personal friend of his and to let me in or he'd "give him a good hiding". He even made the man, who by now was badly shaken, apologise to me. I had never before in my life have a white person defend and protect me.'

But once inside the ground, Albert shivered in the bitter cold as insults continued to be hurled at him from all directions. Sadly it continued for some years, from Stoke to Everton, from Sheffield to Swansea and beyond.

Billy Bremner continued to be a good friend to Albert, perhaps because Billy himself knew what it was like to be away from your homeland and living in a strange land. 'Don't be scared to speak out, Albert,' Billy once said. 'Just ask one of us, someone will help you, we're all in this together, a team.'

Three months later, Albert was shaking like a leaf when he was summoned to Revie's office to discuss his trial. It was Tuesday, 4 April 1961, the day after Leeds had played away at Scunthorpe where, despite two goals from Jack Charlton, they had been beaten 3-2. Johanneson had already come to the conclusion that Revie did not rate him and that he would soon be on his way back to South Africa. He gulped hard as he sat down at Revie's desk.

'How do you think you have done in your three months with us, Albert?' asked Revie.

Albert shuffled nervously as he replied, 'I always do my best, Boss, I love the club and I desperately want to stay.'

Revie stood up and parted the window blind with two fingers, peering out over the Fullerton Park training pitches where Syd Owen and Les Cocker were busily putting the players through their paces. Without turning around, Revie then said, 'I've been watching you out there, as have others, and I am amazed at your skill and pace. Your balance is majestic and the way you leave players in your wake is bewildering.'

Revie sat back down, looked at Albert and continued, 'You are a nice man, Albert, and very polite, but I don't want that from you. I want you to get stuck in where it hurts and never give in, can you do that for me and for Leeds United?'

Albert nodded his head furiously, 'Yes, Boss, yes, yes I can!' He then burst into tears.

'Right then, Albert,' said Revie, 'I want you here at Leeds United. You have got yourself a contract. Now stop your snivelling and get back out there. People will look up to you so act accordingly. Remember, this is *my* Leeds United and you are my first ever signing, so don't let me down – or else. Enjoy Leeds United.'

Revie later admitted that he had been swayed by Cocker into signing Johanneson. And, unbeknownst to Albert, two First Division clubs, Newcastle United and West Bromwich Albion, were very keen on signing him.

Four days after his meeting with Revie, Johanneson made his debut in a home game against Swansea Town, where another brace from Charlton earned United a 2-2 draw and another point towards preserving their Second Division status, with four games to go.

Watching Albert that day was 19-year-old John Booth, from Hunslet, who had gone to the game with his cousin Craig, a Swansea fan staying with him.

'My cousin Craig came up with his mum and dad (my dad's brother Ron), who lived in Swansea. We stood in the Lowfields Stand right next to the Scratching Shed, where the noisy set of Leeds fans stood behind the goal. Craig was really scared of the atmosphere but he was also mesmerised by Albert Johanneson running up and down the wing. He had never seen a black player before. I remember that the Leeds fans took Albert to their hearts from that day. He became a big hero.'

I watched Albert Johanneson for the first time in 1966. I had been to my first Leeds game against Blackpool at home on 26 March, two days short of my tenth birthday. But I first saw Albert play on the left wing in a home game against Everton the following month. He scored the final goal in a 4-1 win.

I watched from the Lowfields Road terrace with my dad and his mate John Hamilton, an exiled Geordie and a massive Leeds United fan. We were stood close to the wall at the halfway line when an Everton defender kicked and floored Johanneson. Suddenly all hell let loose and we were jostled as the men around us surged forward, swearing and raising fists at the guilty defender, who disappeared pretty swiftly. I was almost knocked to the ground as Dad and John held me up, but even at just ten years old I enjoyed the atmosphere immensely. In fact I loved it (at the Watford away game at the end of the 2021/22 season, Leeds fans celebrated a second goal and I ended up beneath dozens of jubilant supporters, and loved it – even at 66 years old. Brilliant, better than anything the Blackpool Pleasure Beach can offer).

Albert was a magician with the ball; I can remember him once going round a player with such speed that the defender just laid on the floor staring at the 'Black Flash' disappearing down the wing. On another occasion he nutmegged a Sheffield United defender, who was so annoyed at what Albert had just done that he tried to rugby tackle Albert and missed him completely. Albert literally showed him a clean pair of heels and continued on with the ball closely controlled at his feet, completely oblivious to the flailing opponent he had left behind, sprawled on the grass. Albert was sublime with the ball and in the days of abhorrent racism, it was difficult to make out whether his beaten opponents were frustrated because he was black, or simply whether he was just class.

Sometimes, in fairness, the racism factor was unintentional. Albert was an integral player for Leeds in the 1960s and during that time they were one of the first clubs to bring out a record, a 45rpm single. The club actually released quite a few, one of which actually reached number ten in the charts, but 'Leeds United Calypso', sung by renowned artist Ronnie Hilton, contains these words about Albert, 'I don't know where he comes from, but I think it's Timbuktu.'

Tony Levison was a young Leeds fan of 11 or 12 years of age when Albert moved into 13 Noster Hill, Beeston, 'I saw my first Leeds game in 1960, and in 1962/63 my dad and I got season tickets. I lived with my parents on Cross Flats Avenue, not far from where Albert lived. I was always going down to watch Leeds players train on Fullerton Park and collected loads of autographs, including Albert's, so imagine my delight when he walked into our house one day in 1962. He had become good friends with my dad, Monty, and started calling at our house regularly. Albert loved playing on my dad's drum kit and his set of bongo drums; it was surreal. In 1963, Mum, Dad and I were all invited to Albert's wedding to Norma. It was at Blenheim Chapel in Woodhouse on Wednesday, 27 February. Most of the Leeds players were there, including Grenville Hair, Noel Peyton, Billy Bremner, Jack Charlton, Freddie Goodwin, Willie Bell and Don Revie. Grenville Hair was Albert's best man.

'Albert's first daughter, Yvonne, was born at the end of 1963, and they moved to Carr Manor in Moortown. Sadly, Albert never visited us at our home after they moved.'

Towards the end of his glorious career at Leeds, Albert would frequent the bars and pubs of the city centre – much to the disapproval of Don Revie. Albert's drinking habits got so bad that in the end Revie shunned the very man he had given the opportunity to to display his talents for all to see. There was always a bottle of whisky in the dressing room, mainly for the benefit of Bobby Collins, who liked a wee nip before 'going into battle', and so too did Billy Bremner. But on one occasion Albert had been substituted late in the first half and at the half-time whistle, the players returned to the dressing room. When the players went out for the second half they left Albert to get dressed. By the time they returned after the game, Albert had finished the bottle of whisky and was laid comatose and fully dressed in the old bath (dry at the time) that was used only by Jack Charlton.

The Nags Head in Leeds was always a favourite boozer of mine. On the junction of the Headrow and Vicar Lane, it was always a busy pub, and was run at the time by Don Leech and his wife Mari, who used to help out at my local pub in Kippax, the Royal Oak, owned by Harry Britten. In the Nags Head we had our own 'Leeds United wall' and in the top-right corner was a great action picture of Albert, just above a photo of Norman Hunter with the PFA Players' Player of the Year trophy, which he became the first winner of in 1974.

Albert would often pop in to the Nags as he was hardly getting a game those days down at Elland Road. Mari always gave him a bottle of K cider. It was strong, and very nice. Don and Mari never took any money from Albert, who was always dressed impeccably, in a nice camel coat with black collar, pink silk tie with gold pin through it. He looked the business, but inside he was a broken man. I have a photo of me and Albert stood in front of the wall with him pointing to his photo.

Nigel Davey also got to be good mates with Albert, and he has some wonderful stories about his time at Leeds, 'I was once out for a stroll with Albert, after a training session on Fullerton Park, and we saw a pram by the side of the road. There was nobody about and without looking in the pram, Albert just playfully pushed it, but it sped off down the road. Just then a car came round the corner and swerved to miss the pram, but just caught it side on, enough to send the baby flying through the air and into the hedge. Albert panicked and ran off in the other direction. The driver got out and just as I arrived, he was picking up the baby – it was a kids' doll! The driver gave me a few choice words and got back in his car, muttering, and drove off. I caught up with Albert who was distraught and crying. I told him about the "kid" but not before I'd had a bit of fun with him.'

Nigel was playing for Great Preston Juniors in 1964 when he was spotted by Leeds scouts. He went on to make his debut at home to West Bromwich Albion in a League Cup third-round tie in October 1965.

Although Nigel made only 20 first-team appearances, he was a valued member of Don Revie's squad. Don famously treated his players, backroom staff, laundry staff and cleaners as equals, creating a unique family bond within the club.

Over the years I have become good friends with Nigel, and his brothers Phil and Andy. Nigel was an outstanding full-back, who played in Europe for United, but he must go down as one of the most unluckiest footballers ever. As if being behind Terry Cooper and Paul Reaney in the pecking order wasn't bad enough, Leeds had reached the 1972 FA Cup Final in 1972 and in a league game at Stoke City just a month prior, on 8 April, Cooper broke his leg. Although tragic for Terry of course, it presented an opportunity for Nigel to make a dream appearance in a Wembley final. But, unbelievably, cruel fate conspired against him as on the very same day that Cooper broke his leg at the Victoria Ground, Nigel, playing for Leeds' reserves at home to West Bromwich Albion, broke his leg too. The first person to visit the downhearted Davey was none other than Don Revie. 'I'm absolutely gutted for you, son,' said Revie as he sat on the edge of the bed. 'As soon as you're well enough, you and Sandra have a nice holiday on me,' he added as he put a stuffed envelope in Nigel's hand.

Sadly, things went from bad to worse for Albert as he struggled with alcoholism. He was transferred to York City in 1970 but it wasn't a happy time. He had lost his pace and was overweight as he freely admitted, 'I'd lost my fitness and my touch. The crowds were much smaller than what I'd been used to and therefore I could hear the racial abuse much more, "fat nigger" was just one of the remarks.'

York released Albert after just two seasons as they deemed him too unfit, and his drinking was becoming a real problem. He lost his house and possessions and his wife left him and took their two children abroad to live. In 1995 Albert Johanneson was found dead, alone, in 16 Gledhow Towers, a tiny flat in Leeds 8.

6

'The Wee Man Cometh'

AFTER FINISHING the previous season in 14th place, Leeds prepared for the 1961/62 Second Division campaign with a couple of pre-season friendlies against Third Division Peterborough United. On 9 August, Leeds won 4-1 at Elland Road with two goals coming from Billy Bremner, and one each from John McCole and Albert Johanneson. Three days later, United travelled to London Road and inflicted a 6-3 defeat on Peterborough – Bremner again getting on the score sheet along with a hat-trick from Noel Peyton and one each from McCole and Derek Mayers.

They opened their league account with two wins, 1-0 at home to Charlton Athletic and 3-1 at Brighton & Hove Albion, Bremner scoring in both games. But sadly that run wouldn't last.

Meanwhile, the relationship between Don Revie and Harry Reynolds continued to blossom and the youth policy initially set up by Bill Lambton was much improved and thriving. Young stars of the future such as Terry Cooper, Paul Reaney, Gary Sprake, Norman Hunter and Jimmy Greenhoff were plying their trade in the Northern Intermediate League under the watchful eye of proud 'parents' Revie and Reynolds. The whole atmosphere around Elland Road was better than it had been for several years, and a glimmer of light was beginning to show at the end of the long tunnel.

Reynolds had assisted Revie with everything he required, financial and otherwise. Revie's personal touch with the parents when recruiting youngsters for the club was impeccable and was without doubt the reason that so many of his future stars came to Leeds, a club that at that time was almost unheard of outside of Yorkshire. But one of Revie's most vital recruits was not a youngster at all.

Bobby Collins, just 5ft 4in tall, was nearly 32 when Revie brought him to Elland Road in March 1962. Collins had a blazing row with Everton manager Harry Catterick, who told him that he was being dropped and was to be replaced by Dennis Stevens, who had recently been signed from Bolton Wanderers. Collins erupted, claiming, rightly so, that he had been and was the club's best player, then he stormed out of Goodison Park. Revie, who had been keeping tabs on Collins and had already spoken with the player previously, acted swiftly, and within hours of hearing about the altercation at Everton he was being driven across the Pennines by Manny Cussins with Harry Reynolds in the back.

On arrival at Bobby's home in Aintree, Bobby was still seething with anger and was sat with his wife Betty. But after long discussions into the night, the three men from Leeds were on their way back home with his signature and the club £25,000 lighter. It later transpired that just across from Aintree, Liverpool boss Bill Shankly had heard about the argument at Everton and moved in to sign Collins himself, but he was too late.

Eyebrows were raised in the footballing world – why on earth would Collins leave a top-flight outfit to go to a club in debt and fighting a relegation battle?

Bobby must have harboured doubts himself because after just a few weeks he asked for a transfer.

Revie had given Collins permission to remain in Aintree and commute to Elland Road, training less than his Leeds team-mates, but Bobby was a fitness fanatic and Don knew that he would train at home when not at Leeds. He was even known on occasion to travel to Majorca alone and train and run solidly for a week before returning home. But Bobby tired of all the extra travelling back and forth and he also began having second thoughts about joining Leeds, who were in deep trouble near the foot of the Second Division. Once again, Revie's sensitive managerial skills rose to the fore and after long talks between the manager and his player, Collins agreed to give it a bit longer, and see how things panned out before he made a decision over his future.

Jack Charlton later recalled, 'With Bobby proving a real inspiration on the field, we started to make progress on the field and Bobby had a double incentive to succeed and make Leeds succeed with him. He also had a fierce, burning desire to prove Everton wrong in letting him leave. Bobby knew that there were many fans at Goodison who felt that he should never have been allowed to leave. He had reigned supreme at Everton for so long. Bobby was definitely driven by an undying desire to take Leeds United up to the top flight and return to Goodison Park to do battle with his old club.'

Eddie Gray arrived at Leeds a year after Collins. He saw instantly the effect that he was having on the team, and the club. Collins had signed for Everton from Celtic, which endeared Eddie to him, 'Bias aside, I have to say that Bobby has never received the praise that he deserved. He was, in my opinion, the most influential player in Leeds United's history.'

Few would argue with that sentiment. Charlton, not one to usually show his emotions, said at a Queens Hotel dinner in 1968, 'His super fitness, his abundant energy, his supreme skills as a footballer made their effects felt upon each and every one of us. Leeds United were being driven by this midget human dynamo, and every one of Bobby Collins's team-mates was responding with a will. So much so that the team spirit became as good as a goal to us; we seldom thought about the danger of defeat – we thought much more of what we were going to do to the opposition.'

The day that Revie had finally retired as a player and handed the number eight shirt to Collins was a very significant point in the history of Leeds United. Collins, from his debut the following week against Swansea (in which he scored in a 2-0 win), would play in all but five games for the next three seasons.

Bobby was a midfield player who could virtually do anything. He wasn't tall but he dominated every match – physically, mentally and technically.

Eddie Gray remembered, 'He was very much the general, and his leadership qualities were especially necessary with all the young players that Leeds were bringing into the team. Bobby did much to prevent Leeds from being relegated in that 1961/62 season. They then finished fifth in the Second Division in 1963, the year I came to Elland Road.'

Making his debut at the same time as Collins was full-back Chris Mason, for whom Revie paid Sheffield United £10,000. Mason played in the final 11 games and was a key member of the team as they battled against the drop to the Third Division.

Willie Bell had arrived at Elland Road in July 1960 and made his debut against Leyton Orient on 7 September. Revie was the inside-right that day and had enough faith in the stocky Scot, who had joined from Glasgow side Queen's Park, to involve him in his plans when he became manager.

On the morning of Saturday, 17 March 1962, the week after Collins had made his debut, apprentice goalkeeper Gary Sprake was enjoying a lie in at his digs. He had already played a couple of games in the reserves but he was due to play that afternoon for the juniors. Then, suddenly, there was a very loud knock on the door; it was a club official, there was an emergency. Sprake was needed to play in the first team, 250 miles away at Southampton. He was whisked by car to Ringway airport, then rushed through security and bundled into a small aircraft where Sprake discovered that there was only one other person on board – the pilot.

As the two-seater flew through the clouds, the 16-year-old was sick, and was drip-white, caused by the flight and nerves. Revie was waiting as the plane touched down at Southampton and the manager hustled his goalkeeper into a waiting car. Revie explained the reason for Sprake's dramatic arrival. First-choice keeper Tommy Younger had been taken ill with tonsillitis and with reserve Alan Humphries unfit, the time had come for Sprake to make his debut.

Unfortunately, a 4-1 defeat put paid to any fairy-tale ending for Sprake, but he had done enough to impress the manager, and the following season he would replace Scottish international Younger as the regular starter. Southampton fan Ian Sinclair was at The Dell that afternoon, 'None of the crowd knew what was happening, rumour was that the Leeds keeper had been taken seriously ill. The kick-off had been delayed and then suddenly the teams emerged from the tunnel, with Leeds fielding this really young keeper with large curly blond hair – although the Saints won fairly easy in the end, young Sprake had a brilliant game to be honest.'

Meanwhile, Leeds' fight for survival continued with a hotly contested 1-1 draw at Bury on Good Friday 1962. It was claimed 15 years later by the *Daily Mirror* that Bury's player-manager Bob Stokoe had been bribed by Don Revie to the tune of £500 to throw the game. All bribery allegations made against Revie over the years were proved to be false and this one was no exception – however, from that day on, Revie and Stokoe would be sworn enemies for the rest of their lives.

Stokoe had insisted that Revie had offered him the cash to take it easy, and when he refused, Revie had allegedly asked if he could speak to the Bury players instead. Stokoe said he then reported it to his chairman.

Author Dave Tomlinson wrote, 'Stokoe was a bitter Revie critic. It's difficult to understand where Revie would have found £500 given United's precarious finances and even more puzzling, why did Bury not report Leeds to the [Football] League and Alan Hardaker or the Football Association?'

Billy Bremner often recalled that Stokoe was an extremely bitter man who had a personal vendetta against both him and Revie, to the point that every time they came into contact, Stokoe would never fail to make a jibe against the pair. On one occasion, Harry Reynolds witnessed one of these verbal taunts and reported it to Hardaker, but nothing came of it. Brian Clough remembered Stokoe calling him a cheat as he rolled around in agony in the Roker Park goalmouth after picking up the injury to his knee that would end his playing career with Sunderland.

Meanwhile, four days later, yet another fiercely fought contest, a 0-0 draw with Bury at Elland Road, set up a nail-biting final Saturday of the season. Bottom club Brighton were on 31 points and had to travel to Luton Town. Bristol Rovers, on 33 points, were at Derby County. Swansea, level on points with Bristol, were at home to Sunderland. Leeds, on 34 points, had to travel to Newcastle United, having won only two previous games on the road all season.

A crowd of just under 22,000 were at St James' Park with around 3,000 from Leeds, most of them with jitters. Vic Stanley was at the game, having travelled up with three mates from Methley. He recalls, 'I remember being pretty nervous. This was a very important game in Leeds United's history and the pressure was on, there was no doubt about that. One of the lads, Mick Atkinson, had just bought a second-hand Triumph Herald; it was a convertible but the vinyl roof had seen better days to be honest. And there was a little hole in the floor in the back, right where I was sat with Melv Miller. Stuart Thorpe was in the front passenger seat. I think we were near Boroughbridge on the A1 when exhaust fumes began seeping through the floor. When we got to Scotch Corner we had to stop for Melv to be sick – we were never sure if it was car sickness, the exhaust fumes or match nerves.'

Vic and his mates stood on the 'Pop Side' and the nerves of all the Leeds fans were settled somewhat as United bombarded the Newcastle goal from the off, but an early goal eluded them – until just after half an hour. Albert Johanneson had been relentless down the left and was a constant threat to the Newcastle rearguard, which was finally pierced when Johanneson cut inside and unleashed a shot that crashed in off the underside of the bar. Forward Billy McAdams, from Belfast, fired in a second in the 65th minute and an own goal ten minutes later secured United's survival. Once again, Bobby Collins had been phenomenal in the middle, with tough tackling and orchestrating United's flowing movement, using Billy Bremner at every opportunity. Bremner had played in all but three games all season.

Keith Johnson, from Garforth, played his part that day too. His mate Brian had been asked by Revie to take Bremner's car to Newcastle, but he couldn't do it, so Keith, about 20 at the time, got the job. This came about because Bremner wanted to take his car to Newcastle and join the team there and then travel up to Stirling afterwards. Revie was OK with him about that, but said he had to travel with the team on the train to Newcastle. So, as a compromise, Revie arranged for Bremner's car to be at Newcastle so that he could then drive to Scotland.

After the welcome win at St James' Park, Billy headed north in his car, a Singer Gazelle, and Keith boarded the train with Revie and his players for the trip back to Leeds. Keith says it was a great experience to be with the players and have a drink or two with them, 'I was sat with Freddie Goodwin and Cliff Mason, it was great. Don Revie bought me a couple of bottles of beer and thanked me.'

Keith had a colourful upbringing. Born in Cheltenham in 1942, he was three weeks old when he was moved to a home in London. Three more weeks later, he was adopted by 'a lovely couple' from Liverpool where they were living and working, and where he would spend his early childhood. While there, he attended the Dovedale Infant School. Keith said, 'One of my classmates was George Harrison, and John Lennon was a couple of years above me, although I didn't get to know them personally.'

In 1952, when Keith was ten, he was taken to Leeds with his parents, who were originally from the city. He says, 'My dad was from the Vinery's off York Road in Leeds and was a sewing machine mechanic, and my mum was from Stoney Rock Lane in Leeds, and had a job sewing parachutes. We moved to Beeston, which is where it all started for me with Leeds United. All around us were the club houses, where the young players stayed under the watchful eye of a trusted landlady, who worked closely with the club. The Leeds players would always come out on to the streets and play football with us younger kids. Albert Johanneson, Norman Hunter, Billy, and a young Paul Madeley were always knocking about on the streets with a football. Also there was Andy McCall, who would have a son, Stuart McCall, in years to come.

'I got to know some of the players well, and me and some mates would go down to Elland Road and watch them training. The Leeds Supporters Club was on Elland Road, and once I was old enough to drink, I'd go in there with my mates and we even helped build the extension room to it, that was near the souvenir shop, and we started using the club as our local. We formed a supporters' club football team, and were allowed to play on Fullerton Park and get changed in the Fullerton Park dressing room. They even provided us with a kit. Not only that, but Cyril Partridge took some of our training sessions as did Freddie Goodwin and Don Revie himself.

'Don always called me "Ginner" but, for some reason, Norman Hunter always called me "Ginge".

'Don Revie usually enjoyed his Sunday lunch and a glass of Carlsberg lager at home with his family, but on this occasion by way of a small celebration, he took the family out for a carvery. But as he chewed on his Yorkshire puddings he scribbled little notes on pieces of paper. I was fortunate enough to meet Elsie Revie on a number of occasions and she spoke fondly about how engrossed and excited Don got about Leeds avoiding the drop that summer and how he relished taking United forward. "Don loved everything about Leeds, but his mind never stopped working and it was our job as a family to 'make' him relax," she said. "We wanted him to win though."'

7

Steak, Sherry and Eggs

DON REVIE'S preparations in the summer months of 1962 included the possibility of bringing John Charles back to Leeds from Italy. Supporters held their breath at the prospect of their hero returning home. The impending transfer also aided another deal that had been in the pipeline since Christmas 1961, after the club's Scottish scouts had spotted a centre-forward playing for Airdrie. Jim Storrie had impressed during a cup defeat to Celtic and they had immediately alerted Revie, who approached Storrie only to be turned down flat on the grounds that Leeds looked like they were heading for the Third Division.

Revie would be back; he was not about to give up, but for now his priorities lay elsewhere.

The strenuous efforts of Revie during the summer months left him little time with his wife Elsie and young children Kim and Duncan, but he did manage to arrange a few days' golfing with Elsie in his beloved Scotland. However, just two days into their break, news reached Don that the Charles deal could be on. On 3 July, Revie, chairman Harry Reynolds and director Percy Woodward flew from Yeadon Airport to Turin. Director Albert Morris flew from his holiday in Monte Carlo. Many European sides wanted

Charles on hearing of his availability, but the Welshman, much to the delight of his wife Peggy, had set his heart on a return to Leeds. His three children were also overjoyed at the prospect. David Charles, who lives in my village of Kippax, said, 'I was so happy that Dad decided to come home.'

But the deal was complicated; Juventus fought hard to hold on to their star. Negotiations moved back and forth, frustrating both sides. Three weeks later Morris drove from Monte Carlo to Diano Marina on the Italian Riviera to meet Charles, who was on holiday there. As a result of the meeting, the two men flew to Turin for the next round of talks. After an hour and a half Morris rang Reynolds to inform him that a deal had finally been struck. After completion of the medical, United handed over a fee of £53,000, another record for them.

But supporters would have mixed feelings about the return. John Walker, who had walked behind Charles with his mates when he left Middleton for games at Elland Road in the mid-1950s, said, 'I never got to see John play when he was here before but I was determined to see him this time round. I had a paper round now as well.'

Pat Connor was outside the West Stand at Elland Road for Charles's return. Dozens of journalists and photographers gathered around the entrance. 'I was right near the entrance and within touching distance of Charles, he turned around and spoke to me, but I haven't got a clue what he said to me,' said Pat. 'But the photographer with me stood near Charles was on the front of a *Yorkshire Evening Post* souvenir newspaper that they brought out, and I've still got it.'

Leeds' existing debt had increased considerably because of the deal, and some unpopular decisions would have to be made by the directors. The fee for Charles, coupled with the signing of Jim Storrie, who had now agreed to join

Leeds, took the combined outlay to £135,000, and, after other spending and months later, the debt was £200,000. While most of this money came from the board, Reynolds pushed for a motion to increase admission prices. The other directors fidgeted nervously around the boardroom table as Reynolds announced, 'We need £83,000 from gate receipts to break even. Our crowds averaged over 13,000 last season and a price of three bob [15p today] would give us 40 grand. John Charles will draw crowds of over 20,000 and at the same ticket price we'd clear £63,000. However, we can push ticket prices up. I reckon the fans will stand seven and a half bob [approximately 40p]. That would raise almost £160,000.'

Most of the directors winced; that would be a hike of 50 per cent. It was said later that Reynolds considered an increase of £1. Leeds were suddenly the most expensive team to support outside London, and the supporters were going to be very angry indeed.

The directors increased prices by the proposed three bob (15p), proclaiming that they were 'giving the public a chance to show the firmness of the promises to support the club if the directors embarked on a policy of teambuilding and bringing top personalities to Elland Road'. Season ticket holders were asked to pay ten guineas (£10.50) for the West Stand and eight guineas (£8.40) for the Lowfields Road Stand.

'It is the first price increase in six years,' said Reynolds, who invited anyone who objected to discuss it with him – he gave certain times when he was at Elland Road for anyone to call and see him. Reynolds claimed that he had already spoken to dozens of fans, and that they had all left agreeing with him. He said that the first two home games would be all-ticket and prices were heavily increased all around the ground. The directors claimed that there had been a lot of enquiries for season tickets, but the fans were far from convinced and the *Yorkshire Evening Post* was inundated with letters of protest. 'We supporters have finally been let down by this outrageous exploitation'; 'We shall not attend any more first-team games'; 'After all the promises, we have to pay these absurd prices'; 'Me nor my son will not set foot in Elland Road again'; 'What a kick in the teeth for the fans'; 'Thanks for bringing back the King – pity I can't afford to watch him'; these were just a handful of the bags full of letters of anger. But Reynolds was unrepentant and instead was absolutely incensed at these remarks, 'We have given the fans what they wanted, if the public do not want football in Leeds, why should *we* bother?'

Some fans were in favour, however. Mr Amer from Hull wrote directly to Charles himself, 'Thar't cost us very dear. Aye, US – We're carrying t'load. But if tha shoves us up. Tha'rt more na welcome at Elland Road!'

Another poetic verse came from Mrs Sunderland of Leeds, 'Come four divisions of the league in arms. We shall shock them, naught shall make us rue. If Leeds United to King John be true!'

But the move would not be plain sailing for Charles – far from it. He was unfit, overweight and way off his physical best. He was deemed too unfit to participate in the pre-season matches, being assigned to special training duties at Elland Road instead. But English football was totally different to the Italian game that Charles had mastered so well.

On 7 August, Leeds kicked off their pre-season schedule with a 7-1 win at Morecambe. Christie Park saw a hat-trick from Ian Lawson, a new signing from Burnley, one goal from another new boy, Jim Storrie, Noel Peyton on the score sheet too, and two own goals rounded off the afternoon. Leeds then had a double-header with Leicester City, going down

4-2 at Elland Road on 11 August and drawing 2-2 at Filbert Street two days later. Storrie scored on both occasions.

Leeds won the first game of the season, 1-0 at Stoke City, with Storrie scoring on his league debut. A scorching-hot day saw two footballing legends playing against each other in the Second Division; Leeds had Charles and Stoke City had a 47-year-old Stanley Matthews in their ranks.

Leeds stalwart Grenville Hair, their longest-serving player at the time by a country mile, was at right-back that day, but more importantly he was a long-time friend of Charles. In November 1948, he arrived at Leeds on the same day as Charles, and they both spent their national service with the 12th Royal Lancers based at Barnard Castle in Durham, and Hair could not conceal his delight at Charles's return to Elland Road.

For the first home match, against Rotherham United, just over 14,000 turned up. Reynolds stormed, 'These people want summat for nowt!' Leeds lost an entertaining game 4-3, and Reynolds made a public apology for his outbursts and verbal attacks on the fans, but three days later the visit of Sunderland attracted just 17,753 – half of what the gate should have been for a game against such opposition. To make matters worse, Charles had made a terrible start to the season. It was quickly apparent that he just wasn't the player he had been during his previous stint at Leeds. He had scored in the defeat to Rotherham, but he was clearly lacking in fitness. The method of play was more relaxed in Italy, suiting Charles's style down to the ground, but he was struggling to acclimatise to his new surroundings. Leeds beat Sunderland thanks to a Billy Bremner goal, but they needed Charles to get more involved. He was never a brilliant trainer, he seemed not to need it, but now, five years on from his departure, he was yards slower and couldn't train to the levels expected. This caused several clashes between Charles and trainer Les Cocker.

Meanwhile, Reynolds issued another public apology and scrapped the price increases. He said in a statement, 'I said a few things out of the heat of my disappointed enthusiasm that I should not have said. I am very sorry. I have been wrong, as wrong as could be … I must take blame for the whole business.' With admission prices now back at a more affordable level, United fans returned – the attendance for the next home game against Bury soared to 28,313.

Charles continued to struggle and, although he scored in a 1-1 draw at Huddersfield, his lack of fitness was painfully obvious for all to see, as well as his tactical awareness as a whole.

Storrie said, 'Italian teams don't train as hard as those in England and as a consequence, sadly, Charles didn't have enough speed or stamina for league football in this country. That particular match at Huddersfield, although he scored our goal, he was always getting caught offside because he couldn't get back fast enough.' This would be Charles's final goal for the club.

Leeds fan James Croft was at Leeds Road that day with his 16-year-old brother John, 'I had celebrated my 21st birthday the night before and I was a little hungover. I said to John something like, "It looks as though Charles was out with us last night." He seemed so lethargic, not quite with it.

'I still live in the same house near Elland Road and these days I watch everybody going past on their way to the games. I don't go these days, although I went to a youth team game a few years ago and enjoyed it. In the 1960s, the reserves would play at Elland Road when the first team was away and if I hadn't gone, I would go to the reserve game. Only the West Stand would be open, but we had some great afternoons. I remember, you could hear all the players shouting and there would be a big thud when the ball hit the wall or the hoardings, something you never heard at first team games.

'I met Paul Reaney recently, just by chance, and I was amazed how well he looked. My brother lives now in New Zealand and I sent him, or rather my son did, the picture of me and Reaney and he couldn't believe it either. Paul Reaney was just breaking through into the first team around 1962, so he'll be a few years younger than me, but even so ... I'm 81 now, and I have all on putting the bins out.'

Storrie had turned out to be far more influential to Revie's plans than Charles – and was yet another example of the manager's persistence. In early August, Revie headed back to Scotland.

Storrie recalled, 'Don Revie and Harry Reynolds came to our house, and when my wife told them I was at work, they came there. They were very persuasive. I listened to what Mr Revie had to say and I was immediately impressed by his sincerity. He laid his cards on the table, I remember him telling me, "The sky's the limit – we're going to be like Real Madrid." Well, I did feel that was a bit ludicrous; Leeds weren't even the best team in Yorkshire then. I had no desire to go to Leeds because they were in the Second Division, near the bottom of the Second Division at that. But Revie told me that they had got Bobby Collins and John Charles and all of a sudden the package looked pretty impressive. When I joined Leeds it was like going into a different world. I found them so much more professional than clubs in Scotland – everything was so well organised that it made you want to work at your game.

'One cannot help getting caught up in an atmosphere like this. All managers like to think that their players are prepared to run through a brick wall for them, but this was so true as far as Don was concerned. He treated us like men, as individuals.

'His attention to detail was remarkable: one morning I happened to mention that my son wasn't well, and he immediately arranged for the club doctor to give him a thorough check-up. Don knew that if I was going on to the field worrying about my little fellow, I couldn't give my best. All this may sound trivial, but you'd be surprised how much these little acts of kindness help to establish a good team spirit and player/manager relationship.

'On the eve of my Leeds debut, I was wandering round the hotel looking for the other players and bumped into Don in the foyer. "If you're looking for the other lads, they're in the bar," said Don. "Go in and have a drink, son." I thought he was trying me out to see whether or not I drank, as managers in Scotland frowned on that sort of thing. But sure enough, I found the lads in the bar, knocking back beer. Don trusted his players not to overdo it – his attitude was, "If they want to drink, I prefer them to do it in front of me rather than behind my back."'

All the talk the next day was, understandably, about the return of Charles. But it was Storrie who took all the glory, firing in a beautiful goal from ten yards out after 40 minutes, which proved to be the winner. Storrie finished his first season as the club's top scorer with 25 goals and continued to play a vital role in the rise of Leeds in the 1960s.

Tony Hill of the excellent website mightyleeds.co.uk said, 'I would call "Diamond Jim" splay-footed and often wondered at his ability to beat a defender, they were probably mesmerised by his feet! He was also the first player I saw do the trick of centring with any force by bringing one foot behind the other to deliver the cross. Many happy memories of the "Pillock from Kirkintilloch" as a friend of mine used to endearingly call him, jokingly rather than with malice.'

Revie earned a reputation in the early 1960s for getting his man, whether it was a much sought-after schoolboy international such as Eddie Gray or Peter Lorimer, or a seasoned professional like Bobby Collins or Eddie Gray.

Storrie, along with Willie Bell and Eric Smith, was a big favourite of long-time Leeds fan Tony Winstanley, of Castleford, West Yorkshire, 'Jim Storrie was one of my first heroes at Elland Road. We got Jim from Airdrieonians and he quickly made his mark to become Leeds United's go-to striker. His nickname "Diamond Jim" was due to Airdrie shirts having a "V" on the front and back. I remember a ditty about Jim that was quite popular, but very tongue in cheek as we all loved the man. It went like this:

> *There is a pillock from Kirkintilloch,*
> *whose name is Jim Storrie,*
> *how we got him, I don't know,*
> *but now we're fucking sorry!*

'Obviously, pillock rhymes with his birthplace, but I never heard a bad word about Jim. Ungainly? Yes. Deadly? Certainly. When I was 15 some fellow Leeds fans started a Sunday league side, which I played a couple of friendlies with. The team played on Scott Hall Fields, Leeds, still do as far as I'm aware. Their name is Kirk Sports, taken after the place, Kirkintilloch. Just the thought of Leeds fans associating one of their players with their local football club shows the affection that they had for him. He ran a newsagents at Hyde Park corner in Leeds before moving back to Scotland to play for Aberdeen.'

Eric Smith, another of Tony's heroes, arrived at Elland Road in June 1960 from Celtic and was another of the unsung heroes in Revie's ambitious plans. Smith was a typical Scottish hardman who would run through a brick wall to get to the ball. He was pivotal for a couple of seasons when we needed that fight and determination to stop the club sinking down the league. But on 15 September 1962 at Elland Road, he clashed with Chelsea forward Graham Moore, sustaining a broken leg that put paid to his career. Tony recalled, 'Such was his commitment that his career was basically ended in that game against Chelsea. It was a horrific break and emanated from a really badly executed tackle that would have resulted in a sending-off had it not been for the fact that it was Eric who committed the lunging tackle and Moore was probably lucky to still be walking.

'As a 12-year-old, watching a man break his own leg to help Leeds United made me realise that no matter how well I supported this magnificent team, I would never be worthy to lace the boots of my heroes. I have a tear in my eye for those players even now.'

Smith played just one more game for Leeds, and moved to Morton in June 1964. Tony continues, 'When I first started watching Leeds United in the early '60s the Scottish tradition was already at Elland Road. The left-back from 1960 to 1967 was Willie Bell. I soon realised what was meant by the term "hardmen". I'm sure that Norman Hunter must have been influenced by Willie Bell. Even the club described him as "hewn from granite". Willie played over 200 times for Leeds and I never heard any criticism of him from Leeds fans. Another of those players that was "side before self" every time he pulled on the white shirt. He was very much a left-sided player but I'm sure that he would have played anywhere for the cause. After a Scotland game against Brazil in 1966, Willie was singled out for special praise by none other than Jairzhino. When he left Leeds he moved on to Birmingham before moving to the USA.

'In a strange twist to the impression given as a football hardman, Willie and his wife formed a religious ministry in America and back home in England. The ministry cares for the welfare of prisoners both in the States and in Britain and now he lives here in Yorkshire. Now in his 85th year, he is someone I will always remember when thinking of those '60s players who shaped my life.'

Gerry Goode met Willie and his wife Mary when they visited him in Fulford Prison, York, in 1996, 'I was 18 and was serving an 18-month sentence for a car theft and both Willie and Mary were brilliant and really helped me through a rough period of my life. We talked about religion, as you'd expect, but also about Leeds United and Willie's career. Before I was sentenced I was a York City fan, but after meeting Willie and Mary on a number of occasions, I became a Leeds United supporter and still remain so. I am married now and my son, Andy, 19, and I are season ticket holders in the East Stand.'

Revie had been keeping a watchful eye on his youngsters; he knew that some of his older charges were getting ever nearer to the end of their careers, but with careful guidance and sensible management a blend of the two could be achieved. Bremner, for instance, was safely under the wing of Bobby Collins, as the pair operated together with Collins dragging Bremner in from the wing, when the need arose, to great effect. For a few years Bremner had been saying to Revie that he wanted to play inside, but the boss had his doubts, thinking that he wasn't quite ready for that role yet.

With thoughts of a return to Scotland still in Billy's thoughts, Revie was monitoring the situation almost by the day. He had been steadily clearing the decks of surplus players; Gerry Francis had gone to York City, Billy McAdams had been taken by Brentford, Tonbridge had taken John Kilford, Bobby Cameron was on his way to Southend United and Bury had agreed terms with Derek Mayers. Revie, as you would expect, saw each outgoing player personally before they left, giving them all something in the way of a small 'thank you'.

Eric Smith had been a stalwart in defence during the 1961/62 fight for survival. Noel Peyton and Grenville Hair both gave excellent service, Hair appearing 443 times over 16 years for Leeds, the only club he played for. He later moved on to manage Bradford City where tragically, in 1968, he suffered a heart attack while taking a training session and died. He was just 36. Peyton was snapped up from Shamrock Rovers and made his debut against Bolton Wanderers on 1 February 1958. He later joined York in July 1963.

The personnel was changing fast at Elland Road and a few days before a fixture at Swansea in September 1962, the reserves travelled to Anfield. United's team that day was one of the youngest ever in what was known then as the Central League. Teenager Gary Sprake was in goal and the side included Paul Reaney, Terry Cooper, Norman Hunter, Paul Madeley, Rod Johnson and Peter Lorimer.

Reserve games used to get attendances of 1,000, sometimes 2,000, and this game attracted 2,966. Leeds fan Andrew Cochrane, from Wakefield, was there. He was working for a maintenance firm doing work on the Mersey Tunnel. Andrew sadly died in 2021 at the age of 81, but his son Rob told me how he followed Leeds all over the country and was 'chuffed to bits' when he discovered that the reserves were playing at Anfield the same week that he was working there. It was a real feather in the cap back then to see a reserve away home; doing so was virtually unheard of. 'Best of it was,' said Rob, 'Leeds won, I can't remember the exact score but he [Andrew] said the Leeds team were absolutely brilliant.

'He said that a couple Leeds players that night won't be long before they are in the first team.'

Andrew would be proved right. The full line-up was: Gary Sprake, Paul Reaney, Barrie Wright, Mike Addy, Paul Madeley, Norman Hunter, Ronnie Blackburn, Rod Johnson, Peter Lorimer, John Hawksby and Terry Cooper. In the dugout were Don Revie, Les Cocker and Syd Owen. The young Leeds team won the game 3-1 thanks to a hat-trick by Blackburn. Alf Arrowsmith grabbed a consolation for the Reds.

Five days later, Leeds were away at Swansea Town, and on the team coach were Hunter, Reaney, Sprake and Johnson – presumably to gain experience of being around the first-team players. But less than an hour and a half before kick-off Revie gathered his four youngsters together and told them that they would all be playing.

Johnson lived in Kippax until his sad death in December 2019 and he told me about that day, 'I nearly fainted on the spot, I couldn't believe it! As it turned out it was my mum who fainted – during the game. Afterwards, the boss was the first to call at our home to see if Mum was OK. He left some juicy steaks behind and made sure I was OK for sherry and eggs, a concoction that he gave to the players. It wasn't the best of combinations, but you got used to it. Revie said it was good for us, so that was good enough for us.'

During early spells of pressure by Swansea, young Sprake held firm. Then, against the run of play, Leeds took the lead with just over ten minutes gone. Fine play down the flank by Albert Johanneson saw him release the ball inside for

Bremner who then put a delightful pass through for Johnson to latch on to and weave through a pack of defenders before firing low and hard past keeper Noel Dwyer. On 15 minutes, following a corner, Sprake was beaten by a low shot from Derek Draper only for Reaney to clear off the line, a trait that would become a trademark for the right-back over the ensuing years. With Bremner and Collins operating superbly in midfield, United began to take control, and Johnson, who had left the field injured earlier, fired against the bar, Noel Peyton hitting the rebound inches wide. In the second half, United added a second with what Phil Brown of the *Yorkshire Evening Post* described as 'the best goal that United have scored this season'. Once again it came from some fine play on the wing by Johanneson, who linked up with Collins. The ball was then fed for the oncoming Bremner to slot home.

After the 2-0 victory, 17-year-old Johnson described an eventful afternoon that literally had it all for him, 'I was in the team because of an injury to John Charles and I scored early on which was more than I could have dreamt of. Then I got injured. I collided with Swansea keeper Noel Dwyer and I was stretchered off unconscious. My parents, Violet and Ron, had travelled down to see me play and were obviously delighted when I scored. But then when I got injured, my mum fainted. When I came to, she was laid on the treatment table next to me! The medical staff didn't know who she was and initially thought that she'd had a heart attack.'

Following that game, Sprake would keep his place for all but three of the games for the rest of the season. Reaney would play all but one game up to the end of the season and Hunter went on to play in every single game of the campaign.

Hunter had been spotted by a Leeds scout while playing for Birtley Juniors in County Durham. He lived at 8 Rosemary Gardens in Eighton Banks, about six miles from Newcastle. The house had four bedrooms but living in it were Norman's mother Betty, her sister Jean, and two of Norman's uncles, Bill and Frank. Norman's father, also Norman, had died two months before the future Elland Road great was born.

The family were delighted when Norman was invited to a trial match at Elland Road. He would be playing for the club's juniors against Bradford Park Avenue at inside-right. On the right wing was Ronnie Blackburn. Leeds won 6-0 and the very next day Norman received a call from the club asking him to join the groundstaff at Elland Road, which he jumped at the chance to do.

But travelling alone on the train down to Leeds, 15-year-old Norman was having second thoughts about moving so far away from home comforts. He later said, 'I arrived at Leeds station very late at night and was met by a man called Billy Leighton, whose mother ran the house where I was to stay in Beeston. "Ma" Leighton was very nice but I was feeling very homesick already, I'd only left my house a few hours ago. But I soon settled in and we were allowed to go home for a few days every six weeks, which definitely helped me early on. Also living at the house was Billy Bremner, who had already signed professional terms and was just breaking through into the reserve team. He too was also very homesick.'

Jack Taylor had been the manager when Hunter arrived at Leeds, and as he approached his 17th birthday he was devastated to be told by Taylor that he didn't think he was 'strong enough or big enough to become a professional footballer'. The boss agreed to keep him on for a further spell to see if he developed. In the meantime, however, Taylor was sacked and Revie became player-manager. 'Don Revie was a great manager,' said Hunter, 'a terrific motivator who possessed a wealth of football knowledge, initially as a player of skill and technical ability, and later as a very successful manager. Albert Johanneson had been Don Revie's first signing and I became his second.'

Coach Syd Owen and trainer Les Cocker had been brought in by Taylor, and player discipline was poor to say the least. Owen and Cocker worked tirelessly with the unruly players, often clashing with each other as to the different methods being used. But with Revie, his authority was immediately felt. He clamped down on the troublemakers and dismissed anyone he deemed as surplus to his requirements. It is well documented how Jack Charlton and Revie fought over various tactics and instructions, but an impressed young Hunter watched on as Revie slowly began to build a team around Charlton and Bremner. One morning on the Fullerton Park training field, Revie said to Hunter, 'In our next reserve game, I'm going to play you as a defender alongside the centre-half.' Hunter, despite scoring an own goal, came through a 2-2 draw impressing Revie so much that from then on he remained a defender, becoming in time very accomplished.

In later years, after Norman had retired, I got to know him really well. We would talk at meetings and events; he really was a great bloke, very pleasant and Leeds United through and through. We once shared a stage at an event in Otley in 2014 for a packed house and the audience was firing questions, mainly at Norman, who by then was as deaf as a post. Every question he would lean into me and ask, 'What did he say?' It made for a long but interesting evening.

One inevitable question was about Norman's encounter at the Baseball Ground in 1975, when he and Francis Lee, then of Derby County did six or seven rounds of boxing before getting sent off, and they then started to fight again as they headed for the tunnel. Norman again asked me what was said, to which I just replied 'Frannie Lee'. 'Oh, that,' he chuckled. 'It all got a bit out of hand [laughs]. I don't suppose it set a great example to the young kids, but it was one of those things. Frannie was a bugger for diving, he won more penalties for his theatrics than any foreign player I've ever seen. This particular incident occurred when he dived outside the box and then got up, sort of, and dived again hoping to reach the box, but it was yards away. He looked like Jackie Pallo, a wrestler in the 1960s who used to feign injury and act as if he was dazed and then attack his opponent who was by now off guard. Anyway, when he went down a second time, I said something to him, and he flicked me with his foot while still on the ground, so I kicked him back. Then he jumped up and then the fracas ensued – almost all players on the pitch were involved.'

Then someone shouted out from the audience, 'Have you ever considered a rematch?' Norman looked at me and said, 'What did he say?' After I'd explained, Norman just said, 'It's all forgotten with me, but I'm not sure about Francis.' With that he winked and we moved on.

I'm happy to report at this point that not long after this event, Norman did obtain a small hearing aid which he used to great effect. We still joked about it years after, and when he saw me he would always pretend to turn the volume up and smile like only he could. What a really smashing bloke he was.

Paul Reaney, who had made his debut alongside Hunter at Swansea, was born in London but always considers himself a Yorkshireman. 'I was born in Fulham,' says Reaney, 'but I was only a fortnight old when I moved with my parents to Yorkshire, so I reckon I'm a Yorkshireman, a local lad.'

Reaney went to Cross Green School in east Leeds, and was always playing football at school and outside of it for different local junior teams, youth club teams – anywhere there was a football to be kicked around really. It was in October 1961 that he was spotted by Leeds United, playing for Middleton Parkside Juniors, and the club signed him as an apprentice. Peter Grimshaw owned a garage in East End Park and at the same time Reaney was an apprentice motor mechanic there. Grimshaw recalled, 'Paul would always come to work with a football in a bag. During his breaks he would constantly kick the ball at the wall behind the garage, sometimes kicking it through one of the old tyres.'

Reaney became a very fit and very fast right-back, and someone who would later be described by George Best as his 'most difficult opponent', but for the time being he was busy establishing himself as part of Revie's developing defence. Rod Johnson also played for Middleton at inside-forward, and three games after Reaney's big break he was also signed up.

Johnson's injury sustained during his debut at Swansea prevented him from playing the week after, at home to Chelsea, leaving the door open for John Charles to return. Leeds won 2-0 courtesy of two lovely goals by Johanneson. Johnson then returned for an away fixture at Luton Town, playing out on the right wing, with Jim Storrie in at centre-forward for Charles. A goal apiece from Storrie and Bobby Collins earned United a draw. Charles returned the following week at home to Southampton, and was outstanding, but in defence – he spent most of the game helping out at the back and United's goal in a 1-1 draw was again scored by Storrie. In the dressing room afterwards, Norman Hunter was full of praise for Charles, as was Jack Charlton, but there was an uneasiness developing between the Welsh star and Revie.

Don's son Duncan told me in 2007, 'Dad once told me that his gamble to bring back John Charles backfired. He only played 11 games, scored three goals, but was unfit and very ineffective. But Dad didn't dwell on this so much as he was moulding a crop of young players that he expected to go right to the top, blending them with experienced players he already had, such as Bobby Collins and Jack Charlton. His only intention with regards to John Charles was to recoup the money, or more, that the club had paid Juventus to bring him back to Leeds. The thing that had ruffled Dad's feathers was a massive row that he had with Charles, which Noel Peyton witnessed. It was after a 3-1 defeat at Bury and Charles said he wanted to go back to Italy as he was missing the life and the sun and asked for a transfer. Dad was blazing and hardly said a word to Charles again, except for a few begrudging words in the dressing room before games. He wanted the directors to deal with the whole business of the eventual sale of John Charles.'

The final game of Charles's career with Leeds came on 13 October at Derby County. Leeds fans Vic Stanley and Melv Miller were there. Vic says, 'We had started travelling to away games on the train for the Huddersfield Town game in September and it was brilliant. We pulled up at Derby train station and hundreds of Leeds fans got off. The crowd was about 30,000 with plenty of Leeds fans there, but the game was a massive disappointment. After a 0-0 draw we were glad to be on the train home, but little did we know that we had just witnessed John Charles's final game for Leeds United.'

The directors were reluctant to part with him, but just over a week later chairman Harry Reynolds announced, 'Regrettably, we have agreed to John Charles's transfer request and are in negotiations with an Italian club.' That club was Roma and on the evening of Friday, 3 November 1962, an amicable deal was struck between the clubs, so Charles flew back with the Italian party and a day later made his debut for Roma against Bologna. Charles made a statement before he left Yorkshire, 'I turned out for Leeds when I wasn't match fit, and every move I made was in the glare of publicity from television, radio and newspapers. Publicity is fine when you are doing well, but I knew in my heart of hearts that I wasn't playing well.'

The outcome gave Leeds a handsome profit. Having sold Charles to Juventus for £65,000, they bought him back for £53,000 and then sold him to Roma for £70,000 which included a deal that involved a friendly between the two clubs, which was eventually played on 5 June 1963 at the Stadio Olimpico. Charles was in the Roma line-up and the team that Leeds fielded was: Sprake, Reaney, Hair, Bremner, Charlton, Hunter, Weston, Lawson, Storrie, Collins, Johanneson. Storrie scored in a 2-1 defeat.

The Southampton game, which had seen Charles perform admirably in defence, had also marked the debut of a 15-year-old Peter Lorimer. Sadly, however, Lorimer was given his debut because of the absence of Bremner, who had once again suffered homesickness and returned to Scotland, and he was refusing to come back. Despite the directors reluctantly agreeing to Bremner's transfer request, Revie once again had to use all his persuasive powers to talk Bremner into returning to Leeds, which he did, scoring in a 3-2 home defeat by the Saints. But Bremner's appearances for the rest of the season were sporadic.

Leeds were still in debt and juggling finances despite the sale of Charles, but Reynolds promised Revie that any requests for incoming players would be given every assistance possible. Bremner's best friend Tommy Henderson, who had also suffered from homesickness during his early days at Leeds, was bought for £1,500 from St Mirren, and the club paid £18,000 to Rotherham United for inside-forward Don Weston.

Lorimer's debut would be his only game for two and a half years, partly hampered by a broken leg in a Northern Intermediate League Cup Final against Sheffield United. He had first attracted the attention of Leeds while playing for Stobswell School in Dundee, where he scored an unbelievable 176 goals in one season alone. Known from an early age as 'The Cannonball Kid', Lorimer would regularly score ten or 12 goals a match. And he was crowned the hardest shot in football, recorded at 76.8mph, beating off all challengers, such as Francis Lee, Geoff Hurst and Bobby Charlton.

As a youngster, Peter lived on Church Street in Broughty Ferry, nestled on the edge of the River Tay estuary just east of Dundee. He lived with his father Peter and mother Janet. Peter senior was in the Royal Navy, later becoming a fisherman, while Janet worked for the publishers DC Thompson. When he was 13, Peter junior played for Scotland Schoolboys against England at Ibrox. Lorimer netted twice in a 4-2 win – he was becoming quite a sensation, prompting interest from almost 30 league clubs north and south of the border.

One of those teams was Leeds, and Revie was so anxious to get his man that he drove up through the night, collecting a speeding ticket on the way. Scores of club representatives filled Church Street, one of whom was Joe Armstrong from Manchester United, who left a briefcase containing £5,000 in the front room. It was a phenomenal amount of money and would have been accepted by almost anyone. Leeds, on the other hand, could only offer £800 – but with a structure that would put Lorimer on more money than any of the kids already at Elland Road. The senior professionals were on over £20 a week; Lorimer, a tall and skinny 13-year-old, would be on £17 a week. The club would also pay for his lodgings and two large steaks a week.

John Quinn, the chief scout at Leeds, went up every weekend to keep tabs on Peter and to give Janet a bottle of Harveys Bristol Cream sherry and a dozen fresh eggs, so as to build up his frame and develop his strength. Peter senior was given £5 a week (half his wage) and Peter junior was given 50p a week. The sherry and eggs, and the steaks of course, were becoming a trademark of Revie's development of his young team, but Lorimer said, 'I used to go to school half-pissed because of the rather large measure of sherry with a raw egg in.'

This continued until Peter left school and travelled to his lodgings in Easterly Road, Leeds. But for all the gifts and sweeteners, Lorimer maintains that it was Revie's attention to detail and his plans to build one of the best teams in Europe that persuaded his parents to let him go to Leeds. He said, 'I always listened to my parents' advice and took heed. As I signed the form in our front room watched by Don Revie, and my mum and dad, I knew I was heading for the big time.'

When Peter signed professional forms, his parents received a further £2,000. He would go on to make over 700 appearances for the club and score more than 200 goals. He continues to hold the record for the only player to represent Scotland at every level – schoolboy, youth, amateur, under-23s and full international.

Just as with Norman Hunter, I got to know Peter really well over the years. I saw him score the majority of his club-record 237 goals, but it was after he retired that I really got to know him. Being in the company of Peter was special. He was special and always had the time to talk about his career, or anything really. I always had a question for him about his career and his reply would be measured and sincere. He was a very knowledgeable man, who liked a flutter on the horses and the odd pint or two. I got to know him in the 1980s when he ran a club in Hunslet called The Trafalgar. It was a sportsman's club and we had many of our own local team's annual events there.

When The Trafalgar closed down and was eventually demolished, Peter and his wife Sue took The Commercial in Holbeck, not far from Elland Road. It was a major attraction for Leeds fans, none more so than the Scandinavian contingent of the United collective. Offering a good pint, accommodation and a hearty breakfast cooked by 'Hotshot' Peter himself, the pub was bursting at the seams on matchdays. During the week, however, it was not so busy.

Save for the odd worker from Kay's, the nearby factory, the place was mostly deserted. But sometimes that's when a pub is at its best. One rainy, dark winter's afternoon I just happened to call in. I had called at a job nearby and thought, 'Why not?'

The wind slammed the door shut behind me as I walked into the lounge. Including me, there were four people in the whole pub. Peter Lorimer was behind the bar and Bobby Collins and John Charles were sat at this side of the bar. It was unbelievable. I walked to the bar and Peter pulled me a pint of Tetley's bitter. Peter, a big horse-racing fan, had the television on and the sports paper open on the racing page. In between races he would switch to Yorkshire TV's *Countdown*. It was unreal. Then it became hilarious. Three Leeds United legends would be arguing about conundrums and mathematics and I was sat there watching them, in awe, with a pint of Tetley's to hand, convinced that I was dreaming it all.

At one point, John piped up with an answer, to which Bobby laughed and said, 'That's nae a word! You've made that up!' I can't remember what the word was, but the two of them must have argued about it for a good half an hour, all the time. Peter was concentrating on his horse selections. Then Bobby put a pint in front of me, I would buy another round, then John, then Peter, then as time moved on those pints were replaced by whiskies. It was dark when I walked into The Commercial and it was dark when I parked my van round the back near Peter's car and rang my mate Webby for a lift home. When he walked in, he just stood staring at the bar where, to be honest, the three Leeds legends didn't look quite as bad as they should have. I just looked at Webby, shrugged my shoulders, and we left. We did have a bit of an argument in the car because I hadn't rang him sooner to tell him who I was with, but, I reasoned, 'How would I have got home?'

Bobby Collins was once described by *Yorkshire Evening Post* reporter Phil Brown as 'five stone of cast iron', and I can personally vouch for that. After his professional career came to an end he continued to play with the Leeds United ex-professionals well into his 60s. I played in goal against him in an exhibition match at the Yorkshire Copperworks ground in Stourton, Leeds, in the early 1990s. During the game our captain Denis Ruddick passed the ball back to me (in those days the keeper could pick the ball up from a back-pass) and I gathered it up as an opposing forward closed in. I was still in mid-air when all of a sudden I was hit by that five stone of cast iron. I hit the ground wincing, but still holding the ball as Bobby ruffled my hair, grinned at me and disappeared back up the field.

Afterwards in the club bar I was talking to Peter, who had also appeared for the ex-players, when Bobby came over and said to me, 'I know we're supposed to swap shirts, but will these do?' He then handed me the shorts that he'd been wearing.

Our left-back, Paul 'Acka' Atkinson, then shouted, 'Hey, Bobby! I should have them shorts. You hit me that hard in the first half you nearly knocked me through the hedge and on to the main road.' Bobby just grinned at Acka. I still have the shorts.

Also playing that day was another Scot who I've got to know fairly well over the years, Eddie Gray, one of the most skilful footballers ever to play for Leeds United. Young Eddie played for the Glasgow Schools representative team alongside his close friend Jimmy Lumsden, who would also get his chance at Leeds. He was about 13 or 14 when he was spotted by the club's trusted scout in Scotland, John Barr.

Several clubs were more than interested in Eddie and Don Revie wasted no time in heading north to talk to him and his parents. He arrived at 14 Cavin Drive in the Castlemilk district of Glasgow, and Eddie and his parents were immediately impressed, like many before them, by his powers of persuasion. Leeds weren't allowed to sign Eddie until he left school, and that left the door open for other clubs to attempt to persuade his parents to possibly weigh up other options. Revie countered this by sending his assistant, Maurice Lindley, to basically act as a minder to Eddie. Revie was particularly wary of Tommy Docherty, manager of Chelsea, who had just been relegated to the Second Division. Of all the managers who wanted to sign Eddie, Docherty was the one who worried Revie the most, so much so that when Docherty did call at Cavin Drive to discuss him going to Stamford Bridge, Lindley was hiding in the bedroom, listening to the conversation. On occasions, there would be two or three rival managers at the Gray house at the same time.

In the end Revie persuaded Eddie that the move to Leeds was the right one. The usual procedure for signing players from school was to give them a two-year contract as apprentice professionals at 15 and, depending on their progress, their first full professional contracts at 17. Clubs could not have more than 15 apprentices on their books at any one time, and could not pay them more than £7 a week for the first year and £8 for the second.

Gray said, 'Leeds signed me as an amateur player and arranged for me to be "employed" by a local printing company, which didn't exist. It was a scam. Don Revie told my father that it had to be done this way because the club had reached its apprentice quota. But I cannot deny that I benefited from it financially. A number of clubs bent the rules this way.

'Another reason for my decision to join Leeds was Don Revie. He had tremendous physical presence and personality. He told my father that "even though you don't know much about Leeds United now, Mr Gray, but in the not too distant future this club is going to be one of the best in Britain" and we believed him. When it came to making people feel special, he thought of everything; he thought about things that I know would go over the heads of most other managers. It was typical of him that, to celebrate the decisions of myself to join Leeds, Don and the club chairman, Harry Reynolds, came up to Glasgow and threw a party for us and our families at the Central Hotel.'

Eddie played with the Leeds United juniors in a tournament in Italy which they won in 1966. Among the promising youngsters were Sonny Sweeney, John Lawson, Paul Peterson, Willie Waddle, John Craggs and two others, called David Harvey and Terry Yorath.

Revie's persuasiveness really came to the fore when, because Eddie wasn't allowed to leave school until the summer, the manager actually went to the school one Monday morning and persuaded his headmaster that it would be in everybody's best interests for him to be released a bit earlier. So that afternoon, Gray and Jimmy Lumsden travelled to Leeds in Don's blue Zephyr – a journey that would lead Eddie to a glittering career of over 580 appearances for Leeds, followed by roles as manager, youth-team coach, reserve-team coach, assistant manager and still, today, club ambassador.

8

Fan-Assisted

ON 4 March 1950, Leeds United played Arsenal in the sixth round of the FA Cup; 15,000 fans headed for the capital by train, plane and coach, leaving the city resembling a ghost town. A similar amount had travelled to Bolton in the fourth round of the same competition, and it was estimated that 20,000 supporters could have gone across to Hull City for a promotion-clinching game in 1956.

This astounding support, however, was only evident for special occasions – it was in the early 1960s that fans began to travel consistently to away games.

Leeds supporters are truly a special kind. The fanaticism, unswerving loyalty and at times blind devotion is evident everywhere Leeds play today and always has been throughout the club's chequered history. But one particular fan was a supporter extraordinaire.

Charles Webster was a member of the select group of fans who saw both Leeds City and Leeds United. Charles, speaking in 1974 when he was 83 years old, said, 'I saw the second ever game played by Leeds City in 1905 – it was against Grimsby Town and I've been coming ever since. I can remember when season tickets were 10s 6d [53p] and even throughout the First World War my mother kept me in touch with what was happening here by sending me copies of *Athletic News*. Apart from my war years I've been coming along to practically every game at Elland Road since 1905.'

Charles was a cloth finisher in Armley before he retired. He had a keenly retentive memory of most of the milestones at Elland Road, 'When I first started coming the pitch was the other way round. I remember the forerunner of the Scratching Shed as an old wooden affair with both terracing and seating with wooden steps inside. Football now is merely a pastime for me. My enthusiasm has become a little blunted over the years. But I still enjoy what I see even though the game is nothing like the one I first started watching all those years ago.

'The best individual performance I've seen over the years was by Russell Wainscoat, who United signed from Barnsley, in a game against West Ham although I can't remember the actual year. It had rained solidly all day and the pitch was in a terrible mess but it didn't affect him one bit – he played better than anyone I have ever seen and scored two or three goals.

'I also used to travel away to watch the team, particularly to all the northern grounds. Obviously, Leeds were never a top side until the last decade under Don Revie, but I still get enjoyment out of watching them. It was always the case that the club had to sell their best players merely to survive. That's why John Charles went. He must be the finest footballer who ever lived – I watched him right the way through to the top from playing in the third team. But football at Elland Road has been my life's interest. I'm a widower now and it's this interest that gives me my incentive to keep coming along every week. Football has given me tremendous enjoyment over the years – football news of any sort to me has always been interesting.

'For 50 years I walked from my home in Barden Mount, Armley, to every game and I was part of the enjoyment. I wish I had a pound for every mile I've covered watching Leeds – I'd be a near millionaire! Football has changed dramatically over the years. Really, it's fallen into three phases. There was a particular part of football played up to the First World War which changed after the hostilities because most of the players didn't return and a lot of youngsters were blooded. Now, since the Second World War it's changed again. It's a passing game now. I remember though when football was a religion for some of the clubs in the north-east. Before the first war, Middlesbrough, Sunderland and Newcastle were three of the country's top teams – local firms used to support them financially because the game boosted the workers' morale.'

Charles was a proud holder of ten £1 shares in the club, and he once challenged Don Revie that if Leeds didn't win the title then he would stop coming to games. Charles said, 'I actually said it as a joke but Revie seemed very concerned. I was actually going to sell my shares anyway, as they're not much use to me financially – but I'm a sentimentalist at heart and have decided to hang on to them and eventually pass them on to my sons.

'Even though United were never successful until more recent times, they used to have some fine players. Willis Edwards was the one I most admired – he was the prince of half-backs. I've never seen a player before or since for his control and accurate passing. Mind you, I'm a firm admirer of Billy Bremner, although he's more of an attacker than Willis was.'

Charles had some highly interesting thoughts on hooliganism at the time, 'It's only developed since the last war and there's a definite reason for it. Youngsters today have too much money and too much time on their hands and have been brought up with too little discipline and no respect. Youngsters in my day were true sportsmen – and my definition of a sportsman is someone who can win a prize or a trophy and immediately hand it back to his defeated opponent. No, youngsters today are too interested in material things. They aren't what I would call real supporters who would follow the team through thick and thin. Sportsmen don't go home if their team is losing ten minutes from time. Leeds United support is good, very good – but it could be better. The trouble is, Leeds is not a footballing city. Rugby was here before football and it was always the case that every boy born was immediately a rugby fan. Look at Bramley RLFC – they've never won a major trophy in 90-year history but the fans still keep going. That's what I call support – true support.

'We always used to come to Elland Road prepared for anything. We half expected the team to lose every week but all the time we hoped they'd win.'

Charles, at the time, was keen to hear from any fan who thought they could match his longevity support record. 'I really don't think anyone could but I want to know,' he said. 'I'd like to meet the chap who could beat it because we could talk for months on end about all that we've seen and experienced. I keep reading of fans who claim that they have been supporting the club for many, many years, but in every case, I've been able to go back some ten or 15 years further.'

So there you have the story of undoubtedly one of the best supporters in the club's history, but Charles Webster had some pretty outspoken views and I'm sure some of his comments regarding the young supporters would be fiercely contested. I can certainly vouch for the loyalty of the vast majority of young fans these days, on the coach I travel away with – the Garforth Whites – and supporters' branches throughout the city, the county and, indeed, the country.

Graham 'Wagger' Wagstaffe, like me, comes from the Kippax area of Leeds, and has been supporting United since the early 1960s. On 5 December 1964 he travelled to Old Trafford to watch the team. There was always a long line of Wallace Arnold coaches in Call Lane, Leeds waiting to take fans all over the country. This particular morning, Wagger was waiting with a few mates to get on the coach to go across the Pennines, 'I would always try and get on the same coach as a lad known as "The Minstrel". I managed this for the trip to Old Trafford and we came back with both points after Bobby Collins scored the only goal of the game.

'It had been foggy all day and it was still misty when we pulled up at a pub on the old road [pre-M62] over the top of the Pennines for an hour. We had just got our drinks when the team bus pulled up outside and in walked Don Revie with the players. Bobby Collins saw The Minstrel and shouted, "Hey, Minstrel, where's your guitar?" to which The Minstrel replied, "It's on the coach." Bobby told him to go and get it and we all had a good old sing-song.'

So, who was The Minstrel?

The word 'unique' is not out of place when referring to certain fans of Leeds United. Back in 1960, an unusual sound, never before heard in a football ground, certainly not at Elland Road, began emanating from the stadium's terraces. A guitar could be heard as an introduction, and then, to the tune of *The Beverly Hillbillies*, a popular television comedy show from the 1950s and 1960s, these tuneful words came belting out from the Scratching Shed:

> *Come listen to my story, about a football team.*
> *They are called Leeds United and for them we let off steam.*

They always play good football, wherever they may go.
And that's why we support them, through rain, wind
or snow.

The man twanging that guitar was a 19-year-old by the name of Philip Dobreen. Otherwise known as The Minstrel, Phil became famous at Plymouth and Preston, Arsenal and Aston Villa, Southampton and Sunderland, at all points north, south, east and west. A ten-hour coach trip of 200-odd miles could be a swinging affair for Phil and his regular choristers, 15 of them in total, who always travelled as a party.

Phil was a tailor and for one of those trips, for example, his coach would leave at 6am, but if the distance was longer than 200 miles the coach would leave at midnight on the Friday night before, sometimes only arriving just in time for the game (no motorways back then).

His first Leeds game was a friendly against Juventus at Elland Road on Wednesday, 2 October 1957. It was a fixture that was set up as part of the deal that took John Charles to Turin. Philip was standing on the open Kop and it was the biggest crowd of the season. Charles was at centre-forward for the Italians and was their captain. Leeds' line-up was: Roy Wood, Eric Kerfoot, Jimmy Ashall, Archie Gibson, Jack Charlton, Keith Ripley, George Meek, Hugh Baird, Bobby Frost, Chris Crowe and Jack Overfield. Crowe opened the scoring for Leeds after five minutes, but just after half an hour Juventus equalised through their new £100,000 signing, Argentinian forward Omar Sívori. Baird put United back in front with a well-executed side-footed shot in front of the Scratching Shed after 40 minutes, then Charles, with socks rolled down to his ankles, tiptoed through the tackles of the Leeds rearguard and was at the end of a great cross from Gino Stacchini to head home brilliantly on 44 minutes – but tempers flared a minute later when Archie Gibson clashed with Bruno Nicole and had to be pulled apart by referee Jack Ellis from Halifax, with assistance from John Charles.

Both teams were putting on an excellent display and there were those in the Leeds crowd certainly who were rooting for Charles, while others were for the hosts. The tempo remained high in the second half and Sívori got his second to put the Italians in front with a close-range header. Roy Wood pulled off some brilliant stops and bravely dived at the feet of Giorgio Stivanello to foil a certain goal, but Charles wrapped things up four minutes from time when he swivelled to hit a rocket into the roof of Wood's net.

Phil remembers the West Stand fire in 1956 but he really started going regularly in 1961, and it was about then he took up the guitar. Before his Leeds adventure began, he was a Leeds rugby fan, often visiting Headingley, and going to the odd game at Elland Road whenever he got the chance. One of his first memories watching United was goalkeeper Ted Burgin. Phil said, 'Burgin was an England B keeper, and I could never understand how an England keeper could get beat so many times!'

It wasn't long before The Minstrel and his singing entourage were getting recognised and applauded everywhere; even Revie and the team became big fans of them.

Phil said, 'We used to go in a group of around 15 lads to all the games. At Elland Road, because I was a programme seller I would come out of the tunnel five minutes after the game had started with my guitar and walk round to the Scratching Shed to the lads who were always in the same spot.

'The lads and me were encouraged by Revie himself to get the crowd going. He loved us, and would do anything to help us whip up the crowd. They were great days.'

On one occasion, against Aston Villa on 12 December 1964, Phil was asked by Revie to try a new song out on the crowd, but unfortunately it didn't go as well as planned. He said, 'I was stood in front of the crowd trying to get a new song over to the crowd, but it didn't go down too well mainly because of the one tannoy loudspeaker at the corner of the Scratching Shed and the West Stand which could hardly be heard.'

Their coach once got stuck in traffic on the way to a vital game at Swansea in 1964 and arrived at Vetch Field 15 minutes in, but they were in time to witness a brilliant display by United and a 3-0 win that clinched promotion to the First Division with two matches to go. After the game the lads had a whip round on the bus and bought a bottle of champagne, and headed straight for the train station. 'We knew the team were returning by train,' Phil remembers, 'and we gave them the bottle of champagne in a pub opposite the station.'

Two weeks later United won at Charlton Athletic and went up as champions. Revie returned the gesture from Swansea and presented the lads with two bottles of champagne at Kings Station before they boarded their train home. Phil said, 'In those days when there wasn't any hooliganism, it was fun going to all the away games and we all had good times.'

Graham Wagstaffe did tell me that he once saw The Minstrel whack a Chelsea fan with his guitar, so naturally I asked Phil about it. 'Nothing much to it really,' he said. 'At the FA Cup semi-final against Chelsea at Villa Park, we were robbed blind by the referee, Ken Burns, who disallowed a perfect Peter Lorimer free kick. On the way back to the coaches, this Chelsea lad was shouting all sorts of crap at us about Lorimer's disallowed goal, so I belted him over the head with my guitar – it made me feel better, although it didn't do too much for my guitar.'

Before one game at Tottenham Hotspur, Phil went to see the team at their hotel. Revie greeted him warmly as did the players. They then took him on their coach to White Hart Lane where a good old sing-song took place. Revie then told Phil that they were staying in London after the game and asked if he could accompany his son Duncan home on the train. 'Of course,' said Phil.

He became good friends with most of the players: Bobby Collins, Billy Bremner, Terry Cooper and especially Norman Hunter, who he would play table tennis with, along with Terry Cooper in the gym at Elland Road before the matches and at the youth club in the Judean Club on Street Lane, Moortown. Bobby used to coach the youth club team, and whenever the lads were at matches in the Rotherham area they would always call at a pub that was run by Jimmy Greenhoff's family – Jimmy would be behind the bar.

Philip Dobreen, the famous Minstrel, is now 77 years old and has been living in Israel since 1967. We thank you for your service, sir.

The Minstrel clearly started a trend in the Scratching Shed as vocal support behind the goal was soon on the rise. The West Stand Paddock was probably the first part of the ground that had vocal support of some description, but was confined to a resounding 'Leeds, Leeds, Leeds' chant. That said, it was an impressive sound and often resonated around the ground and can still be heard today. I clearly remember a lad with a beard and a woollen Leeds hat playing the flute at games and I still seen him around today. But two brothers made a real impact after the mid-1960s.

Neil and Keith Peniket lived on King Edward Avenue, Horsforth, and they started another trend at Elland Road.

Dubbed the 'Leader of the Scratching Shed', Neil stood up on a crash barrier to conduct his flock; 5,000 would pack the Shed, and the siblings made up several songs for the fans to sing. But there was a problem. Some people in the crowd would add filthy words to the lines. This annoyed Neil and Keith so much that they protested about it, and vowed to do their best to stop it.

Keith said, 'When I get up in front of the crowd I tell them straight that I want no swearing. But you can always hear swearing at any football ground. It starts mainly by people who have had too much to drink before the match, one or two start swearing and the others join in. Once that sort of thing starts, it is difficult to get control. The crowd are excited in the Shed and get carried away.'

Neil and Keith promised to continue their campaign about bad language and after being told by the *Yorkshire Evening Post* that they would win many admirers if they succeeded, Neil said, 'We'll certainly keep trying.'

The pair began looking ahead when plans to improve Elland Road emerged. The Spion Kop on the opposite end of the pitch to the Scratching Shed was a large, uncovered terrace at the time and under the new proposals a new covered stand would replace it. The two agreed that when this happened it would become the new home of the 'Shedders'. Keith said, 'At the moment the Kop is dead as far as the crowd is concerned, but when they build a new stand with a roof, the "Shedders" will move in there.' Keith even started a breakaway group that went on to the open Kop to try and 'liven the crowd up and get them cheering for United'.

Tony Winstanley knew the Peniket brothers and met his future wife through Neil. It was 5 November 1966 and Leeds fans had taken the North Bank, the home end at Arsenal. Rather cheekily, as soon as the gates opened about

500 visiting supporters strode in. The Arsenal fans found themselves in a bit of a pickle and the police immediately threw a ring around the Leeds fans who were right in the middle of all the home faithful.

Tony recalled, 'During the game, Neil Peniket was on one barrier and I was on the other, but I saw the police coming and jumped down, but it was too late for Neil and the police grabbed him and arrested him. I had been talking to a girl who was with Neil and after the match we all left Highbury and went to the police station and they released Neil.

'Poor old Arsenal, not only lost their home end, they lost the game too, as big Jack Charlton fired home to give Leeds a 1-0 win.

'The next morning I was on the first bus out of Leeds to Cross Gates where I lived at the time and the girl who was with Neil was on the same bus. We had travelled back from London on the night train and Neil and his gang were on the coach all night. It turned out that Neil and this girl were only friends, so I asked her out and four years later we were married.'

It seems that Tony got around a bit in the 1960s. The Minstrel mentioned a pub they used to go to that was run by the Greenhoff family – well, Tony has been there too.

'It was called The Morning Star,' confirms Tony. 'We used to call there whenever we'd been to Sheffield or Derby. It was in Barnsley and the locals used to get in after the dog track closed about 9pm and old Sydney got on the piano for a good old sing-song. We got to know Jimmy Greenhoff's dad really well and Jimmy was often in the pub helping out behind the bar. His mam and dad had a terrace house at the top of the street.

'One day on our way home from somewhere, we called and Mr Greenhoff was swamped. He asked me to go up to the house and tell Jimmy to hurry up and get down to the pub to give him a hand. I took Sue, who was now my fiancée, and she was all of a wreck because she fancied him like hell. Jimmy's girlfriend at the time let us in and he was there combing his hair in the mirror. "Won't be minute," he said, and we were off down the street. Brian Greenhoff used to kick a ball around in the street and we would often have a kick about with him. They were a really lovely family, but Brian was told by his dad and Jimmy that he wasn't good enough to play for Leeds!'

The slightly worrying aspect of this brilliant story of Tony's is that he mentions that his fiancée, Sue, was besotted with Jimmy. But I'm not entirely convinced that she was the only one. Remember, this was in the mid-1960s and Tony, bless him, can still recall what car Jimmy drove. 'It was a Singer Gazelle,' said Tony. 'Registration number – FUA 504D.'

Sadly, after retiring, Jimmy put most of his money into a business venture backing his friend, but it transpired that this so-called friend actually conned Jimmy out of all his money. He was jailed but Jimmy lost everything, ending up having to get a job as a forklift driver in a warehouse near Wombwell.

Many older fans will remember the man who was dubbed as the original 'King of the Kop'. Bramley lad Kenny Wilson, or 'Wilkie' as he was also called, was well known at Elland Road and at away grounds. He was nearly always dressed in a suit, and he carried a walking stick, but it was not to aid his walking. At 68 years old he was the first pensioner to receive an ASBO, for threatening a neighbour.

On 31 October 1964 this article appeared in the programme for the home game against Sheffield United, praising the behaviour of Leeds fans the week before away at Burnley. It was under the heading 'Compliments on our following' and ended with a 'but', 'We would like to thank you fans once more for your orderly behaviour away from home. The chairman, Mr Harry Reynolds, and the board and all the staff are so proud of the good name that our following has earned and been given all round the country, and you lived right up to it at Burnley last week, and in a "Red Rose" county despite the closeness and rigour of the match. In fact we also got a tribute from Burnley about those of our followers who went by rail that we shall always treasure because of its rarity and its absolute genuineness.

'The inspector in charge at Burnley Central Station, Mr J. Cowperthwaite who supervised the departure of the many trains for Leeds wrote to us of his own accord. He told us that they were that they were the best-behaved and most orderly crowd that the Burnley station people had had so far this season. It had been a pleasure to control the loading of the trains, so courteous and obedient had the Leeds people been. He hoped that we would let you know how appreciated it all was at Burnley, so here you are – our warmest compliments.

'Please try to keep it up too. We have plenty of places to visit yet, and the more you can spread our good name the better it is for everybody, including yourselves, both on the away ground and in the away city. [But] if the few toilet rolls that appeared on the pitch at Burnley were thrown by Leeds hands then we would ask you to cut that out completely everywhere. It is one of the most stupid and unsightly pieces of litter lout conduct that we have ever known in football, and we want none of it from our crowd, home or away, please.'

An interesting advertisement appeared in that same match programme in 1964, aimed at United fans heading for the forthcoming away game at West Ham United.

Nov 21 United v West Ham – London
MAKE A WEEKEND OF IT
160 Bedrooms
3 Luxury Bars
Radio in Every Room
Television
Theatre , Bookings
1sr Division Food

Stay at the Mandeville, one of London's friendliest hotels and make the most of your weekend. Fri. night to Sunday inc breakfast and lunch Sat. and Sun – only £5.15s 6d inc tips or Sat. to Sun inc lunch both days, accom. and bkfast – only £3.17s.6d inc tips.

Don't miss out, write for brochure and special offers to:
MANDEVILLE HOTEL
WIGMORE STREET
LONDON
W.1

Around 1966 and 1967, with United now in Europe, supporters began embarking on trips across the continent. They were called the Globetrotters, and I was pleased to travel with them myself later down the line. One of these early 'European pioneers' was Henry Stogdale, then in his mid-40s and the landlord of the Black Horse pub in Mabgate, in the centre of Leeds. 'There was a wonderful atmosphere among the fans on these trips,' said Henry. 'Apart from seeing the matches it is a wonderful way of going to places that you would not normally visit. Before the start of away matches the Leeds team would find out where the fans were sitting. Then when they took the field, the players would acknowledge their fans with a special wave. When we got to these away grounds we would go hunting for souvenirs and we'd mingle freely with opposing fans swapping stuff – on one trip I gave away my scarf and tie. I had a Dinamo Zagreb scarf behind my bar for years.'

One person who would definitely have been a Globetrotter was 51-year-old Arthur Dunhill, a fan with an amazing record at the time. Arthur lived on Hough Lane, Bramley, and ran a newsagents there. He saw every match home and away for seven successive seasons. At first he never used to tot up his mileage, but then he started keeping a careful check. From 1965 to 1967 Arthur clocked up 58,638 miles. 'I sometimes had to hire a taxi to get to some far-off places,' he said. 'Sometimes on some grounds I have been the only United fan there, like Plymouth Argyle on 7 December 1963, when Albert Johanneson scored the only goal of the game.' This claim, however, is disputed, in a friendly sort of way; Clive Richards laughs, 'I was at Plymouth with my son, Graham, for that game in '63. I didn't see Arthur there, but I'm pretty sure he would have been there. He was beginning to build up quite a reputation.'

Clive and Graham took a day and a half to reach Devon. 'Arthur and me became good friends as we trawled up and down the country and beyond, watching United,' says Clive. 'The only difference between us was that Arthur would often go see other teams play; I could only ever watch Leeds United.'

Arthur in fact saw every team in the Football League play in three seasons. Watching United, Arthur travelled to Scotland, Holland, Luxembourg, Italy, Spain, Yugoslavia, Hungary and East Germany. And there was a time when he was the only Leeds fan at a game. Arthur had turned up to watch Leeds play at Partizan Belgrade, where he was spotted by a United official and given a first-class stand seat and brought home with the official party.

Arthur, who just missed out on becoming Britain's number one fan in 1968, was a bachelor and would rise extremely early to sell his newspapers and cigarettes before closing his shop and heading to wherever Leeds were playing that day. Not having a car, Arthur would make a careful study of the fixture lists, the weather forecasts and the railway timetables, and then he worked out how to get there.

In the morning, after many an away game, Arthur had arrived back in Bramley around four o'clock, got straight down to the job of sorting out the papers for the day, snatched three or four hours' sleep before lunch, and then set out to watch yet another match that evening because, as well as being an avid Leeds fan, he watched hundreds of other matches not involving United.

As with Charles Webster, Arthur placed a strong emphasis on sportsmanship. He used to say, 'I try to be fair in my assessment of a game. Of course I love to see Leeds United win, but only if they deserve to do so. West Ham defeated Leeds 7-0 in a League Cup match and the football in that match really was superb.'

Somehow I don't think that David Harvey, the Leeds goalkeeper that evening, would agree with Arthur. But Arthur's own record was impressive. He watched Leeds in league and cup matches, European fixtures, friendlies and West Riding Cup games – he even watched the reserves in the Central League. But he saw all 92 Football League clubs for three consecutive seasons. He kept a detailed logbook of his travels and in 1966/67 he watched 157 matches, travelling 27,175 miles. The following season he saw 185 matches and clocked up 31,463 miles.

Following football all over Britain back then cost Arthur on average £400 a season. He used to freely admit that there were United fans who saw more games than he did, but he was watching Leeds long before the war, and was running a junior team called Leeds Wanderers in the local Red Triangle League right up to the time he began to follow United week in week out. And even with the Wanderers, his record was phenomenal – he missed only two games with the juniors in 25 years.

Arthur started watching Leeds in the doldrums of their history and was rewarded with seeing the emergence of Don Revie's team and beyond. He once said, 'Don Revie and his players deserve tremendous credit for the terrific job he and his backroom staff have done. And the great thing is that Don and his backroom team have built up a situation where the future of the club is assured for many years to come. Most of the first team are still young, and good for several seasons' service, and there are other youngsters, plenty of 'em, who are ready and waiting for their first-team chance.'

Bob Liddle, from Castleford, met up with Tony Winstanley and some other lads in December 1965, 'I went on the football special train to Northampton to watch Leeds United play Northampton at the County Ground which was a three-sided ground that Town shared with Northamptonshire County Cricket Club. It was quite a wet day and the game was called off to protect the cricket part of the pitch. The football special didn't return to Leeds until about 6pm so we had lots of time to go on the rampage in the town centre. Loads of lads got their veg for their Sunday dinner from the local market.

'Back on the station I got talking to a lad called Steve Simpson and then another lad called Barry Goodhall joined in as well. On the train on the way home the three of us sat together and really hit it off. There was this annoying little shit sat near us and he was fucking about jumping on the tables and generally making a nuisance of himself and

White Swan pub, with the top of Well Lane to the left and Kippax School on the horizon. – Edgar Pickles

Royden Wood, aged 92, pictured in front of himself in the 1950s Leeds team. – Vicky Powell

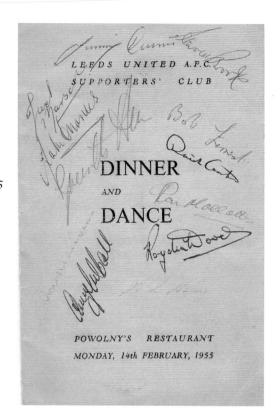

Supporters' Club Menu 1955 signed by Roy Wood, Raich Carter, John Charles and others – author

Albert Johanesson with Tony Levison in Tony's kitchen – Tony Levison

Monty (Tony's dad, with Albert and Tony Levison) – Tony Levison

Albert plays on Monty's drums – Tony Levison

Billy Bremner enjoys a pint and a ciggie with friends – author

The Northampton 6, Gordon, Bob, Barrie, Steve, Tony and James –
Tony Winstanley

Leeds players relax in Blackpool mid-1963/64 season – author

Philip Dobreen – The Minstrel. – Philip Dobreen

ning has the First Word on scenes like these

The climax to the troubled game at Elland-road — both teams are lectured by the referee.

Bremner, of Leeds, puts out a restraining hand as team-mate Lawson brushes with Singleton, of Preston.

Newspaper cutting of a bruising battle between Leeds and Preston in 64 – author

The open kop at Elland Road in 1963 – Tony Levison

Rod Johnson signs for Leeds United in 1962 watched by Don Revie –
The Johnson Family

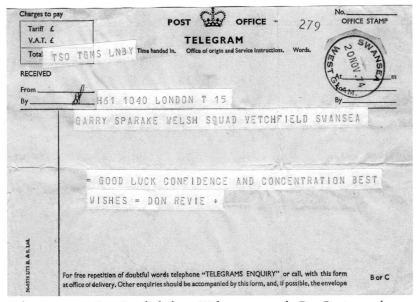

Telegram sent to Gary Sprake before a Wales game, sent by Don Revie – author

Sprake, Reaney and Hunter with Leeds fans after winning the 1964 Second Division championship – author

Original team photo from 1964 – The Johnson Family

we told him to fuck off. Anyway, we three decided that the following Saturday we would meet up before the home game in the American coffee bar on Wellington Street in Leeds. The little shit on the train had been earwigging in on our conversation and he turned up as well. That's how I came to meet Tony Winstanley and I've been trying to get rid of him ever since, ha ha. All four of us are still friends to this day.'

Tony says, 'On 18 December 1965 Leeds United were away at Northampton Town, or at least they should have been. Little did I and several other Leeds fans realise what a momentous day it would turn out to be. About one hour before kick-off, a cloudburst broke over the County Ground in Northampton and the game was postponed. We Leeds fans were left to make our way back to the railway station having experienced a blank Saturday. The "special" soon filled up for our early return to Leeds.

'In the carriage near me were a couple of friends from Selby and others from Leeds who I had just met there on the train. I butted in on their conversation and because I was a bit younger than them, they told me to "fuck off". Needless to say, I didn't and although none of the parties knew each other at that moment, by the time the train arrived back in Leeds, they were making plans to all meet up for the next game. My attempts at joining their gang were still being rebuffed but I refused to go away and to this day we are all still great mates and see each other. We have attended each other's weddings, birthdays, etc. and our kids have grown up knowing each other. Just a few weeks after Northampton, another Leeds fan became friends with us and he also, although having lived in Spain, and Cumbernauld, near Glasgow, is still in regular contact and visits have been made regularly over the years – all this due to supporting Leeds United, a true family club; Tony, Bob, Steve, Baz and Gordon (Big Man).

'By the way, when the game at Northampton was eventually played on 5 March 1966, the Mighty Whites scored through Mike O'Grady – unfortunately, they scored two. Fuck it!'

Another Leeds fan who didn't have a car was Terry Hopkins. He 'thumbed it' to every away game. This was before the M1 motorway, says Terry, 'And most of the time I used the old A1.' I know a few fans who used to hitchhike to games. Roy 'Collar' Coles, from Leeds but now residing in Southampton, was well known for hiking and has stood at dozens of roundabouts and service areas up and down the country. Gaz Noble from Kippax was a long-distance 'thumber' in the 1960s, but once his thumb must have been a bit too far outstretched and a big truck hit and badly damaged his hand. On the plus side, he was easier to spot next time as his white bandaged hands could be seen for miles.

But Terry's record of hitchhiking will certainly take some beating as for three seasons in the mid-1960s he thumbed his way to every single away match that Leeds played. One time, however, he clocked up more miles than he anticipated, 'I went to West Ham one Saturday in 1963 or '64 – I used to work nights at a bakery at Sherburn just outside Leeds and after my shift finished at 5am I walked to the A1 and almost immediately a van stopped. I told the driver that I was heading to London and he said he had deliveries elsewhere but could take me about 40 or 50 miles down the A1, which sounded perfect. I had to get in the back as there was a lot of boxes and some papers on the front passenger seat. In the back it was covered with piles and piles of sheets of material.

'Having worked all night I was soon fast asleep, it was so comfortable. I awoke hours later and it was still dark, or so I thought; I had crawled under some of the material and once I put my head out, I quickly saw that it was daylight. "All right, mate," I said to the driver, who was so surprised to hear me that he almost veered off the road. He pulled the van up and turned around. He told me that he had stopped at a garage on the A1 and had gone to the toilet. When he returned he had looked in the back and because he couldn't see or hear me, he assumed that I'd got out and began walking. We were now heading across country to Wales to make his deliveries. I had to hitchhike almost 40 miles back to the A1 to continue south as I didn't really know any other route.

'Courtesy of a motorbike with sidecar and a very noisy wagon, I arrived at Upton Park a quarter of an hour into the match. I didn't arrive home until Monday morning. But a fortnight later I was threading my way through Sherburn and worming my way along the A62 to Old Trafford.'

Ken Brown, former employee at the Tetley's brewery in Leeds, used to enjoy hitchhiking to United's games, 'There used to be a few of us and we'd split up into pairs. We'd wait at the side of the A1 close to the Boot and Shoe pub in between Micklefield and Fairburn, and two would get in the first car, and then the next and so on. Sometimes other lads from another group would try and get in ahead of us, so they had to be persuaded to wait their turn.

'One time we arrived at Fulham and it had taken so long to get there, me and my mate slept all the way through the game at the back of the Leeds open end.'

Trevor Rushworth brings creature comforts into this fan's episode with a delightful intervention during a crucial encounter at Elland Road as the 1961/62 season drew towards a close. As Leeds and Bury were knocking seven bells out of each other in the final home game of the season, a scruffy black and tan mongrel dog entered the stage via the gap between the West Stand and the Spion Kop. It began by simply running up and down the perimeter track in front of the West Stand dugouts but then, seemingly bored at being ignored by the crowd who were watching the vicious events on the field, the dog then decided to enter the field itself. It went straight for the ball, which it got with the greatest of ease, then using his nose he started dribbling the ball all over the pitch while being chased by players of both sides and a pretty useless copper. Then it ran over to Leeds goalkeeper Tommy Younger and just rolled over in front of him wanting to be tickled. Younger then picked up the little scamp and handed it to the useless copper who was trying in vain to convince everyone that he had everything under control. As he approached the corner where the dog had first appeared, Trevor told the policeman that the dog was his. To his surprise he was handed the dog and was told to accompany the policeman.

'All three of us went into this little room under the stand, with the dog wagging its tail and furiously licking my face, we sat down,' said Trevor, 'and at this stage I wondered to myself why I had said that the dog was mine when it wasn't. But I instantly fell in love with the dog and when the officer asked why I didn't have him (I knew by now it was a him) on a lead, I instinctively said that he'd pulled the lead out of my hand and that it must have lost it in the crowd.'

After filling in a form, Trevor was allowed to leave with the dog on a bit of makeshift rope and take it home to nearby Beeston. Initially Trevor said he felt guilty at taking the dog but that he also thought that its owners had been irresponsible at letting this little mongrel run free. He was prepared to give it back if needs be, but admits that he was getting quite attached to the dog, who looked about two years old and who he had now called Tommy, after Younger. The story soon hit the local newspapers.

Trevor said, 'The *Yorkshire Post* and the *Evening Post* both ran stories and photographs of us and Tommy and I lapped up the attention. At the back of my mind I was aware that the original owners would see the photographs and come forward to claim the dog. But they didn't. Tommy became a star down at Fullerton Park training ground and had his photograph taken with fans and players on numerous occasions.

'My wife, Pat, didn't want Tommy at first, but he lived with us until he was 15 years old and after he died nobody shed more tears than Pat herself. We are both now in our 80s, still in the same house and we've had a couple of great dogs since – but Tommy the pitch invader really stole our hearts.'

The next addition to our collection of Leeds fans is an odd choice in that he is in fact a passionate Manchester City supporter! But he's probably seen more Leeds games than most. Dr Raymond Ashton was brought up in Guernsey but finished his secondary education in the north of England, Leeds to be exact, bunking off school at any opportunity. A City fan since the age of eight, Raymond's love of football extends to clubs and individual players at all levels. He only went to Elland Road because the school orchestra rehearsed on a Saturday morning and as a result he was only able to get to Elland Road rather than Maine Road, in order to see the kick-off. Over the years he has seen several hundred Leeds games and got to know most of the players personally. One vivid memory Raymond has of his 'trial' at Elland Road was on the old Fullerton Park training ground behind the West Stand. Billy Bremner was the first out for training and immediately told Raymond to go in goal. Bremner then fired the ball straight past the stranded goalkeeper, who says with a large grin on his face, 'It was at this point perhaps that I decided to take my studying seriously!'

Raymond is a Guernsey Advocate and Public Notary. He is also a member of the English Bar, with chambers at 9 Stone Buildings, and is a member of the Law Library in Ireland. Raymond's priceless insights into Leeds United and fascinating anecdotes are threaded throughout this book. His Elland Road hero is undoubtedly Bremner.

He says, 'The one constant during my years watching Leeds United was the presence of my idol and role model, Billy Bremner. He simply did not know when he was beaten and served as a benchmark. After a few short months at school, a teacher asked me what I wanted to do when I left school; I said, not surprisingly, football reporter, to which the teacher replied, "You have to have O levels for that, lad." Later I asked another teacher for a reference to university to which he said, "It's a degree, lad." After several degrees no doubt he would have taken "egg from his face". Throughout, the late Billy Bremner and his fighting qualities have been my personal inspiration. It was often said that there would be no ball that Billy wouldn't go for, a mantra I have applied into my studies and life.'

Raymond has written numerous articles and books, including a few on Leeds United, which are excellent, but there isn't one on Manchester City. For the third edition of his books on Leeds, Paul Reaney wrote the foreword in which he says, 'I commend this book which is written by my friend who knows so much about the Leeds team and the players even though his heart is with another great team, Man City.'

Raymond was an admirer of Don Revie and of the team he began building in the 1960s, 'Revie started to construct a brilliant defence in the early 1960s with big Jack Charlton outstanding holding everything together with Cliff Mason, Grenville Hair and Freddie Goodwin. Leeds spent a lot of money getting out of that division and it was Harry Reynolds who backed Don. We [City] bid £5,000 more than Leeds for Johnny Giles but didn't get him. The most spectacular of Revie's buys was Alan Peacock. Great guy who fitted in with the team and he was great in the air. Peachy's knees had gone by then but he was the finishing touch to that team at the time.'

One man who has been in Leeds United's employ easily longer than anyone else is Peter 'Stix' Lockwood, the player liaison officer. He was on the groundstaff when he was just eight years old in the early 1960s. As well as an employee, he is an ardent supporter. 'During the 1960s, if you were attending a game,' says Stix, 'you had to get there very early to get a good viewing spot. Sometimes, we even took a wooden box to stand on to try and see over the adults stood in front of us. But no matter really what time you got there, at kick-off time you were like sardines. Absolutely massive crowds. All big men compared to us little legs. But we found a great vantage point to watch the match, me and my friend, and it was in the south-east corner. It was metal and surrounded by a barbed wire ring and right at the top of it were 55 lights. And yes, it was one of the floodlights. Me and my mate, with much practice, learnt to get over the barbed wire and we were then able to climb partly up the pylon.

'In those days they did not have stewards like they do now, there was just a handful of police inside the stadium, and they were to control thousands and thousands of people. Eventually, a copper would see us up the pylon and come over and shout at us and tell us to come down – but of course, there was no chance! And he certainly wasn't going to risk climbing up to us so we had our own private viewing spot for many a game.

'Close to that was the Scratching Shed; it had a long barrel-shaped roof and stood where the South Stand is these days. Once that stand was full, you were literally packed in like sardines. But no matter what time you went in to the Shed, be it before or after kick-off, the young lads were always allowed to go down to the wall at front – your father still had to stand at the back, but you were allowed to go down to the front. And the blokes stood behind you, would put their arms around you and put their hands on the wall to take the stress of the crowd when it surged forward, so that the little ones at the front did not get crushed against the wall. I vividly remember, as if it was yesterday, six lads stood in a group behind me sharing one cigarette between them because it was packed and so tight in there that they couldn't get their hands in their pockets to light one up, so they shared the one that was already lit.

'I also have a memory that will make every parent cringe, because as a kid, irrespective of whether we were behind the north or the south goal, my friend and I had a ritual that took place after every game. Gary Sprake, our goalkeeper at the time, was a great advertisement for Wrigley's spearmint chewing gum! During that period of a match, he must have consumed four packets, easily. He used to take a long piece out of the packet, take the paper and silver off it, throw that in the back of the goal and chew away merrily. Once it had lost its flavour, he went back to his pack and repeated the same procedure, but this time removing the piece already in his mouth and throwing it into the back of the goal. This procedure was carried out during the first half, then he changed ends for the second half. Once again, it was mainly police in the stadium and not stewards like it is now, so once the final whistle went, it was a race between me and my mate to get over the wall, get into the back of the net, get hold of the tasteless chewing gum, pop it into our mouths and merrily chew away ourselves! We'd have been about 13 years old. RIP Gary Sprake.'

The first Leeds United game that Les Wakefield ever saw was at home to Leicester City in September 1964.

He said, 'Dad had told me and my younger brother, Eric, how well Leeds had been playing lately. I had taken an interest in football when I was 11 and still at school. My dad asked me and Eric if we wanted to go to a real football match. As we'd only ever seen local teams at amateur level, we jumped at the chance. Then, he gave us a choice of two games, Sheffield Wednesday v Liverpool or Leeds v Leicester City. The decision wasn't that simple as most of my classmates and a few members of the family were Sheffield Wednesday fans. This might have (or should have) had an influence on our decision; however, Dad reminded us again of the good start that Leeds United had made in the First Division and that they were only a young team.

'Putting friends and family aside I asked Dad if we could go to the Leeds v Leicester game as Gordon Banks was playing in goal for Leicester and he was already an icon in football, who almost everyone knew of. My brother Eric nodded his approval so all was settled.

'When we arrived at Elland Road we stood at the top of the open Kop end. Along the top was a wide track which fell away down an embankment to the bottom. From there, looking back, we had a view of Gelderd Road, Lowfields Road and the city of Leeds. The atmosphere was something that I'd never experienced before. Thousands of Leeds fans chanting "Leeds Leeds Leeds"; needless to say, we joined in.

'The game itself, as I remember, was pretty quiet in the first half with Leicester scoring two goals before going in at half-time. Even though it was my first game, being 2-0 down at half-time gave me a sinking feeling in my gut – it would be something I would experience many times. The second half was totally different with Leeds constantly on the attack. One player who stood out was the captain, Bobby Collins. He seemed to be everywhere with the ball. I also remember the old-style boots he wore which covered his ankles.

'A little red-haired bloke scored for Leeds to make it 2-1 and then the same red-haired bloke got another to make it 2-2. This was to be my introduction to Billy Bremner. Again, the crowd erupted and I remember an old bloke wearing a flat cap and a raincoat running up and down the track at the top of the Kop, he was throwing his arms up in the air pointing two "V" signs depicting 2-2 towards the city of Leeds. The crowd were going absolutely crazy. It was something I'll never forget, seeing grown men emotionally and totally excited. It has resonated with me ever since.

'I didn't realise that the best was yet to come – Leeds kept pressing for the winner, the crowd was deafening, "Leeds Leeds Leeds" rang out all around the ground and from all corners. Then, late in the game, Albert Johanneson scored with a left-foot drive to make it 3-2. The crowd went mental. I was hooked and so was my brother, Eric. In one afternoon we became Leeds United fanatics. Albert Johanneson became my favourite player while my brother chose Billy Bremner as his. It was a day that changed my life forever.

'Huge thanks go to Gordon Banks because without him I could easily have become a Sheffield Wednesday fan as they beat Liverpool that same day. I've got lots of great memories from that season; the next game at home we were 1-0 up and lost 2-1 to Nottingham Forest, but it didn't matter, I was a fully fledged Leeds fan. Once you're Leeds, you're always Leeds.'

This chapter began with an FA Cup tie at Arsenal in 1950. Frank Birch was there with his dad, 'It was a present for my 12th birthday. I remember it because my sister Mary is my twin and she was upset that for her 12th birthday she only got a second-hand bike. We went on a coach from the corner of Elland Road. Mary was so angry that she became an Arsenal fan and refused to ride her bike. I didn't know that she was now an Arsenal fan until we arrived home early the next morning. We lived behind the Astoria on Roundhay Road in Leeds and our house was right outside the bus stop. When we got off the bus, I noticed some red trousers or slacks hanging from Mary's bedroom window and although I thought it a bit strange, I didn't realise at the time that this was Mary's protest and she was showing Arsenal's colours out of her window.

'Dad and I sat in the kitchen eating some toast while my mam told us the whole story, how they had both sat and listened to the game with Mary shouting her support for Arsenal and how she had said that she doesn't want her bike and that it wasn't fair that I got to travel 500 miles to London and all she got was a bike that had rust on it. I went to bed for a couple of hours and when I got up Mary was sat in the front room with those red slacks on and a reddish jumper. She sneered that she was glad that Leeds had got beat and she wished that our coach had broken down. At least she didn't say that she'd hoped it had crashed. Thankfully, her spiteful love affair with Arsenal was brief and she was soon riding her "new" bike. In later years she even went to Elland Road with her boyfriend as a Leeds United fan.

'We are in our 80s now and we both live close to our old house and Mary can actually see her old bedroom from where she lives. To this day whenever Leeds play Arsenal, we still have a joke about that day back in March 1950. I continued to follow United all over the country until I was about 70 years old.'

These fans were the foundation of, what I believe, to be one of the strongest, largest and most loyal brands of supporters that exists today. With a massive fanbase that spreads across the entire globe, a fanbase that actually increased as the team's status declined, there will never be a shortage of support from the terraces, be it vociferous, financial or downright unswerving loyalty, and I am in no doubt that it will always be there.

Meanwhile, however, it was the summer of 1963, and Don Revie was busily plotting his assault on the First Division.

9

Summer of '63

WHEN JOHN Charles signed for AS Roma in 1962, part of the deal included Leeds playing his new club in Italy and receiving a fee of £10,000. So on 5 June 1963, United arrived at the Stadio Olimpico in Rome to face Roma. Leeds had travelled with a strong squad a couple of days ahead of the game. Gary Sprake, Paul Reaney, Grenville Hair, Billy Bremner, Jack Charlton, Norman Hunter, Don Weston, Ian Lawson, Jim Storrie, Bobby Collins and Albert Johanneson would be the starting line-up, but they had several squad players making the trip too, one of whom was Rod Johnson, 'I was delighted to be travelling as part of the party, I wasn't expecting to play given the strength of the squad that had travelled, but I was determined to enjoy the experience.'

Joe Brook, a Leeds fan, travelled on the same plane as the team, 'It was the first time that I'd ever been out of Leeds, let alone abroad! Me and my mate Les, who lived a few doors from me on Dib Lane in Leeds, decided just a week before to go to Italy. We were a bit surprised to discover that the team were on the same plane as us. After we'd taken off from Yeadon we chatted with the players on the plane and Don Revie was fantastic. He kept saying if there was anything we needed just ask.

'There were a few other Leeds supporters on the plane too, one of whom was Arthur Dunhill who at the time was known to be Leeds United's number one fan. He was very quiet, he just sat doing his crossword puzzle in his newspaper. But he kept nodding across and was very polite. There were a few fans on the plane and I remember talking to one from Wakefield but I can't remember his name. I seem to recall that he was a mechanic. I have photographs of us in a group at one of the matches somewhere.

'I was sat behind Paul Reaney and we were just chatting about Leeds United in general. Some years later I took my family to Butlin's on holiday and Paul Reaney was taking a football coaching course for young budding footballers. My son Mark joined in and my wife Linda and I chatted with Paul afterwards and I asked him about our trip to Italy in 1963 and if he remembered speaking to me. He replied, "Yeh, course I do." I'm not sure whether he did or not, but that didn't matter to me. My mate Les died only a few years ago and we still talked about that trip to Rome in '63. We were kind of proud, that we were one of the first fans to travel abroad to watch Leeds United.'

Johnson told me that there were some Leeds fans on the plane to Italy with them, 'There weren't too many of them, maybe about ten or so, but I do remember that they wanted to buy us drinks on the plane and even again when we saw them in Italy.'

A 10,000 crowd at the Stadio Olimpico saw a hard-fought contest, with Roma coming out on top 2-1, Ian Lawson scoring for Leeds. Charles, of course, was centre-forward for Roma. Prior to the game, there had been a minute's silence in honour of Pope John XXIII, who had died two days earlier.

Three days later, Leeds headed across to the Stadio Danilo Martelli in Mantuna to play a Cremonese Select

XI, but they fared no better, losing this encounter 2-0 to goals from Rossini and Tassi. Albert Johanneson went closest for Leeds after latching on to a cross from Tommy Henderson and delivering a spectacular overhead kick that goalkeeper Bottoni did well to just tip the ball over the bar. Cliff Mason, a reliable left-back, got a well-earned run-out in this game. Because of the emergence of Terry Cooper, his appearances had been limited for United, but he earned praise from the Italian manager and also from the winger he faced, Pasinelli, who replaced Del Negro when he couldn't find a way round Mason.

The third and final game of the Italian tour saw Leeds face AS Prato at the Stadio Lungobisenzio. Grenville Hair was in at left-back instead of Mason, and Johnson finally got his chance. In the first five minutes, Johnson hit the bar and just moments later he produced a world-class save from the Prato keeper, Capascutti. Then a one-two between Johnson and Bobby Collins resulted in Johnson being brought down just outside the box. Johnson had to go off for treatment but returned to muster up another United attack. Unfortunately for Johnson, the injury he sustained was too severe for him to carry on and at half-time he was replaced by Jim Storrie. The game itself ended in a 1-1 draw, with Willie Bell getting United's equalising goal in the 78th minute.

Johnson said, 'Don Revie told me in the hotel the night before that I would be playing against Prato and I was so disappointed that it ended with my injury, and that I'd only played 45 minutes, but afterwards Don Revie assured me that I was still part of his plans for the club. Every player at the club, whether he was playing regularly or not, was made to feel that he was needed. Growing up in Wortley, I would look down at Elland Road from Wortley rec and think, "One day

…" I was just happy being a Leeds United player. Nothing compares with wearing the white shirt of Leeds.'

The tour of Italy had been largely unsuccessful on the field. However, it was significant for the fact that it saw Don Revie convert Billy Bremner into a right-half, a position he would relish in for the rest of his career. United had lost two games and drawn one, but with £10,000 to come from Roma on top of £6,000 already owed by Juventus, at least they would benefit financially. Or so they thought.

On their return from Italy, Leeds continued with their pre-season preparations. On Tuesday, 13 August they entertained Peterborough United in the first of their two friendlies at Elland Road. Just before half-time, a superb through ball from Collins allowed Storrie, the previous season's leading scorer, to open his account for the new campaign.

Three days later, Eric Stanger wrote in the *Yorkshire Post*, 'Leeds United's supporters are a good deal more certain about promotion this season than the officials at Elland Road. Mr Don Revie, the team manager, is realist enough to know that despite the progress made last season, especially by his young players, there are still obvious weaknesses in the side. While the policy at Elland Road remains to build up a reservoir of young talent so that when promotion is achieved again the club will have ample resources to stay in the First Division, they will not hesitate to buy ready-made players from time to time. There may even be a signing before the season starts.'

The following night Leeds took on Fourth Division Bradford City at Elland Road and were met by an extremely resilient team who seemed determined to put one over their ambitious neighbours. Only the previous year City had to be re-elected to the Football League after finishing in 23rd place – but all that looked in the distant past as they took on

United with a renewed vigour. Manager Bob Brocklebank had brought new players in and a new goalkeeper had been acquired from Hull City in Bernard Fisher, who after just ten minutes saved a penalty from Collins after Lawson was pushed over in the box. And seven minutes later Wragg put City ahead. Storrie equalised within two minutes but Stowell restored City's lead with a calculated 25-yard screamer. Unfortunately for Bradford, Leeds got a second equaliser and then Lawson grabbed the winner with just four minutes remaining.

With the 1963 pre-season programme completed, Revie began preparing his troops for what he believed would be a strategic operation in pursuit of promotion to the First Division. He knew in his own mind that there was still work to be done and loose ends to tie up, and most importantly, more signings were needed. He knew who he wanted and he was determined to get him.

Then, just as the vests and cones on Fullerton Park had been cleared away ready for the start to the much-anticipated new season, a most unusual blot on the landscape appeared.

Just over a week before the big kick-off, Bill Mallinson wrote for the *Yorkshire Evening Post*, 'United want £16,000 – So Charles can't play.'

Just over a year after Leeds had sold Charles to Roma, Cardiff City signed the Gentle Giant and returned him to his homeland. There was, however, a problem: Leeds were still owed £10,000 by Roma and £6,000 by Juventus. That money was not forthcoming and as a result the Football League would not accept Charles's registration as a Cardiff player.

Mallinson wrote, 'John Charles cannot play for Cardiff City for the time being – and they need him urgently for their opening match of the season at home to Norwich City next Saturday. Cardiff manager, George Swindin, was understandably furious, "We are being unjustly victimised. We shall appeal against the League's decision, unless they change their minds. The decision means that Charles cannot play for us until the matter is settled."

'The League secretary, Alan Hardaker, issued a statement, "The Football League have not accepted the registration of John Charles for the time being. Leeds United have not received satisfaction from Roma FC."'

Leeds chairman Harry Reynolds said the complaint arose over United's close-season tour to Italy, 'The £10,000 is the sum we were guaranteed to play two matches out there. We have made the tour but have not got the money. Roma have not kept their part of the agreement which was that they should make payment within seven days of the second match. Roma have completed the transfer payments as contracted but not the tour guarantees. We have written four letters to Roma Football Club to which we have had no reply. We had no option but to complain to the police.

'Also, Juventus have not fulfilled their contracted obligations either under the deal which brought John Charles back to Elland Road for a 93-day spell during which he played 11 matches for United. In that deal, we paid £53,000 for Charles and Juventus agreed to play a friendly match at Elland Road. This was arranged for 7 November, but Juventus cried off. Nothing came of a suggestion to play the friendly in the spring or of a move to play Juventus in Turin on the pre-season tour of Italy. There is quite a lot of ongoing correspondence with Juventus. They have recently responded, but that matter is now with the League and the FA, who will take it to FIFA although I do not know whether it has gone as far as that yet.'

Cardiff manager George Swindin was unmoved, 'I just cannot understand this cock-eyed thinking. It is pushing us for something which has got nothing to do with us. If Leeds United have something owing to them from an Italian League club it is up to the League to notify the Italian League and not take it out on us. Our business with Roma has gone through very smoothly and we are paying John Charles. Why should Cardiff City fight to get Leeds United's debt cleared?'

The Roma secretary, Dr Valentini, also weighed into the argument, 'Leeds cannot stop the transfer; as far as Roma are concerned the player has been transferred to Cardiff City.'

When asked if Roma still owed money to Leeds from the original transfer, Dr Valentini simply said that it was an internal matter for the club. One United director, however, said, 'We did not ask for the transfer to be held up, we only told the League what has transpired. We hope that Charles will settle at Cardiff and do well for them. I personally wish him the best of luck.'

Meanwhile, Alan Hardaker maintained that not only was Charles banned from playing for Cardiff for the time being, but he was also banned from playing football anywhere, for anybody, 'Let it be said straight away that the reason is purely legal or administrative. But the fact remains that in football law, in any country, let alone Britain, the big Welshman is out of the game for the time being – at least on paper. The reason is that, apart from the League's holding up of his registration with Cardiff, the Italian FA have not cleared him. Until they do so he cannot play for any club under FIFA anywhere in the world. That is international football law.'

But Hardaker did offer some comfort to Cardiff and Swindin when he said that he hoped the whole saga could be settled in a few days. He said that he had cabled the Italian League asking for action and said that it all depended how fast the Italian FA and the Italian League reacted, 'Charles might be able to play against Norwich after all, but they will have to be quick, without action by them Charles cannot play. We are being blamed for holding up the registration but the amazing thing about that is the League Management Committee were merely doing their duty under the known regulations, and had no alternative.'

Then Hardaker, who was not known for his affection towards Leeds, said, 'Unlike Leeds United, who correctly informed the League step-by-step, when they got Charles from Juventus last year, Cardiff City had done nothing as far as the League is concerned until they submitted Charles's registration. They did not follow known rules, otherwise possible snags might have been pointed out to them. United came into the affair only because they were trying to get a debt settled by Roma by requesting action through the League, and they had nothing whatever to do with the hold-up on Charles's registration. That was the League's affair.'

But then Leeds found themselves in the firing line, facing accusations that they had taken the action they had to 'get their own back' on Charles for his short-lived return to Elland Road. Reynolds immediately hit back. Hotly denying the accusation, he said, 'Far from getting our own back on Charles for his failure at Elland Road, we wish him and Cardiff every success and a quick solution to their snags. My board are behind me completely in that wish. The decision to hold up recognition of his registration was not ours. It was the League's, and only after they had given full recognition to the matter. We did no more than report to the League, as was our duty, what we want is merely our £10,000. We can use every penny of it. We did not want Charles's registration to be held up for a moment, and we had anticipated that our claim on Roma would have been settled much earlier. It is not our fault it wasn't, I can assure you.'

Thankfully for all parties concerned Leeds eventually managed to prise the money out of the Italians, and, subsequently, the Football League's suspension of Charles was lifted and he was allowed to resume his playing career at 32 – but not before a lot of bitterness had been passed around.

Leeds opened their league account with a home fixture against Rotherham United. Twelve-year-old Rotherham fan Keith Alwood was there with his father, Fred, for his first away trip with the Millers, 'It was the first game of the season in 1963. Me and my dad stood on the big open end behind the goal and I couldn't believe the atmosphere. I had heard nothing like it before; admittedly I had only been to a few games at Millmoor, but I'll never forget the home crowd that night, they were buzzing. A few weeks later, we played Leeds at home and me and my dad always sat on a wall near the ground to eat our pies. Some Leeds fans came out of the pub across the road and got into a small van, but it wouldn't start. We helped to push them off and it started and the lad in the front passenger seat gave me a shilling.

'We lived in Canklow near Rotherham and my dad worked at Rotherham Main Colliery; he was a massive Rotherham United fan watching them home and away. Rotherham Main had closed when I was very young and dad went to work at Wath pit.

'The season before, Rotherham had done the double over Leeds, but my dad was raving about their centre-forward John Charles who scored in both Leeds defeats. I went to Leeds a few years later, not sure what year, for an FA Cup replay but when we arrived it was thick of fog and the game was postponed. I couldn't go when it was played and we lost anyway.

'My dad died of bronchitis in 1980, he was 54. I now live in Stafford with my wife Kate and at 71 years old I don't get up to Rotherham as much as I'd like, but I still like to see the Millers whenever I can.'

Terry Buxton was 13 and still at Blenheim High School in Leeds when he went to that Rotherham game. It was also his first match, 'All my friends were Leeds fans and kept on at me to go to Elland Road with them, so I saved the money from my paper round and took the plunge. I hadn't a clue who the players were, I just remember we won 1-0, but that was me hooked, and the start of my 60-year journey following Leeds United.'

Terry's mate Dougie Reid also remembers his trips to Rotherham, 'We used to enjoy ourselves in the Tivoli End when I had left school. It was Rotherham's end but there was always a lot of Leeds fans in there. My first Leeds game had been the season before in 1962. I stood in the Boys' Pen at Elland Road for the friendly against Italian side Juventus. It was played to mark the return of John Charles to Leeds United.'

In August 1963, Don Revie made arguably one of the club's best ever signings. It is fair to say that Johnny Giles wasn't a happy player at Manchester United and never really saw eye to eye with manager Matt Busby, who insisted that Giles play on the right wing, a position not suited to the Irishman.

John Doherty was one of the famous Busby Babes and he said, 'Giles and Busby clashed over Busby's insistence that Giles played on the right wing when Giles's greater skill was in midfield, as he later proved at Leeds where he became a world-class performer in that role.'

Giles said, 'In the case of Busby, I and other players often wondered what he actually did. Assistant manager Jimmy Murphy seemed to do all the important things, with his excellent knowledge of the game and the time he spent developing the young players. It was Jimmy who would tell Matt when he thought a player was ready for the first team. On more than one occasion he had mentioned the possibility of me operating in midfield.'

John Carey played under Busby in their postwar side, captaining them to a 1948 FA Cup win. In 1956, when Giles first arrived at Old Trafford, Carey quickly saw his potential, which appeared to be suppressed by Busby. When Carey's playing career ended he eventually went on to manage Everton where his faithful lieutenant was fiery, pint-sized, Scottish midfield dynamo Bobby Collins. Concerned that discipline standards were slipping, Collins thought that too many players were taking liberties. He believed that Carey should have cracked the whip more but that was not his style. Instead, it was down to Collins to fire up his recalcitrant colleagues on the pitch, and his influence became crucial as Everton narrowly avoided relegation to the Second Division in 1960, before he went on to help revive Leeds under Don Revie.

In 1963 Giles began considering his options, 'Busby was a charming man. He never lost his temper. His greatest attribute was patience even after heavy defeats. If we were winning by a solitary goal with ten minutes left, he preferred that we went for a second goal, even if it backfired – he would say, "It was the right thing to do." Yet there was more to Busby than charisma and a bent for adventure and innovation. He could be ruthless. If someone needed to go, they went. I once saw an interview by Jeff Stelling with Alex Stepney, Denis Law and David Sadler where he asked, "What were Busby's main attributes?" They all answered, "His man-management."

'I honestly thought his man-management skills were poor; in fact in my case he must have had a man-management bypass.'

At the start of the 1963/64 season Giles played in Manchester United's 4-0 defeat at Everton in the FA Charity Shield and was left out of the team for the first league match – a 3-3 draw with Sheffield Wednesday at Hillsborough. He immediately asked for a transfer, 'In football, if you ask for a transfer and the manager wants you to stay, he will do his best to talk you out of it. On the other hand when he wants you to go, he'll tell you he's going to put your request before the directors. When I asked Matt for a transfer, he said, without any hesitation, "I will put it to the board." The general perception that Matt Busby wanted rid of me was only half right because I wanted to leave just as much as he wanted me to go. A team-mate of mine at Old Trafford, Wilf McGuinness, approached me in the car park after he heard that I'd asked to be placed on the transfer list. "Go back up and see the boss," he said to me. "He might change his mind."

'"He might," I replied, "but I won't change mine."'

Giles went on the Old Trafford transfer list on the Tuesday and signed for Leeds just two days later. Busby had told Giles that Leeds had come in for him and that the clubs had agreed terms. He then said, 'Don Revie is on his way to see you.'

Giles had admired Revie as a player at Manchester City and knew in great detail what he was doing at Elland Road. Leeds were in the Second Division but the previous season they had finished fifth in the league after a brilliant second half to the campaign.

Giles made his Leeds debut against Bury and all the talk was about this young Irishman from Old Trafford. The forward line was being labelled 'cosmopolitan'. The *Green Final* newspaper said, 'There can be no more cosmopolitan forward line in the Football League than the one which

Leeds United fielded against Bury at Elland Road this afternoon. The introduction of new signing Johnny Giles means that four different countries are now represented in the United attack.

'Giles was born in Dublin, Don Weston in Rotherham, Scotsmen Jim Storrie and Bobby Collins in Kirkintilloch and Glasgow respectively and Albert Johanneson in Johannesburg, South Africa. Of course, had John Charles still been here, United could have boasted a truly international attack.'

Giles had signed for a club with a rich Irish tradition. For more than 30 years Leeds had always had internationals from Ireland on their club register, and at times, their Irish colony had been the biggest in the Football League. During the previous close season it had looked as though the last of the links with Ireland had been broken when Noel Peyton had been transferred to York City. But Giles now awaited the affection that Leeds fans have been showing for fighting Irishmen ever since Harry Duggan had first worn the green shirt for his country 33 years earlier.

In addition to Duggan, in pre-war years there had been goalkeeper Jimmy Twomey, wing-half Bobby Browne and one of Leeds' biggest favourites of all time, David Cochrane, the man who filled the outside-right position that Giles would be taking on his debut against Bury. After the war, Cochrane was joined by Con Martin, who played in so many positions for club and country, and wing-half Jim McCabe. Then came other Irishmen such as Tommy Casey, Eddie McMoran, Billy Humphries, Peter Fitzgerald, Noel Peyton and Billy McAdams. Of the later contingent, the greatest crowd-pleaser was battling Wilbur 'Billy' Cush, the little man who played such a big part in Northern Ireland's development in international football. At 5ft 3in, Cush proved himself good enough to play for his country at centre-half. For Leeds he played in six different positions.

So as Giles went into action there would have been many tales told on the Elland Road terraces of Irish stars of the past. He could be sure of the special welcome that Leeds puts on for the Irishmen.

Against Bury, there was a slight problem with the scheduled referee. Mr S.B. Stokes of Nottingham had to pull out with a pulled muscle and so for the second consecutive week, the unfortunately named Mr Fussey had to step in. In his previous game against Ipswich he had a quiet afternoon, but against Bury he walked headlong into controversy right from the off. He incensed the crowd when he refused a blatant-looking penalty, after Albert Johanneson, who had been put through by a shrewd through ball from Giles, was floored by the Bury goalkeeper Harker right in front of the large open Kop. Then in the second half he disallowed goals by Bobby Collins and Don Weston for offside, then he bizarrely allowed a goal by Jim Storrie that did look offside.

In the end Leeds triumphed over Bury, whose strong, stubborn defence consisted of Elland Road nemesis Bob Stokoe as well as two brilliant full-backs in Gallagher and Eastham and two brilliant half-backs in Turner and Atherton. In a game where, because of United's fluid style, Giles often found himself working in midfield, Collins so often was United's standout player. 'Stop Collins and you stop Leeds' was beginning to be the motto in the Second Division, but after half an hour Collins surprised a retreating Bury defence by pressing forward with the ball and up the middle and surprised it even more by beating Harker with a beautiful dipping shot from 25 yards. Storrie's second-half goal settled the nerves and Johanneson rounded things off with a third, minutes from time.

United then stuttered to a 2-2 draw at Rotherham and four days later, after going 1-0 up at Maine Road, they lost 3-2 to Manchester City, badly missing the injured Collins.

Leeds had finished fifth the season before and promised to do even better in the new campaign – but that looked in serious doubt after a shaky start. But they then went on a 20-game unbeaten run which saw them assume the division's top spot. During this run, a 3-1 win at Elland Road over Portsmouth saw the revival of the famous 'Yelland Roar'. After a lean spell from the terraces which had seen the ground less than a quarter full, even Billy Bremner came in for some stick. He had been barracked by sections of the crowd when he played at inside-forward, but now an unbelievable transformation took place when he moved into the right-half slot. So after the game with the Yelland Roar still ringing in his ears, Don Revie said, 'These fans have contributed to our team's 100 per cent home record this season.'

The next visitors to Elland Road were Swindon Town and their bright 21-year-old on the right wing by the name of Mike Summerbee, who would go on to enjoy a glorious decade with Manchester City and was indeed a serious target for Revie, who came tantalisingly close to signing him.

But it was the Swindon defence that grabbed the headlines as they kept a rampant Leeds at bay and secured a 0-0 draw, despite loud and vocal support from the home crowd who constantly chanted the rousing 'Leeds Leeds Leeds' chant from the Paddock. Two more draws then followed as United took to the road.

A hotly disputed penalty at Portsmouth saw United trailing at 50 minutes. Grenville Hair was adjudged to have brought down Portsmouth winger McClelland, but Les Cocker immediately ran on to the field to protest. He was promptly booked by referee Leo Callaghan, and so too was

Hair. Cocker was absolutely livid when he retook his seat in the dugout, before order was restored ten minutes later; a free kick by the quick-thinking Bremner allowed Tommy Henderson, in for the injured Albert Johanneson, to grab the equaliser with a perfect header. Both teams had opportunities to take the points, and the crowd of 12,500 witnessed a truly bizarre moment when Hair, in an attempt to clear the ball, hit his own post and, when it then bounced right in front of Saunders, he ballooned it over the top of an empty net. And just for good measure, Paul Reaney had his name taken too in the closing stages.

In the crowd that evening was Martin Browne, 'My father, Roger, was in the navy and stationed at Portsmouth, and any chance at all to watch Leeds United was taken. We had moved there from Outwood near Wakefield a few months earlier. My father had taken me to a few Leeds games at Elland Road, and after we'd moved to the south coast during the previous season, we went to Southampton away. That Portsmouth game, unfortunately, wasn't too brilliant, but at least we got a point and I'd seen Leeds play again, so it was a win really.'

A dour goalless draw at Cardiff City four days later, with John Charles at centre-forward, was memorable only for the superb display by young Leeds keeper Gary Sprake who was being watched by two Welsh selectors ahead of their forthcoming international against England. Charles appeared to beat Jack Charlton in the air but he and his forwards drew a blank in front of goal.

After a routine 4-1 win over Mansfield Town in the League Cup second round at Elland Road, Leeds were at home again as they got back on the league winning track the following Saturday against Norwich City. United swept into action and held a two-goal lead at half-time thanks to a brace from Weston, after two fine pinpoint crosses from Johanneson. Then as Storrie bore down on goal he was tripped from behind by Norwich defender Phil Kelly, and Bobby Collins converted the ensuing penalty. Norwich did pull two goals back thanks to their prolific young centre-forward Ron Davies, after which Leeds had a chance to restore their two-goal cushion when they were awarded a second penalty, but this time Collins failed from the spot. But Johanneson added a fourth for United after a brilliant solo run cutting in from the left ten minutes from time. The only blot was a mistake by young Sprake, who again was under the scrutiny of Welsh international selectors, as his error led to Davies, who was also being watched by the selectors, to score his side's second.

The following Tuesday, United secured their first away win of the season at the County Ground of Northampton Town. Described by journalist Charles Harrold as 'The Revie plan, 1963 style – ten men in defence and the occasional swift break-out', Leeds choked Northampton with a very well-worked system. Throughout the first half, they defended in such massed strength that wingers Giles and Johanneson were continually back in their own penalty area, and Collins was back with them too. The defence was so firm, particularly Freddie Goodwin who was once again deputising for the injured Jack Charlton, and his two wing-halves, Billy Bremner and Norman Hunter, that for all Northampton's pressure it was not until two minutes from half-time that they forced an excellent save from Sprake who pushed a 25-yard drive from Mills round the post.

It was on the break that Leeds were particularly skilful, so much so that they scored twice in the first half from only half a dozen attacks. Centre-half Branston was the only Northampton player in his own half when after a quarter of an hour Bremner launched a long pass to Weston and as inside-right Ian Lawson came alongside him, Weston pushed the ball ahead and past Branston. Lawson went through with it and hammered a shot through the legs of Town's reserve keeper, Coe. Then, another 15 minutes later, United broke for a third time when Weston, in for the injured Jim Storrie, was on the end of a perfect cross from Johanneson and headed home with the unfortunate Coe out of position.

Northampton had no idea of how to find a way through and were far too slow in midfield. There was no sharp movement from their wingers and they remained sluggish into the second half. Leeds came close on a couple of other occasions before Collins sealed the match with a third goal direct from a corner in the last minute.

The following day, Revie was arranging trials for two more black South Africans. United's Goodwin, also an FA coach, had spotted two players while coaching in Northern Rhodesia in the summer, who he thought looked useful enough to be given a chance in England. Kenny Banda, a 21-year-old centre-forward or wing-half, and 26-year-old Ginger Pencil, an inside or centre-forward, were the two names that Goodwin handed to Revie on his return. They were due at Elland Road for trials within a week.

Leeds fan Tony Rawlins was at United's next game, at Scunthorpe, 'My dad first took me and my brother, Ron, to a Leeds game in May 1963 at home to Luton, but our first away match was away at Scunthorpe United the following season. We were really excited at travelling to an away match as Ron and I said it would make us proper Leeds United supporters. So at six o'clock on a damp and drizzly October morning, me and my brother climbed into my dad's sidecar, and he got on the bike. It was called a combination I think, and Ron had ridden on the back of the bike with Dad before, but with it being a fairly long way and raining he said that he should ride in the sidecar, so I crammed into the back seat and we was in the front, and off we went. We travelled down our street, Hough Lane in Leeds and before we got to the main Stanningley Road at the bottom, I had slid my perspex window open just enough so I could stuff my woollen Leeds scarf out; now we really were proper fans! I think it took 'bout three and a half hours or so to reach Scunthorpe and when I pulled my scarf in it was like a drowned rat, and as it squeezed in through the window, loads of water spilled down our Ron's back – he wasn't at all happy. Then Dad said that I couldn't wear the scarf to the match as I'd catch my death of cold. I was gutted!'

It was a hard game for Leeds as they struggled to break down a plucky Scunthorpe defence and an in-form goalkeeper, Ken Jones. Leeds plugged away at a side still seeking their first win of the season and sitting at the bottom of the table, and roared on by a following that was easily half of the 10,000 attendance, they finally made a break through in the 64th minute. Jones, who had been outstanding, made an error that let in Lawson to score the only goal of the game.

Leeds then began to control the game, prompting *Evening Post* journalist Phil Brown to say, 'Collins as usual was the leader of the Leeds band; but this win was due essentially to teamwork. The defence was superb with Goodwin at centre-half. Bremner, who was booked, was otherwise faultless in midfield and now that Johnny Giles is settling down and more attuned to what is wanted, and how fast it is in the Second Division I can say that I have not seen a faster-moving forward row in the whole division. Finally, Collins's pace on a short burst is astonishing for a man over 30 years old. He strung off another valuable game at inside-left, and he seems able to get United on the attack from any part of the field, so good is his eye, his reading of the field, and the accuracy of his pass.'

Tony said, scarf was still soaking wet when they returned to their motorbike after the game, but he wasn't too bothered, 'It had been a great day out and me and my brother hoped that it wouldn't be long before we could go again.'

Jack Charlton returned to the defence for the game against Middlesbrough at Elland Road. He had fully recovered from a particularly nasty bout of tonsillitis and Revie had the job of telling Goodwin, who had performed admirably at centre-half in Charlton's absence. Club captain Goodwin had been flawless in the previous games and Revie, after his usual practice of having a talk with the dropped player, said, 'It has been a most difficult decision for me, but Fred has taken it splendidly. He is the complete club man as far as I'm concerned, and I am most thankful and grateful for seeing him take this decision so well.'

It was not known who would be opposite Charlton on the night. The usual centre-forward for Middlesbrough, Alan Peacock, was said to have dropped out of selection with a knee injury. Boro's manager, Raich Carter, said, 'I have not decided on my side following the grim news about Peacock; we will be bringing 12 players and will decide when we arrive at Leeds.'

Before the game, a group of fans paraded around the pitch with a banner proclaiming 'Leeds For Division One!' The crowd, 36,919, the highest of the season so far at Elland Road, roared loudly as Leeds kicked off towards the Scratching Shed and Boro's Knowles immediately fouled Weston. It was to be a tense and bitter affair, and it wasn't long before referee Mr Seddon from Southport had taken the names of Charlton, and Middlesbrough's Bryan Orritt, and throughout the game he gave 33 free kicks for fouls,

18 of which were committed by Middlesbrough with two of them costing them goals. After 20 minutes, one of those free kicks was tapped into the path of Norman Hunter, who unleashed a glorious 25-yard drive straight into the top corner of Connachan's net. Leeds added a second early in the second half when Collins let fly with one of his speciality dropping shots from fully 35 yards that sailed over a packed defence and over the hapless Connachan, with everyone on and off the field watching on in amazement.

The 2-0 win stretched United's unbeaten run to eight games and moved them into second place, a point behind leaders Swindon Town.

Next up for United saw a short trip up the A62 to Leeds Road, home of Huddersfield Town. It was an ill-tempered match and the first three fouls in the first half and five of the first six in the second were committed by the visitors. Huddersfield, weaker in direction, in spirit and in the will to win, were lured to their own destruction by retaliating. For the *Yorkshire Post*, Richard Ulyatt wrote, 'There were 40 fouls and a similar number of toilet rolls thrown on to the pitch at Huddersfield. The fouls were almost evenly divided; it only seemed that Leeds United were the greater offenders. Morally they were much more to blame. They started the roughness.

'The bad impression created by Leeds on the field was maintained on the terraces and on the trains carrying the supporters. It is inconceivable that these imbeciles who throw toilet rolls as streamers buy them; they must be stolen in transit and so few spectators these days go far to watch Huddersfield Town, it is reasonable to assume that followers of Leeds United carried them. Thus what ought to have been a memorable day for Leeds United turned sour.'

The win was Leeds' fifth in succession, and in that time only Norwich City scored against them. It took Revie's team to the top of the table with a formidable goals record of 24 scored and nine conceded in 13 games.

But in the game itself, Huddersfield certainly looked tired, planless and without enterprise. They did not seem to have been told with sufficient emphasis that football is a hard game. The great difference was that Huddersfield gave in too easily, whereas all the Leeds players wanted to be in the game at all times. Huddersfield's strange decision to play the left-winger Mike O'Grady on the right because he ought to have been able to beat Willie Bell was a complete failure, and in the end it was discarded. O'Grady with the ball at his right foot was not happy and he was unable to dominate the enthusiastic Bell. Huddersfield also had no player as adroit as Johanneson and he and Weston tormented Huddersfield relentlessly. Bremner and Hunter were tireless, Charlton dominated the middle, Reaney kept Stokes at bay and Bell battled away against the quick darts of O'Grady. The atmosphere generated by the Leeds fans, despite the few moronic participants, was absolutely brilliant, sounding at times to be as loud as 50,000.

The game was admittedly littered with needless fouls and the referee, Mr Jones from Liverpool, could not have been criticised for getting his book out more often – but the talent and pure skill shown by Leeds that afternoon should not be overlooked. A brilliant goal from Giles, his first for Leeds, and a further goal from Weston earned a comfortable win, giving the impression that they could move up a gear if needed, but because of a very lacklustre Huddersfield they never had to.

In between the Huddersfield fixture and the upcoming encounter with Derby County, the Leeds board came under a bit of pressure relating to a game that was weeks away. This was mid-October yet fans were wanting tickets for the Sunderland clash on Boxing Day, more than ten weeks in the future. With just two points currently separating the two teams at the top of the division, the anticipation for the game was already rising and Leeds were forced to offer a statement of intent. The club's general manager, Cyril Williamson, said, 'We've never known anything like this. We have had ticket demands already from both Leeds and Sunderland fans. There have been so many inquiries about tickets that we have had to ask the printers to rush them through within the next few days so that we can get them on sale. There seems to be tremendous interest in this game. Some of the ticket requests have come from outside Leeds and Sunderland. I cannot recall any demand as early as this for a league game, but it is most gratifying to know that we're stirring up such interest.'

Derby arrived at Elland Road not expecting a great deal, but within 20 minutes they were two goals up against a team that were top of the league and had only conceded three goals at home all season. Among the stunned crowd of 30,000, a small family feud was developing in the corner between the Lowfields Road Stand and the Scratching Shed as two brothers stood side by side. Terry and Graham Anderson lived with their parents on Foundry Lane in Leeds. Terry was a massive Leeds fan, but Graham supported Derby. 'We shared a bedroom,' said Terry, 'and I had loads of Leeds players' pictures on my wall, including a big one of Jack Charlton above my bed. Graham had posters of the Beatles near his bed. One day I noticed a team photo from a magazine of Derby County at the side of his poster of George Harrison.'

Graham explains, 'I was never a Derby fan as such; I had seen Terry's pictures of Leeds United when we were both about 11 or 12 and liked the colour of the shirt, but I didn't want to be the same as him, so I'd seen that Derby County were also in white shirts so I put their picture up at my bed, much to my brother's disgust!'

Graham told me that he had never been to a Derby game and had probably seen them on the television once, if that. But he didn't want to just follow his brother. 'This all changed that day at Elland Road,' said Graham. 'Derby went two goals up and I didn't feel happy at all; in fact, I started feeling sorry for Terry and I could see the disappointment on the Leeds fans' faces.'

Leeds struggled to find a way back into the game but slowly began asserting themselves and gradually Charlton inspired a comeback. His flair for joining in attacks was given full scope before he moved up once again to head home a Giles free kick ten minutes into the second half. Charlton had previously shown unusual signs of unsteadiness, to say the least, in his defensive work and this goal must have been welcome to him in more ways than one. The Leeds equaliser came a quarter of an hour from the end when Weston headed in a Collins free kick.

Graham said, 'I became a Leeds fan that afternoon. I had seen the passion of the fans, my brother and others around him and I couldn't suppress it any longer. When the equaliser flew in I grabbed hold of Terry and we danced around like we had never done before.'

Terry confirmed, 'I couldn't believe it when Graham grabbed hold of me and hugged me when we scored, but it was great. We went home and the first thing Graham did was to take down his picture of Derby County. I gave him one of my Leeds pictures, but he soon had plenty of his own. The two brothers, now both in their late 70s, told me that they had really enjoyed reminiscing over that day.

Terry said, 'I still have that Derby team photo somewhere, it reminds me of a day that changed my life with my brother. We both followed Leeds United home and away from that day.'

After the draw with Derby, Richard Ulyatt, often a critic of Leeds' robust style of play, wrote in the *Yorkshire Post*, 'To Leeds United and their increasing community of supporters this result probably rankled. In terms of promotion to the First Division, a home draw ranked almost as a defeat. But on reflection it may be found to be more satisfactory. It illustrated two important points – one that Leeds have the ability to recover without the use of unfair force and two that crime does not pay because both the Leeds goals came from free kicks for fouls committed by Derby.'

Phil Brown added in the *Evening Post*, 'The 30,000 crowd had an exciting if trying afternoon, and the cheer of relief when Weston equalised would have run a power station.'

A couple of days later, Leeds were back on the League Cup trail with a home third-round tie against Swansea Town. Revie viewed the game as a chance to have a look at two of his promising youngsters. Sixteen-year-old Scottish amateur international inside-right Peter Lorimer, from Dundee, and 17-year-old right-half Jimmy Greenhoff, from Barnsley, had both made their league debuts the previous season, but neither had figured since. Lorimer was unlucky not to score in the second half when Swansea keeper Noel Dwyer did well to turn away his dangerous close-range flick, and young Greenhoff delighted the crowd with his constructive efforts. In the end, Leeds eased by their Welsh visitors with a Lawson header after just six minutes and a second goal to make it safe ten minutes from time when Storrie converted a great cross from Johanneson.

It was then back to league business as Leeds travelled to the south coast and The Dell at Southampton. In a cringeworthy match report that was certainly a sign of the times, Mike Langley wrote in the *Daily Express*, 'They call him "the Black Flash" although he's really the colour of milky coffee. They cry "Johnson, Johnson" from the terraces, although his name is really Johanneson. But there is no disagreement at all that Albert Johanneson, 22-year-old left-winger from Leeds United, is the fastest man in football since Jackie Milburn. Once, he flicked the ball past Stuart Williams, Southampton right-back who captains Wales, and regained it eight yards further on while Williams was still turning round. I half expected Reg Loynton the Solihull referee with a needlessly itching pencil to book him on the spot for speeding.

'Johanneson, who joined Leeds from South Africa two years ago, looks like the twin of the famed Zulu flyweight Jake Tull. But even Tull never scored a faster KO than Johanneson's second-minute goal. Southampton's defence remained glassy-eyed for the next half hour and were four down before they came round. Superbly trained, Leeds astutely generalled by little veteran Bobby Collins, and with a potential England left-half in leggy 18-year-old Norman Hunter, have achieved great teamwork despite several substandard players. Slap-happy covering and utter lack of authority or inspiration at wing-half and the speed of Johanneson destroyed the Saints.'

After Johanneson's early strike, when he latched on to a superb 35-yard pass from Collins and shot down the middle to score a brilliant goal as goalkeeper Godfrey came out, Lawson added a beautiful second, followed by a headed Johnny Giles goal before Lawson added his second and Leeds' fourth within 33 minutes. The match became ill-tempered in the second half as Southampton's England winger, Terry Paine, was booked along with Lawson, Hunter and Bremner for Leeds, but even though the Saints pulled one back from Kirby the result was never in doubt.

Yorkshire Evening Post reporter Phil Brown rounded up the afternoon's events, 'If Leeds United hurtle on as they are doing they could become the Beatles of the Second Division, as crowd pullers. "Come and see your team buried" could go on the bills of opponents' grounds. United have now won four times in a row away from home, they have played eight away games, won four, drawn three and lost one. Top off with five home wins, two draws and no defeat and you can see why today they are top of the Second Division for the second time this season in spite of Swindon Town continuing to play well. The pulverising of Southampton could have easily been 6-1 and was United's best win yet for me. It had everything, a deadly cutting edge, fire and flourish. And another Revie-planned system of defence held all Southampton could muster with ease.'

Revie singled out Lawson afterwards, saying, 'This is the reward for two and a half years of hard work by all at Elland Road. This has been earned by effort. We're at the top because we've done all we can on and off the field to get there. Ian Lawson got two goals out there and he's a typical case. This lad has not stopped training and working on his game since the end of last season. He kept at it right through the summer and has never slipped back. Now he's playing in the form I knew he was capable of, and we're delighted.'

United stuttered slightly when Charlton Athletic were the visitors to Elland Road the following weekend. The football correspondent from *The Times* arrived to cover the match by train and jumped into a taxi, later writing, 'The future always is a question of faith. However, the Leeds taxi driver, trundling me to the kick-off amid the grey tide of traffic and humanity – some 35,000 to a man – seemed to lack it. "Unit'd have flattered us befoore," he said in a broad accent. "They mucked abaat wi' John Charles and failed to put wood in t'ole." He talked further about not being a turncoat, but it transpired he was a rugby league man. Perhaps the nose had suddenly been put out of joint by his local rivals at Elland Road, who, at the moment, were leaders of the Second Division.'

From the start, Leeds struggled to find the form they had shown almost throughout the season so far, but Charlton did look a well-organised side and it came as no surprise when they went ahead through Matthews after 15 minutes, going in at half-time with that lead intact. Luckily for Leeds, they were level just five minutes into the second period when Jack Charlton went up for a corner. Giles took it and Charlton met it perfectly but goalkeeper Rose parried it, and with everyone in the box seemingly rooted to the spot, Big Jack seized on the rebound and slammed it home to give Leeds a point.

On Bonfire Night, Millwall contacted Leeds to enquire about Freddie Goodwin, who they wanted as their player-manager. They were turned down but immediately began preparing a second bid. United had said they needed Goodwin as cover for Charlton who was suffering with a recurring knee injury. Millwall chairman Mr Purser said that his club had offered a new bid and were prepared to wait but after a meeting at St Annes between the chairmen of both clubs, his Leeds counterpart Harry Reynolds said, 'Any recommendations to the United board would rest with Mr Revie.' Purser then issued a statement from Millwall, saying, 'The deal is off – for the moment. Leeds will not part with Goodwin as they want him for the first team, but we have not given up hope of getting him. Naturally we will consider other applicants, but we are still interested in Goodwin and will see what happens in the future. We are not desperate to make an appointment at this time.' Revie said, 'Our need for Freddie is certainly greater than Millwall's at the moment. The club is bigger than any individual and must come first in all matters.'

Goodwin stood in once again for Charlton for the visit to Grimsby Town three days later. United fans in their droves poured into Grimsby and Cleethorpes, with many staying over the night before. The familiar chant of 'Leeds Leeds Leeds' pounded out to sea. Supporters continued to descend on both towns throughout the morning, including Mick Downs and a few mates from Halton Moor in Leeds, 'It was absolutely scorching hot for a November day and everyone was in high spirits. When we got into the ground, over half the crowd was Leeds, there were United banners everywhere. My mate Stan had brought a flag but had left it on the train. We hoped that someone had taken it to the ground and we could get it back, but we never saw it again.'

Lawson, lining up at inside-right but playing much further forward, opened the scoring for United when he raced on to a low cross in from Johanneson and cleverly diverted past Wright in the Grimsby goal. United remained pretty much on top throughout; although Sprake was called on to perform a couple of smart saves, Weston wrapped things up three minutes from time to send Leeds home with both points and back on top of the division.

Preston North End arrived at Elland Road for what was certainly the most ill-tempered game of the season so far. Fraught with nastiness, 'hard-fought' has never been used before so aptly as a description. Afterwards, *Sportsmail* wrote the following account, 'So much violence erupted over the playing area at Elland Road on Saturday that a fight between two grandstand patrons when Preston conceded a penalty served almost as light relief. But it was not the tragic sight of grown men who play football for a living trying to knock lumps out of each other which disturbed me. It was the apparent resignation, almost condonation, of officials that this had to be when two teams met while fighting for promotion.'

Eight Preston players needed the trainer's attention – centre-forward Alex Dawson also needed an X-ray which revealed a cracked bone in his left wrist received when he was bundled into the boundary wall – compared with two in the Leeds team. Both managers, Gordon Milne and Don Revie, however, appeared afterwards to accept this as an inevitable sequel to a promotion campaign. Bremner was lectured early in the second half and booked a few minutes later. Then referee Eric Jennings called all 22 players into the middle of the field and basically told them all to calm down and to cut out the rough stuff. Following that, a foul on Lawson resulted in a penalty which Johanneson stroked home with ease. After an hour had gone the fighting and fouling seemed to peter out and both teams realised that points were far more important and some good football was played. Then in the closing stages Preston equalised in bizarre fashion – Willie Bell hit a back-pass to Sprake far too gently and the ball then bounced off the goalkeeper's knee, hit Preston striker Holden in the face and flew into the net to make it 1-1.

Preston fan Dennis Higgins was at Elland Road that day, 'It was much better when both teams stopped brawling and fighting and began to play some good football between them.'

Dennis has been a Lilywhites supporter since 1958, when he was ten years old. He said that he had been to Elland Road with Preston three times in the 1960s and watched from three different parts of the ground, 'First time was in the Scratching Shed, then in the Paddock area where the players come out and then opposite end to the Shed on the big open end.'

After the game, Revie made the decision to take the players away for a few days to relax away from all the tension that appeared to be building up. It was a decision welcomed by all.

The boss said, 'It took only 53 points to win promotion last season. Everything points to a tougher fight this time around. Whoever goes up is going to have to be good. We hope that will apply to us. After five away wins in a row it is clear that we have been playing more relaxed football away from home. At Leeds the tension has mounted. In their attempts to give some wonderful supporters the results they deserve, the players have tried to force the play too much at home and it hasn't gone right.'

Goodwin admitted, 'There's been a lot of tension creeping into the game. With some of the out of step fans it's a bit like Beatlemania. Everybody wants to get in on the act. With players the tension tends to get a grip on things. A good side becomes an ordinary side from the day it turns from inspiration to desperation. It is the taut and tense side that gets desperate. That's why a side needs the right sort of relaxation.'

Trainer Les Cocker added, 'When a trainer has got his men fit, tension is the main problem with which he has to cope. In a tight Second Division like this, somebody will crack and we're attempting to ensure that it won't be us.'

So on the Monday, Revie took his boys away to Blackpool to rest and regroup. Rod Johnson said that it did the players and staff the world of good, 'We trawled around Blackpool pretty much free to do what we wanted – within reason. Me and some of the lads went for a game of snooker and a pint for a couple of hours. Some went to the pictures. And some just went for a quiet drink. We had to be back at the hotel at a certain time and we'd gather in a room and generally have a chat amongst ourselves. It took a lot of pressure away from what had been going on with the football. And by the end of a few days away, we were raring to go again.'

The first game after the break was down in London against Leyton Orient. Apart from the goalmouths being heavily sanded due to incessant rain, the overall pitch was in good condition. Before the match, the Orient fans were warned of their behaviour over the tannoy and in the match programme. At the previous home game, against Northampton Town, crowd trouble had occurred and a dart was thrown on the pitch. Police patrolled in the crowd throughout this time.

The strong wind spoiled a lot of the play and the score was 0-0 at half-time, but the game sprang into life four minutes in when a 25-yard free kick from Collins flew past stunned keeper Mike Pinner. The ball was still rising when it approached the goal and sailed into the top corner.

Then with just under 20 minutes remaining, Hunter threaded a delightful ball through to Johanneson to put Leeds two up and end any hopes of an Orient comeback. The eventual 2-0 win equalled Leeds' 1931/32 club record of 15 league games unbeaten.

Towards the end of November, the club learned of some good financial news. Fred Marshall, a former chairman of the 100 Club, which was affiliated to Leeds United and who three years previously had proposed a vote of no confidence in the board, said at the annual meeting that he was now one of the club's greatest admirers. Mr Marshall, on being told that United's directors were not only lending the club £10,000 each but were also covering the £84,000 overdraft at the bank, said, 'I think it is magnificent. They are to be congratulated on standing cover to over £160,000. Leeds should know about this – the man on the popular side should know about it. It is a fantastic amount. Very few club boards would do this.'

Albert Morris, United's finance chairman, said, 'It is nice of you to say so, but the directors have not finished – if Leeds United want any players and they are for sale, the club would find the money.'

Revie missed the meeting because of a chill, and his report was read by hhis secretary, Cyril Williamson, on his behalf. 'One can never guarantee success,' said Revie's report, 'but I do wish to convey to you that the playing staff are giving 100 per cent effort – and this, together with our coaching, training, scouting and administrative side, make us a formidable combination. We hope it will bring the desired success.'

Harry Reynolds responded, 'We are blessed with one of the finest managers in the game in Don Revie. With the spirit he has created we as a club are going somewhere. He spared no effort and worked day and night. His inspiration had brought loyalty throughout the whole staff. We want to be one of the best clubs in England and in Europe.'

In turn, Sam Bolton, a former chairman of the club, paid high tribute to Reynolds for his drive and enthusiasm which, he said, had played such a big part in putting the club in its present position. He was the man who said Revie would make a good manager.

Leeds played Swansea at Elland Road for the second time that season on 30 November, and won a tight game 2-1 with goals from Johanneson and Bell. The following week saw a long journey to Devon to meet Plymouth Argyle. Despite a round trip of 600 miles, United had a fair-sized contingent of supporters. They were seeking to extend their record-breaking unbeaten run to 17 games and were also looking for their seventh consecutive away victory, to set yet another club high. Without the ever-reliable scorer Lawson because of an injury in training, Storrie stepped in without hesitation. Cocker had to treat Sprake after just 90 seconds after a collision with Carter but he was OK to carry on.

Leeds took the lead on 15 minutes after a throw was worked to Johanneson, who took on almost the entire Argyle defence before driving a beautiful right-footed shot into the back of the net. As the team ran back to the centre for the restart, the chant 'Albert! Albert!' rang out from the supporters. But on the hour, Plymouth's Lord collided with Sprake who stayed down. Cocker, Revie and reserve Eric Smith all ran on to Sprake. A stretcher was called and the ambulance men carried Sprake from the field. Storrie pulled on Sprake's blue jersey.

United did not fall back on defence as a result and instead kept trying to pin the hosts in their own half. Then five minutes later Sprake was back on the pitch with his right leg heavily strapped just above the knee, still limping. Storrie returned to the attack and Leeds headed home to Yorkshire with two vital points and another record. As well as being unbeaten in 17 games and having won the last seven away games, they were also unbeaten in their last nine away matches, conceding just two goals in the process. And they remained top of the division.

Then once again United faltered in their next home game, against Northampton. They were looking for their first double of the season, having won 3-0 at the County Ground on the first day of October, but it just wasn't to be and that became evident when Leeds were awarded a penalty, after Town defender Everitt, stood on the goal line, used his hands to stop a goalbound header from Giles. Unfortunately, Johanneson hit a really poor penalty which keeper Harvey saved easily without even moving his position.

A disappointing 0-0 draw prompted a subdued Revie to make a public apology to the fans. He said in a statement, 'After Saturday's match I can only ask our supporters, easily the best in the division for me, to please be patient, to forgive and forget, and to back the lads up all the more through this strange home slump. The short answer is that they try too hard at home. They start too tense, going in for the early goals we used to get so often, get worried when the goals don't come, and get worse.

'They were missing their men with the simplest of passes on Saturday. At least seven men played badly. The lads all know this, but it is hard for a young side to understand and to swallow, and it is greatly bothering them. Those of you who have been to an away match this season know they can play ever so well. But let there be no mistake about this – while I am pleading for tolerance of the team as it plays at Elland Road I am still intensely proud of them, taken overall, and I hope and trust to be prouder still before this season is over. This home jinx will go. The team will one day snap out of it and really play well at home. I am sure we are getting through this mood, and the continued backing of our supporters will help to kill it. I am asking for that for the lads.'

Then, as if as a footnote, Revie added, 'News from Old Trafford via a newspaper report indicates that we are interested in buying Nobby Stiles, who apparently wants a transfer. I can say categorically there is not a word of truth in it.'

Leeds didn't have to wait long for that elusive double. They had beaten Bury 3-0 at home in the second game of the season and after the disappointing draw with Northampton, their next fixture was away to the Shakers at Gigg Lane. The match was played at an extremely brisk pace from the start. No quarter was asked or given and there was an abundance of incident and a fair ration of good football from both sides.

Leeds began in the mood of division leaders, moving the ball about quickly and precisely and had the Bury defence, including Revie's nemesis Bob Stokoe at centre-half, in all sorts of trouble. The visitors really should have gone ahead when Weston's early shot went inches wide. A bottleneck in a side road near to the ground meant that many Leeds fans arrived late, and some were still coming through the turnstiles when Lawson scored after 20 minutes. It came from a long punt from Sprake down the middle which initially eluded both Lawson and Stokoe, but the forward was quickest to recover and slid past Stokoe to race through and score with a spectacular crashing drive.

Then Lawson found himself with an open goal in front of him when defender Turner mis-headed, but Lawson lobbed the ball over the crossbar. The miss proved costly when five minutes before the interval Alston scored with a 20-yard shot to put Bury level. Leeds survived a few goal-line scares with Sprake coming to their rescue. And when a draw seemed the most likely outcome, the wily Collins, who had played what was for him a very minor role, broke away and laid on the chance from which Weston got the winner with nine minutes left on the clock.

The long-anticipated clash against Sunderland finally arrived on Boxing Day and a crowd of over 41,000 squeezed into Elland Road. The game had been in doubt because of the terrible weather and only a 40-ton blanket of straw spread over the pitch saved the day. The conditions were treacherous. Pools of water were all over the penalty areas and peat blackened the goal areas; underneath the slimy top the ground was hard from the frost. It was obvious that there wouldn't be a great deal of 'pretty' football played. Sunderland took the lead after 55 minutes and for a period Leeds' unbeaten home record looked in danger. Then the normally dependable Sunderland goalkeeper Jim Montgomery made an uncharacteristic error when he fumbled a through ball and Weston touched it through to Lawson who slipped home the equaliser. It remained at 1-1 and although United were disappointed that they hadn't won, they could take consolation that their unbeaten home record had remained intact.

Jim Keene was at the return game at Roker Park just two days later, 'I left my house in Seacroft in Leeds and walked the short distance to South Parkway to meet a friend, Robert, and soon we were picked up by Kevin Spence in his car and we headed north to Sunderland. It was a bleak day and the weather all the way up was really poor. We arrived at Roker [Park] and the queues outside were unbelievable. We didn't get in until 20 minutes or so had gone and we were already a goal down. There was a Leeds fan who we recognised stood near us on the steps and we asked if he'd seen their goal. He just said, quietly to us, "Sprakey dropped another bollock." We knew it wasn't going to be our day when Sunderland scored again within minutes of us getting in.'

The match was littered with fouls, and Storrie was carried off on a stretcher. It was game over for Leeds and they had finally lost their unbeaten run. Their lead at the top had been narrowed to one point; Sunderland were now level with Preston in second place and with Charlton Athletic three points behind in fourth, promotion looked to be down to these four clubs.

A forthcoming FA Cup tie against Everton was a welcome diversion from league football. Almost 50,000 people crammed into Elland Road for the third-round encounter. It was a fairly scrappy match but had plenty of highlights. Lawson put Leeds ahead just before half-time and as the game progressed it looked as though one goal may be enough to put them in the hat for the next round. Then as the game entered its final ten minutes, there was controversy when Everton were awarded a penalty after Bremner was adjudged to have brought down forward Alex Scott as he entered the box. The Leeds fans were incensed, and Revie was fuming, later claiming, 'If Bremner's tackle on Scott was worthy of a penalty, then so was the foul on Bremner by Labone when our man was clean through on the edge of the six-yard box.'

But there was still more controversy to come. Scott dusted himself down from the foul and took the spot kick himself which Sprake saved magnificently. As he was mobbed by his team-mates, referee Tom Langdale interrupted the celebrations by ordering the penalty to be retaken because, said Mr Langdale, Sprake had moved. Scott was reluctant to retake it himself and it was left to Roy Vernon, who made no mistake and sent the tie to Goodison Park for a replay. But in the few days before that replay the FA issued a warning to Bremner over his poor disciplinary record. Bremner's booking against Everton had been his fifth of the season and the FA had already sent a letter to Leeds in December after his fourth caution. So even though he had never been sent off, Bremner faced a carpeting by the FA Disciplinary Committee. Immediately, the press were all over it, whipping up hysteria. 'Leeds fear ban on the bomb' was typical of the kind of headlines that were being put around. *Daily Mail* journalists Don Hardisty and Ronald Crowther presented this joint article, 'Billy Bremner, the Leeds redhead who goes through each game like a bomb, often with explosive results, steps into tomorrow's white-hot replay at Goodison with the threat of suspension hanging over him. How will this affect his powerhouse play, so vital to Leeds, in the feverish atmosphere of a Goodison crammed with 60,000 roaring fans? And the anxiety to stay out of trouble could take the edge off his powerhouse play. These are some of the possible flashpoints: 1 because two other players were booked at Elland Road along with Bremner – Everton's Jimmy Gabriel and Alex Scott. 2 because of the dramatic, twice taken penalty which Bremner conceded and which kept Everton in the Cup. 3 because of the mystery rumour that someone tried to punch the referee at Leeds, Tom Langdale from Darlington, after the match and that he had locked himself in his room for an hour with a policeman, apparently standing guard outside, added strength to the rumour.'

But Langdale rubbished these rumours, saying, 'I have no complaints at all about my treatment at Leeds. Nobody attacked me or said anything out of place. Why did I stay in my room? I certainly wasn't sheltering from anyone. I listened to the cup results and reports on the radio. I have no reason to submit a special report to the FA. The only report I will send will be about my booking of the three players.'

Bremner, by now 21, spoke out about the accusations of too rough play which had been made against him and the club, 'I really can't understand what all the fuss is about. I play hard, yes, but I don't grumble when opponents play hard against me. The trouble is that when you're top of the table, like Leeds, players, crowds, and, in some cases, referees single you out for that special treatment. You have to take it. Football is a man's game, and is meant to be played hard. But I never set out with the deliberate intention of injuring an opponent. Any professional player who would do that is crazy. When I first earned my place in the Leeds side as a teenage forward, I was often described as another Denis Law. I never was and never will be another Denis Law – he's a great player, but I must admit that perhaps it all went to my head a wee bit in those days. I was impetuous, inclined to flare up and retaliate. But I was younger then and you soon learn your lessons in professional football. Ideally, I would like to play at inside-forward again, but if the gaffer, Mr Revie, thinks it's best for the club for me to play right-half then I have no complaints whatsoever.'

Talking about Leeds' chances of promotion, Bremner said, 'I have never doubted that Leeds will win promotion. There is still a long way to go, of course, but we'll do it. Of our opponents this season I rate Charlton, Southampton and Preston as the best teams we have played. In fact watch Southampton as promotion candidates if they get off to a good start next season. On a more personal note I'm hoping to get into the Scottish under-23 international side to play England at Newcastle in February. But I have been disappointed so many times when I have been tipped for an under-23 cap in the past, that I really don't hold out much hope.'

A disappointing 2-0 defeat in the replay at Goodison Park meant that Leeds could now return to more important league matters, with Bremner at right-half.

A crowd of 34,000 turned up at Elland Road on 11 January to see a close battle with Manchester City and the only goal of the game, scored by Weston, got United back on track. Next it was a tricky-looking encounter away at Swindon Town. Goals by Giles and Hunter earned a point, but again United lacked the power up front. They did, however, receive praise and admiration from an unlikely source – Swindon's manager. The renowned journalist Ken Jones wrote in the *Daily Mirror*, 'Leeds, the team with the toughest reputation in the League, can now offer in defence the unsolicited comment of Swindon Town boss, Bert Head. There was only admiration from Bert for the method and spirit of a team who look certain to ride to promotion on a wave of hysterical criticism.'

Head was quoted as saying, 'They play the game as I like it to be played. They play hard and they never give up fighting.'

Jones continued, 'I left this game satisfied that Leeds have faced and played in front of too many cowards this season. They are tough and, at times, awkward. But they always have one saving grace: They are honest. What they do they do openly. And if they come off second best, there are no squeals. The knife-edge tackling of right-half Billy Bremner is undoubtedly the most controversial issue in any Leeds performance. Bremner, reminds me of Spurs' Dave Mackay. Both are tremendous players with tremendous natural talent who underline their skill with great heart.

'Swindon, moving sweetly early on and two goals up through inside-left Bill Atkins, felt the full fury of the now-famous Leeds fightback. A Giles header put Leeds back in the game just before half-time, they got a deserved equaliser in the last minute from Hunter.'

Cardiff City were the next visitors to Elland Road. Bell had to deputise at centre-half for both Charlton and Goodwin, and put in a solid performance, but the problems for United were in the attack, where they had been all season. Pathetic finishing by the forwards had left nobody in any doubt as to why they had the worst home scoring record in the top half of the division. Leeds had enough chances to have been three goals up before Mel Charles gave Cardiff the lead after 18 minutes with a fine left-footed drive that went in off the bar. And later Leeds had at least another half a dozen chances to sink the far-from-formidable Welsh side, who had too many casual strollers in attack.

Johanneson missed from five yards out and Giles missed from two yards, and then there were loud groans from the Leeds fans when Weston incredibly put the ball over the bar from just one yard out. Then when Leeds looked as though they would never score, Johanneson forced the ball through a crowded goalmouth in the 40th minute to save United's home record. But an incident occurred involving trainer Cocker that would linger into the following week. Cardiff manager George Swindin claimed that Cocker had rammed his elbow into the Bluebirds' Barry Hole's ribs as he went past the player to attend to Lawson during a stoppage. Swindin reported it to the FA, whose Disciplinary Committee then issued a statement saying, 'We will consider this report in due course, the Committee at present is labouring under its work for this season, and has heavy agendas for its only occasional meetings for some time ahead.'

Cocker, who was preparing to be once again England's under-23s trainer at Newcastle the following day, said, 'The whole complaint is ridiculous. I merely bumped into Barry as I was turning, I apologised to him, and that was heard by the linesman.'

Revie strongly defended his trainer, 'Swindin is completely wrong and unjustified, but he has made an official complaint. The referee said he saw nothing because he was booking Williams of Cardiff at the time, and has to report that of course. Neither Cocker nor I are worried about the upshot of this, because no offence was committed. But we both resent this latest sneer on Leeds United very greatly, built up as it is a mistaken conclusion by Swindin out of nothing. Cocker will vigorously defend any charge, should there be one, and I will be glad to give any evidence that is required.'

Revie had other pressing matters after yet another lacklustre display by United's attack. He had to rectify the situation if United's promotion hopes were to be fulfilled. Chairman Harry Reynolds, at Revie's request, sanctioned the funds to sign Alan Peacock from Middlesbrough. On 5 February, Leeds offered Middlesbrough £50,000 for the centre-forward. Then, just after 1pm, Revie announced that the clubs had agreed terms and with that he was on his way to Ayresome Park, along with his trusted chairman, to complete the deal. Revie was delighted to be finally getting the man that he had wanted for months but because of a cartilage operation the previous autumn, the deal had been put on hold. Peacock expressed his admiration for Revie, who added, 'I am happy Peacock will be joining us for he is a player for whom I have always had the highest regard.'

On arrival at Teesside, however, Revie and Reynolds were met with a small problem – Peacock was nowhere to be found. Middlesbrough manager Raich Carter had searched the district for over two hours before Peacock was finally located on a local golf course. Revie was relieved and delighted. The fee, which would rise to around £53,000 with add-ons, was the highest ever received by Middlesbrough, and also over £10,000 more than they paid Sunderland for Brian Clough, whom Peacock had succeeded at Ayresome Park. Peacock would go straight in for the trip to Norwich.

The deal with Middlesbrough had been organised with Revie's customary precision, wrapped up in two minutes flat at Elland Road after a specialist had pronounced Peacock 100 per cent fit.

With the ink still drying on the transfer forms, Peacock said, 'From the moment Leeds agreed terms it was always at least 10-1 on my moving. In fact, I was so keen that my wife Margaret and I didn't even get around to picking out a house in Leeds. We looked at a couple of estates and Albert Johanneson let us look over his house to get a general picture of the type of accommodation that Leeds United gave their players. It's certainly good enough for us.'

Then came the question from Leeds fans everywhere, 'Will Peacock get us promoted?'

Raich Carter had already been asked that. 'Who knows?' he said, 'but at least the boy has got some pretty useful operators – like Bobby Collins, who is the best inside-forward by far in the Second Division – to help that push. Peacock is good in the air and he takes his chances on the ground. And his prize asset is that he can score goals. What more could anyone want?'

With his signing in the bag, Revie said, 'Alan Peacock won't guarantee promotion for us this season, because football knows no such guarantee. A manager could sign five top-class players all on the same day, and even this wouldn't necessarily do the trick. But a chap like Peacock is the type I'd always prefer to have playing for me rather than against me.'

A considerable contingent of Leeds fans made the trip to Carrow Road, no doubt wishing and praying for a vast improvement in the attacking formation, or indeed the lack of.

In defence Revie brought back the young Paul Madeley in at centre-half, and six forwards, as well as Peacock who travelled with the party. With Sunderland at Cardiff and Preston at Huddersfield, a Leeds win at Norwich was vital. Unfortunately, however, United had to be satisfied with a point. Yet despite the comparative disappointment of one point instead of two, which had looked within grasp, Leeds' play was more than promising. Most important of all, Peacock got off the mark with a goal on his debut. It was a trademark header, but the rest of his play was intelligent against a defence led by one of the best centre-halves in the division for the past three years, Barry Butler. Elsewhere on the pitch, the half-back line of Bremner, Madeley and Hunter was solid, Collins and Giles worked non-stop and although he had a relatively quiet game, Johanneson provided the telling cross that enabled Peacock to score.

After the 2-2 draw at Norwich, Leeds were second in the table with 29 points from 42 matches. Sunderland were top on 44 from 30, with Preston third on 41 from 29, and Charlton fourth on 36 from 28.

The *Evening Post*'s Phil Brown was upbeat, "'Roll on next Saturday! They'll paralyse Scunthorpe at Elland Road!" I heard one of Leeds United's band of young followers at Norwich call to another. Without being as ecstatic as that, there should nevertheless be a good deal of truth in the remark. United looked on the upgrade again. It was just the improvement we all wanted for the hard road ahead after the sometimes rough road since those Sunderland games at Christmas.'

The following week, Leeds didn't exactly paralyse Scunthorpe United, although they did get two very welcome points. But, alas, they did make hard work of winning at home. Peacock, making his home debut, definitely had the right ideas, but his team-mates needed to buy into them – and quick.

Madeley, once again at centre-half, was cool and tidy, and could hardly have been bettered by the men for whom he was deputising. Johanneson scored the only goal of the game.

Another team in danger of having the double put over them were Huddersfield Town who arrived at Elland Road and were under intense pressure from the first minute. They did concede a goal after seven minutes but stuck doggedly to their task. It did look as though that one goal by Storrie would be enough to give United two much-needed home points, but once again there was a mistake by Sprake, when he dropped a ball from Town centre-forward Derek Stokes to let in Lewis for a cruel and costly equaliser five minutes from time.

Off-field events dominated Leeds United, the draw with Huddersfield. The transfer deal which would have taken Lawson to Scunthorpe for £25,000 seemed to have fallen through when the club and player failed to agree terms. Scunthorpe manager Dick Duckworth said that after Lawson had been shown two club houses and had talks, the requirements he demanded didn't sit easy with Scunthorpe, 'Unless he changes his mind it is unlikely he will sign for us.'

One outgoing player was full-back Cliff Mason, who had played a major part in Leeds United's fight against relegation in 1962. He did sign for Scunthorpe. Revie was full of praise for him, 'Cliff gave us two years of brilliant service after we signed him from Sheffield United. He nobly did his stint towards getting us clear, he was a very valuable player for us.'

Meanwhile, following on from his warning in December, Billy Bremner was suspended for three games by the Football Association. It was a very severe and unprecedented punishment for a 21-year-old considering that he hadn't been sent off. Leeds closed ranks and regrouped. Revie told the press, 'We are very, very disappointed at this decision, but our blow will be softened by the return of Willie Bell, who has recovered from a deep chill on the chest.'

United suffered a loss in their next game, 2-0 at promotion rivals Preston North End. In front of 36,000, Preston outmanoeuvred Leeds on the night. Both teams were two points behind leaders Sunderland yet Leeds were in second on goal average. Leeds, missing Bremner who was starting a three-match suspension, tried hard to take the game to their hosts. But for the stubborn resistance of Charlton, Hair and Sprake, it could have been a heavier defeat. There weren't many good points for United that evening; they had suffered only their third defeat of the season, but it would also be their last.

Four days later, Leeds entered the final ten games of the season in great style with a 3-1 win over Southampton at Elland Road, watched by a very special guest, the England manager Alf Ramsey. Lawson was back in the line-up and scored. Ramsey was there to look at United's two talented teenagers, Hunter and Reaney, for the England under-23s, and it was beginning to look as though he had chosen the wrong day. A nasty thigh injury forced right-back Reaney to limp at outside-right for 40 minutes. And in a major reshuffle by Revie, left-half Hunter had to take on the toughest job in the defence as the full-back set to face Southampton's only really troublesome forward, Terry Paine.

But the spirit in which these two 19-year-olds took on these makeshift roles must have created a good impression as Ramsey watched Leeds round off the game with a long-overdue surge of power. When Lawson opened the scoring after just one minute, they looked well set to swamp Southampton. And, for all the stubborn defensive efforts of the Saints' Tony Knapp and Tony Godfrey, they should have done so with plenty to spare. But once again their patient fans suffered agonies of frustration before the forwards managed to shake off the tension that had played havoc with their finishing at a critical stage in the promotion race. After an unmarked Johnny McGuigan had been allowed to equalise with a soft touch goal for Southampton in the 35th minute, Paine missed a great chance to lunge Leeds into serious trouble in the 63rd minute. But ten minutes later Collins bluffed his way round the defensive screen for the goal that broke the spell. And, after giving Stuart Williams the runaround all afternoon just as he had done at The Dell, Johanneson then struck to make it the biggest home score by Leeds for five months.

Alan Peacock lined up against his old club for the first time when Leeds visited Middlesbrough in mid-March. Giles returned from international duty with the Republic of Ireland against Spain in Seville.

This was United at their best. On a rain-soaked, greasy pitch they regained the leadership of the Second Division with a display of fast, attacking football that delighted their followers – all 30 buses of them. The half-back line of Greenhoff, Charlton and Hunter was magnificent. Greenhoff, in particular, gave a polished exhibition of football. Aged 17, he worked tirelessly in attack and defence and one thrilling dribble, in which he beat six men only to be foiled at the last moment, deserved what would have been the goal of the match. Lawson scored for Leeds and at half-time the game was 1-1.

In the second half, with the wind and rain at their backs, Leeds, inspired by Collins, launched attack after attack. Middlesbrough's right-back kicked off the line and Charlton thumped the crossbar from 25 yards as Leeds pounded the Boro defence. Then four minutes from the end Peacock celebrated his return to Ayresome Park by emerging from a ruck of players to head Leeds in front for the second time. Three minutes later, Giles scored a magnificent third with a powerful shot from a difficult angle. Revie said afterwards, 'The players did very well indeed this afternoon, especially in such spoiling conditions. Once again they gave the lot, and you cannot ask more. But I am not sure whether our supporters at Middlesbrough didn't do even better for us. I thought the weight and the enthusiasm of our followers on such a terrible day were fantastic. Our players think so too. Our supporters were wonderful from the cheer we got as we came out right up to coming off.'

For the visit of Grimsby Town to Elland Road the following week, Revie had a dilemma. On such brilliant form how could he leave Greenhoff out? Yet Bremner was available again after his suspension. In the end it was Bremner, recently chosen for the Scotland under-23 squad, who got the nod over the unlucky Greenhoff, who Revie assured would figure in his plans.

Grimsby fan Ian Mitchell was heading alone to Leeds by train, unhappy at his team's prospects. There was a strong possibility that both sides could be leaving the Second Division; Leeds by promotion, and Grimsby, unfortunately, by relegation. Ian had met up with some Leeds supporters at the reverse fixture in early November, 'I got chatting with some Leeds fans in the pub in Cleethorpes when they came down to watch Leeds United at Blundell Park. We hit it off and one of them, Mark Green, had suggested that when Grimsby play at Leeds, I should go up and have a night out with them. So I took them up on their invitation.

'On the day of the game I met Mark and a couple of his mates, Keith and another lad whose name I can't remember, at a pub near the station called The Peel, I think. At the match I stood with them in the stand opposite the players' tunnel, but it wasn't a good day for my team, we lost 3-1, and that sent us closer to relegation, although I remember we did play well that day. After the match we went round the pubs in Leeds and considering the result, I had a great time. Later we ended up in a nightclub, can't remember the name, Tiffany's? It was in like in a shopping centre. Anyway, I got drunk and missed my last train home. I slept on Mark's settee. Mark died a few years ago, and I never returned to Leeds again, but we always kept in touch.'

Leeds kicked off their Easter programme on Good Friday at St James' Park to play Newcastle United. Giles scored the only goal of the game close to half-time and although the visitors had other chances to increase their lead, they also had to defend well too. One such incident was described splendidly by journalist Eric Stanger, 'Sprake made the save of the match from the fierce shooting of inside-forward McGarry, tipping over a real whizz bang of a drive from 20 yards out.'

With two more valuable points in the bag, United then travelled to Derby County the following day. With ten minutes, to go Peacock headed home for Leeds. Then just as it looked like another two points, Cullin, Derby's inside-right, took a speculative swing at a dropping ball with his back to the goal. Somehow he managed to hook the ball over his shoulder and it went in off the post with Sprake completely baffled. There were just 90 seconds left and the game finished 1-1.

On Easter Monday Leeds played Newcastle for the second time in three days. Over 40,000 people packed into Elland Road to see Weston and Johanneson triumph in a tight game to stay top of the division. Revie remained cautious. 'One match at a time please,' he said. 'The side did a great job over Easter with five points out of six. The win at Newcastle was particularly splendid, I thought; after that we had to travel down to Derby.'

Leeds played host to Londoners Leyton Orient next up and didn't put in their best performance of the season, but once they had broken down the massed visiting defence of Orient, Giles scoring after half an hour, they settled down and played more relaxing football, although high winds and a dry pitch made that difficult at times. Leeds remained in overall control and Weston put them two up just two minutes into the second half, but a late goal by Orient tested the nerve of the 31,000 crowd. Eric Stanger wrote of Orient's goal, 'Sprake failed to cut out a corner from McDonald. Sprake may not have been entirely to blame, but for a young goalkeeper of such high promise he has been dreadfully prone to simple error of late. Possibly in this instance it was due to lack of concentration through being underemployed for most of the game.'

Results elsewhere now meant that Leeds were just one point from promotion with three games still to play. But before he left for another junior talent-hunting trip to Scotland, Revie stressed, 'We still have to get that point. But, there seems no reason why the lads shouldn't now raise their sights towards the Second Division championship.'

Leeds then had a brief break from League duties and that all-important final three games, with a friendly against Juventus at Elland Road. A crowd of 19,000 turned up and they were entertained by a fast and skilful display by both sides. Absentees for United were Reaney, who was making his debut for the England under-23s in Rouen, and Giles, who played for the Republic of Ireland in Dublin against Spain in the European Nations Cup. Barrie Wright and Tommy Henderson deputised for the international pair and did not disappoint. Leeds certainly held their own and Juventus were under siege for long periods. Young Terry Cooper came on for Bell, Storrie replaced Peacock, and Lawson took over from Weston. With a quarter of an hour left, Giancarlo Bercellino hammered a 25-yard free kick hard at Sprake who failed to hold it and Silvino Bercellino put in the rebound. But with six minutes remaining Henderson crossed for Storrie to score with a fine header and make it 1-1.

Leeds returned to Second Division business with a trip to South Wales and an encounter with Swansea Town. Revie gave Cooper his league debut. Cooper, a 19-year-old from Brotherton, three miles from Castleford, was originally due to travel as a standby left-back, but in the end he played on the left wing for the injured Johanneson, missing only his fourth league game of the season.

Thousands of United fans converged on Swansea, some arriving two days before the game itself. Every United director was also present and the club issued this rousing statement, 'The present board is ambitious to make this club one of the best half dozen in the land and if their ultimate goal of being able to take part in the European Cup seems unduly ambitious at the moment, that is surely better than being merely content to stay in the First Division for as long as possible before inevitably relegation comes once again. Too often in 44 years as members of the Football League, Leeds United have suffered from that restricted outlook.'

The fans, Leeds easily outnumbering Swansea, stood enjoying the mild sunshine as the teams strode out on to the surprisingly well-grassed pitch. The cheers for the visitors were almost deafening as they sensed celebration after a long, hard season. Bremner was lectured in the first minute following a foul on keeper Roy Evans. Then Leeds began to show a superiority over the home side, cutting Swansea's defence open with swift attacking play out to the wings, and defensively they crushed any countermoves. Then Peacock scored two deadly goals within four minutes, and when Giles added a third on the half-hour mark the United fans were delirious. The score remained at 3-0 without the need for further goals. With promotion now in the bag, Revie said, 'There will be no easing off by us. We want that championship flag flying over Elland Road next season.'

GREETINGS TELEGRAM

H11 GTG 10.20 LEEDS T 31 GREETING

GARY SPRAKE SWANSEA TOWN FOOTBALL CLUB
VETCHFIELD SWANSEA

= KEEP THE SCORE THE SAME AS YOU ALWAYS
HAVE DONE IN WALES BEST IF LUCK GARY =
DIRECTORS AND STAFF OF LEEDS
UNITED +

GARY SPRAKE + +   LS 0

Telegram of best wishes to Gary Sprake (Wales) from the directors and staff at Leeds United – author

Willie Bell is carried off by Les Cocker and Johnny Giles at The Battle of Goodison – Jim Keoghan

Unusual rosette from the 1965 FA Cup Final, depicting the black Leeds player Albert Johanesson. – author

Rod Johnson with the Leeds players' golf trophy in 1965 watched by Rods wife, Margaret and runners-up Gary Sprake and Jimmy Greenhoff (right) – Johnson Family

Programme from Leeds' first ever game in European competition. – author

Leeds players board the plane for the club's first ever competitive game in Europe in 1965 – author

Trainer Les Cocker tends to the injured Jim Storrie in Budapest in 1965 – author

Leeds United Juniors in Italy in 1966, featuring David Harvey, Terry Yorath and Eddie Gray – author

A Soccerex card belonging to the founder, Duncan Revie – author

The home of Don and Elsie Revie in the late 60s and early 70s – author

*The house where Don and Elsie retired to in Kinross, Scotland, in the mid 80s –
Steve Cooke*

*Jack Charlton personally signs
his book to his 'mate' – author*

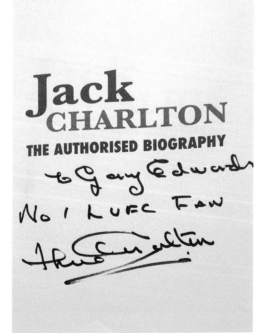

Jack
CHARLTON
THE AUTHORISED BIOGRAPHY

to Gary Edwards
No 1 LUFC Fan

GPO ● GREETINGS TELEGRAM

H64 GTG 2.52 COLLINGHAMBRIDGE LS 24 GREETING

SENT
84

Paul Reaney

MR GARY SPRAKE BIRMINGHAM CITY DRESSING ROOM

HIGHBURY STADIUM LONDON =

JUST SHOW THEM HOW GREAT YOU REALLY ARE ALL THE BEST

= PAL PAUL +

Telegram of best wishes on Gary Sprake's debut for Birmingham against Arsenal from his 'pal' Paul Reaney – author

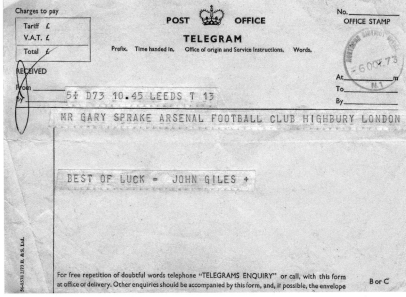

Charges to pay		POST 👑 OFFICE	No.
Tariff £			OFFICE STAMP
V.A.T. £		**TELEGRAM**	
Total £		Prefix. Time handed in. Office of origin and Service Instructions. Words.	

RECEIVED

From

By   5½ D73 10.45 LEEDS T 13

-6 OCT.73
At   m
To   N.1
By

MR GARY SPRAKE ARSENAL FOOTBALL CLUB HIGHBURY LONDON

BEST OF LUCK = JOHN GILES +

For free repetition of doubtful words telephone "TELEGRAMS ENQUIRY" or call, with this form at office of delivery. Other enquiries should be accompanied by this form, and, if possible, the envelope

B or C

Johnny Giles sent this telegram to Sprake after Leeds sold him to Birmingham City – author

Gary Sprake surrounded at his wedding by his Leeds team-mates during better days for the keeper – author

The author chats with the keeper who replaced Gary Sprake, David Harvey – author

Gaining promotion meant Leeds had to pay Middlesbrough a further £5,000 on the Peacock deal, but I wouldn't imagine that bothered the club too much.

Leeds would win that championship title if they took three points from their final two games. Sunderland lay two points behind United on the same amount of matches played, but with a better goal average.

The penultimate fixture, against Plymouth Argyle, was a disappointing anti-climax if truth be told. Jack Charlton said, 'We were all a bit lethargic, it was as if we'd won it already. It was hard to lift our game. It didn't feel right, I can't really explain it. We'd more or less achieved promotion with four games still to play. Before this game against Plymouth the Leeds players did a lap of honour to give our fans something to cheer about. It was about the only thing they did have to cheer about too, for the 90 minutes of this, our final home game, were probably the worst we had served up all season. It was one long boring yawn for fans and players alike.'

Nevertheless, Leeds earned another point towards that title. They went in front after 20 minutes courtesy of a 30-yard drive from Bell, but Plymouth drew level after an hour when Sprake made another of his far too frequent simple errors. This time he allowed a gentle shot from Jennings, the young left-winger, to slip out of his hands. Sprake found himself on the spot too often and Eric Stanger remarked, 'For all his Welsh international caps Sprake still has a lot to learn and his unreliability recently is not balanced by his occasional brilliance.'

Plymouth fan Tom Craven was at Elland Road that afternoon, 'When I was 14 years old, I travelled up to Leeds to watch Argyle play Leeds United at Elland Road with my father, Bob. We had travelled by train to London and then by bus to Leeds. It took us almost a full day there and the same back to Devon. We were watching the game from the halfway line on the terraces right opposite the tunnel. I had a big green and white woollen scarf that my mother knit for me. It had all the Argyle players sewn on in green in the white blocks on the scarf. It was my pride and joy. I then felt my father pull up my jacket collar to hide my scarf. A Leeds fan, who was smoking a pipe, was stood behind me. He then tugged at my scarf and I thought he was going to steal it, but he pulled it up above my coat collar so that it was showing. He then said something along these lines, "Therz no need t' hide thi scarf lad, thaz among friends 'ere cock." I don't know if they'd have been as friendly if they hadn't just won the league, but I got the impression, certainly, that they were genuinely friendly people.

'After the game, hundreds of Leeds fans piled on to the pitch in celebration, and we set off back to our digs for the night. We were staying in a guest house not far from the Yorkshire cricket ground, Headingley. Some years later, I married a "Yorkshire lass" and I often wonder if my experience at Elland Road swayed my judgement when it came to love.'

Even before the last game, Leeds fans were hit in the pocket. The club announced that admission prices for the following season would go up by a shilling (5p) to stand, two shillings (10p) to sit and two guineas (£2.10p) for season tickets. But Harry Reynolds emphasised that rising costs, and not promotion back to the First Division, were the cause for the increase. 'Even if we had not won promotion, we would have had to put up our admission prices. The board is sure that our supporters will appreciate that it is their whole endeavour to get a first-class football club in Leeds and we anticipate wholehearted support.' The 18 London and district clubs had already lifted their minimum admission, and Arsenal had raised all their match ticket prices.

As Leeds headed to Charlton for the final game of the season, there were various scenarios. If United won, then they would be champions. Sunderland were their only title rivals and they played at Grimsby Town, the bottom club but not yet mathematically relegated. Anything but a victory for United would leave the question of the title dependent on the result at Grimsby.

Charlton were in fourth place but with no chance of anything but a top-four finish. United were at full strength and with everything to play for, but Charlton had every intention of stopping them getting a result. That was echoed by their captain and legend Eddie Firmani. But in the end Leeds put the finishing touch to a great season by winning the Second Division championship for the first time in 40 years. And it seemed like the whole of the city had descended on south-east London to witness it. Jack Roberts, from Rawdon, Leeds, arrived early with two friends, Mark and Bob, 'We travelled down through the night to be there, it was only about 8.30 in the morning and Leeds fans were everywhere you looked. A group of fans were asleep under a huge Leeds banner near a bush by the side of the road, others were just walking about aimlessly.'

Within the first few minutes United were firing on all cylinders and had several times been dangerously deep into the home defence. The game never drifted from that early pattern and Leeds stayed on top throughout. Roared on by the massive hordes of their supporters, Leeds stormed into the lead after 36 minutes; using quick long passes to counter the heavy pitch, an incisive move paved the way for Peacock to head home. Then on 70 minutes it was all over as Cooper put a fine cross in and Peacock finished it with a neat header. If United had a star, once more it was Bobby Collins. Covering every inch of the field, he and Bremner controlled the game from start to finish. And, once all the dust had settled, the top of the table read Leeds on 63 points, Sunderland on 61, Preston on 56 and Charlton on 48.

At the bottom, Grimsby were relegated with 30 points along with Scunthorpe on 32. Plymouth Argyle also finished on 32 points, but their goal average was 0.672 compared to Scunthorpe's 0.627. That's called cutting it fine.

Meanwhile, the fans from Leeds were in seventh heaven, yet two years ago to that very weekend those same supporters had been picking themselves up off the floor. In their last match of the 1961/62 season, United had won at Newcastle and held off relegation, finishing fourth from bottom.

Leeds had certainly come far in those last two years; their average crowd went up from 13,000 to 30,000 and with First Division gates to come. There was one key reason behind this transformation – Don Revie. His progress from the apprentice manager in 1962 to that of one of the most respected figures in the game had been phenomenal, and at all aspects of managing.

Journalist Phil Brown wrote, 'Granted the new faces and the new financial resources on the board; granted the inexhaustible enthusiasm of chairman, Harry Reynolds; granted the six-figure spending; and granted the wonderful leadership given the side on the field by Bobby Collins. But I have to cite Don Revie for having given United their new exciting lease of life. He has not only built a winning team, which isn't easy even if you have money, but he has totally reorganised the nursery and the scouting system likewise at all levels. And they start at school level. His drive has gone right through a loyal training staff and a devoted playing staff. His leadership and planning of what was a rocking club when he took over has been nothing short of brilliant, and at just 36, his best years as a manager are surely yet to come.'

A civic reception, to celebrate United's success, was given by the Lord Mayor and Lady MAyoress of Leeds, Alderman and Mrs E.J. Loy Wooler, at the Civic Hall in Leeds. It was attended by the players, their wives, the club's directors, officials and their wives. Revie addressed to crowd, 'I am glad we have won the championship for the players' sake. They certainly deserve it. When you think, it has been a fantastic performance to go through the season with only three defeats. The credit goes to the boys. They have trained hard, worked hard on the field and carried out their instructions to the letter.'

Revie said that the team had done so well that each man would be given his chance to make his mark in the First Division and that Leeds didn't contemplate making any big close-season signings.

The boss had no previous experience of management prior to taking over at Leeds, only a wealth of football knowledge and ideas gathered from some 15 years as a player, and from the outset he proved himself to be a person of strong character. He insisted from the start on full control of the playing side. He asked for five years in which to build up a really good team and felt that was not unreasonable considering the state of the club's playing register when he took over. He stressed that no club could be successful unless it built from the bottom, and that meant signing the best of schoolboy talent as junior professionals, coaching and teaching them so that as footballers they grew up with the club. This was a long-term strategy which paid off much earlier than expected.

Just how many miles Revie had travelled in search of young talent only he knew, but few managers, if any, could have shown such an infinite capacity for hard work. The benefit of Revie's overall plan was that players could step from the junior side to the reserves and to the first team knowing exactly what was required of them. The club's style and general tactics would be ingrained in them.

But in United's case, before it could be fully operative, there had to be a lot of improvisation and a lot of make and mend in the first team if relegation to the Third Division was to be avoided. Of the signings, none turned out to be more important than that of Bobby Collins in March 1962. It was thought by some that his best days were behind him at 30, but he not only led Leeds to safety that season but his shrewd generalship and leadership were decisive factors in taking them back into the First Division. Very few inside-forwards worked harder than Collins and his influence both in the dressing room and on the field were incalculable.

Collins certainly had an input in making Billy Bremner into one of the best wing-halves in the country. The pair formed the hub round which the team revolved. They were responsible for the quick transformation from defence to attack. But Leeds' success was not due to any one or even two men; it stemmed from a happy boardroom, a happy executive and happy players. Man for man, position for position, no other club could boast a better team in the full sense of the word. Every man was prepared to pull every ounce of his weight, to shoulder extra burdens to help out a colleague in trouble. Individual glory was readily sacrificed for the good of the whole, which was true team spirit and enabled many a game to be won when victory seemed unlikely. United were not always an attractive side to watch, in the sense of providing a glittering spectacle, but they were a mighty efficient one.

Once all the euphoria had eventually died down, Revie took his family – Elsie, Duncan and Kim – away for a short break while Syd Owen took charge of a squad of players behind the Iron Curtain to embark on three games in East Germany. The trip had been designed by Revie to test his young charges against relatively unknown foreign opposition. On 14 May, United lined up against East Germany Olympic in front of 60,000 at the Walter-Ulbricht-Stadion. But Storrie's goal after half an hour wasn't enough to prevent a 3-1 defeat. Charlton had his name taken by referee Herr Kopke, for a foul on Viogel, just after he had scored for Olympic. Leeds then went on to play SC Turbine Erfurt two days later, when this time a Storrie goal was enough to settle matters. The final game took place the following day, Weston scoring in a 1-0 win over Dynamo Dresden. On their return, Owen passed Revie a rather favourable report on his men in Europe.

10

The Battle of Goodison (Dirty Leeds)

LEEDS HAD ended their championship-winning season with an unusual summer tour of East Germany. And as the team prepared for perhaps the most important campaign in the club's history, back in the First Division, they began their pre-season programme with a trip to Northern Ireland. Leeds accepted an invitation to play Linfield in a benefit match at Windsor Park for the Blues' Ken Gilliland. Don Revie's men ran out 3-0 winners in an entertaining game with two goals from Don Weston and one from Bobby Collins, who was lectured by referee Jack Adair for remonstrating with a small section of the crowd who appeared to throw something on to the pitch after he had scored.

On 7 August United travelled to Castlereagh Park to take on Ards. Leeds ran riot with a brace each from Ian Lawson and Jim Storrie, the 6-0 rout completed by Johnny Giles and Collins. Their next destination was North Wales to take on Wrexham at the Racecourse Ground. In a close tussle United took the honours 2-1, with Ian Lawson again getting on the score sheet and the brilliant young Paul Madeley scoring the winner after 74 minutes. When the clubs met again at Elland Road three days later the crowd were thrilled by a very high-scoring match indeed. There can't be many 8-4 scorelines on record, but that was precisely the outcome. Albert Johanneson opened the scoring after just 30 seconds and went on to get a hat-trick, as did Storrie, while Ian Lawson and Collins grabbed a goal apiece. Referee Jack Luty, from Leeds, commented publicly afterwards on such a 'fine game'.

It was while on this trip to Northern Ireland that Revie had learned of the *FA News* report on the club's disciplinary record, which led to the 'Dirty Leeds' tag. Revie was philosophical, 'Although we don't agree with many aspects of the report, we will endeavour to monitor our behaviour. The strain of the 1963/64 season is now over and I hope that we will not be offenders to that extent. Many teams had far worse records than us and that is fact that cannot be disputed.'

But the directors took greater exception, chairman Harry Reynolds writing to the FA, 'We wish to register a strong protest regarding the statement and implication in the *FA News* that Leeds were the dirtiest team in League Football. We consider that this matter was purely a domestic one between the FA and the club, and should not have been for publication, as this was a bold statement without any details and apt to give a false impression. We would point out that we have only had two players sent off in the last 44 years. We maintain that the "Dirty" tag, which was blown up up out all proportion by the press, could prejudice not only the general public but the officials controlling the game, to say nothing of the minds of spectators, especially some types who are watching football today. It could lead to some very unsavoury incidents.'

Revie's Leeds had hoisted themselves into the First Division and were determined to make an impression – and they certainly did that. They kicked off the 1964/65 season with three consecutive victories winning many admirers, but they gained enemies along the way too. The opening game had been at Aston Villa, but Billy Bremner remembered initially having doubts about United's ability to survive, 'We were like greyhounds out of the traps … we launched attack after attack in the first quarter of an hour and ran Villa ragged. You can imagine how we felt when they opened the scoring … I don't often panic but I distinctly remember a dark cloud of self-doubt passing over. "We're not going to be good enough," I thought. The boss couldn't wait to get us back in the dressing room. He didn't shout at us, but he told us quite firmly that we were to stop running about like a set of madmen and get down to playing calm football. That moment was another big step in our growing-up process. We went back out and played exactly as he had told us and Albert Johanneson equalised … Jack Charlton then put us ahead and that is how it stayed until the end of the game. We had won 2-1, taken maximum points and had grown up a little, all in the space of one game.'

The Minstrel, Philip Dobreen, was at Villa Park and also recalls being somewhat nervous about United's return to the top. 'I was a bit sceptical as this was the first time I saw the First Division and I was convinced that it would be too fast for us, but I was totally wrong. We won that game and the next two games too, Liverpool and Wolves, so it looked too easy,' he laughs.

A little over 36,000 were at Elland Road for the next game, against reigning champions Liverpool. The ground was more than a third empty as Harry Reynolds had opted for a return to his premium pricing policy, having relaxed it for the previous season. Liverpool were always struggling and centre-half Ron Yeats put through his own goal, before Roger Hunt equalised for the visitors. With Bremner and Collins pulling the strings in midfield, Weston put Leeds back in front before Bremner added a third. Bremner then put Giles through with a superb ball to put Leeds 4-1 up. Gordon Milne pulled one back from a penalty rebound after Gary Sprake had saved his spot kick, but Leeds had drawn a defining line in the sand.

People began to take notice of the division's newcomers. Brian Kempton wrote in the *Yorkshire Post*, 'I am tired of reading about Denis Law. Granted, he's a good inside-forward, but because he's a great showman with magnetic visual appeal, I'm sure sports writers and spectators believe that he is better than he actually is. And his ability is greatly exaggerated. How many times have we read of comparisons between Law and Puskás, Law and Pelé, etc? Rubbish! He isn't even the best in England. Bobby Collins of Leeds United is a far superior all-round player. Law cannot control a game as well as Collins, he cannot pass a long ball as accurately, cannot "read" the game as well, is not as mature a player and, above all, cannot shoot as well. The Leeds fans are still laughing about the feeble £40,000 offered for Bobby by Aston Villa. If Law is worth £115,000 then Collins is worth £200,000.'

And the Old Pensioner, a 78-year-old regular contributor to the letters page of the *Yorkshire Evening Post*, wrote, 'In my time, I have seen many fine left-wingers – Bastin [Arsenal], J.R. Smith [Huddersfield Town], Alan Morton [Rangers], and Bobby Charlton to name a few – and there is not one playing at the present time as good as Albert Johanneson of Leeds United. He has fine ball control and can beat a full-back by both speed and body swerve. Everton have a useful player in Derek Temple, but I rate Johanneson the finest left-winger in Britain – and I'm including Scotland. Johanneson's ball control is comparable to that of Stanley Matthews, the daddy of them all, and he is fair in all he does.'

Leeds made it three wins out of three just three days later with a 3-2 home win over Wolverhampton Wanderers. With Collins out injured, Giles operated admirably in midfield and although Wolves twice went ahead, two goals from Storrie and one from Jack Charlton secured the win. But the fine run came to an end with a 2-1 defeat at Anfield.

Philip Dobreen was also there at Anfield with his guitar; his reputation was gaining nationwide acclaim and he featured in the renowned *Charles Buchan's Football Annual* from that season.

His popularity was such that he was swamped for autographs everywhere he went. While outside Anfield, a young Scouser said to his mate, 'There's that guy from the telly with the guitar – let's get his autograph.' Phil obliged of course and provided a little strumming on the old guitar along with it. Phil said, 'In those days there wasn't any hooliganism and it was really fun going to all the away games and we all had great times.'

Suddenly, shockwaves swept through Elland Road and the city of Leeds. Don Revie was considering a move to Sunderland. An emergency board meeting was hastily convened. It was revealed that Revie had considered the option of heading to Roker Park, after being refused a five-year contract, after two directors had threatened to resign if he received this new deal. Harry Reynolds, an ally of Revie, was in hospital following a car crash, but said from his bed, 'Mr Revie will not be leaving Elland Road.'

Revie had asked for a five-year contract but had been given one for only three years. And Reynolds said, 'I myself have fought to get Don's contract amended to five years. Other directors are behind me, but we are not strong enough to carry it through. But even if Don wants to leave Elland Road, his present contract is binding both ways.'

Reynolds lay in hospital with 64 stitches in his head following a car crash near Barnsley. Inside-forward Don Weston had been in the car with him. They were travelling back from a game between Rotherham United and Portsmouth. Weston said, 'We collided with a motorcyclist and then glanced off on to a wooden electric pole and ended up in a ditch.' Weston was unhurt but shocked.

The motorcyclist was 20-year-old Maurice Hollins, of Barnsley. He broke a leg and remained in hospital in a poorly condition.

Revie had said that he too would have been in the car, but following the abortive discussions with the directors he decided to take himself off to the game between Bradford Park Avenue and Bradford City instead. From his hospital bed, Reynolds threatened to resign if Revie went to Roker Park.

Phil Brown covered the story in the *Evening Post*, saying, 'Mr Revie is a firm believer that money is not everything and he is not holding a financial pistol at United's board. He has intense pride in the tremendous improvements he has made at Elland Road and I am not without hope that there may be a change of heart and decision which would enable him to stay.'

Meanwhile, the players were in a state of shock. Collins said, 'It has come to a great shock to us all. Mr Revie is a great manager, and if he goes, he will be missed – United's tremendous progress in the last two years is due to Don Revie.' Jack Charlton, who had worked with four Leeds managers, said, 'Don Revie is the best manager I have served under. I can hardly think of him leaving now.'

These sentiments echoed through the squad. Willie Bell said, 'I can't believe it. He's doing so well here,' and Jimmy Greenhoff added, 'It's awful, I cannot understand it at all.'

Billy Bremner, who had more than most to be thankful to Revie for, said, 'This is a terrible thing. It will be a bad day for United if he goes. He set high standards. I can't see life being the same.'

In the absence of Reynolds, Alderman Percy Woodward presided over another emergency directors meeting that lasted an hour, after which he issued the following statement, 'I wish to make it clear that this has been the first and only meeting to discuss the manager's contract, it was not even discussed at the last meeting. It has been the unanimous decision that Mr Revie remains with Leeds United and he is happy with that. He has the five-year contract and the salary he asked for. He is happy to carry on with the work he has done so well at Elland Road, and we will remain as we were – out for success and a happy club.'

Revie responded, 'All the time in my heart I did not want to go. One does things in the heat of the moment probably that one regrets. Leeds United have a great future, although it will take another two years before we really see the full results. We have made a great start in the First Division, but I don't want people to expect too much. When I was first appointed in this job three years ago, I said it would take five years, I still hold to that opinion. I would find it intensely difficult to leave all the progress and all the promise achieved at Elland Road. And now we can move on.'

So it was back to business as usual with a visit by Blackpool to Elland Road, who arrived with the talented Jimmy Armfield, Tony Green and Alan Ball. And in goal was Tony Waiters, who was in superb form throughout. Leeds won 3-0, but he brilliantly saved two powerful penalties from Bremner.

After two defeats and a draw, United bounced back with a fine 3-2 win at Stoke City which included a penalty save from Gary Sprake. It was a result that signalled a consecutive run of seven victories. A 3-1 home victory over Tottenham followed, watched by a crowd of 41,464, the highest Football League attendance of the day. An uncharacteristic mistake by goalkeeper Pat Jennings allowed Rod Belfitt to put Leeds ahead in just the second minute. Tottenham struggled to get into the game and four of their players, Cyril Knowles, Cliff Jones, Jimmy Robertson and Ron Henry, were all booked in quick succession. The outstanding Jimmy Greaves pulled Tottenham level with a superb effort and his overall performance prompted the *Daily Express* to report, 'Greaves caused gasps of astonishment with the precision of his passes.' But Leeds went back in front with a goal from Giles and a penalty from Willie Bell and continued on a brilliant winning streak.

Just a few years previously, Greaves had suggested that the 1959/60 season had brought football's so-called age of innocence to an end, with open, attacking football giving way to defensiveness, aided and abetted by specialist coaches and tacticians. This fitted a description often given to Leeds by some quarters in the world of football and it was a label that was justified for a period. But as Charlton often said, 'If you wanted a battle, you got a battle. If you wanted to play football, we would play football. But Don made it clear that we weren't there to enjoy the game, we were there to get results.' And Leeds found it difficult to win admirers, who were reluctant to heap any sort of praise, however small, on the newcomers. Norman Hunter said, 'Don never lost his temper with us, but you knew when he was unhappy. I used to get carried away at times and try to nutmeg opposing players, but he would make it clear that was not to happen again. He would say, "Win the ball and give it to those who can play."'

Revie did eventually 'let Leeds off the leash' and crowds and TV audiences were astounded by the new-look team as they slaughtered all before them. Paul Reaney said, 'Most people say we are a more attractive team now than we were a season or so back. But I reckon we're going to have to work out a compromise between playing it tightly and playing it brightly.'

Meanwhile, sandwiched in between an impressive seven-win run by Leeds was a game that would become known as the 'Battle of Goodison'.

On 7 November 1964 United travelled across the Pennines and into Merseyside for an encounter with Everton. Brian Crowther of *The Guardian* set the scene: 'Like an exasperated teacher walking out of a class of unruly boys, Mr Ken Stokes, the referee, left the field in the 38th minute of the match at Goodison Park. And, like sheep who at last realise they have gone too far, the players followed. Ten minutes later, Mr Stokes restarted the game, a concession that was abused by players and spectators. Amid the alarms and excursions, there was a sort of football game in which Leeds United beat Everton 1-0.

'Since this reportedly was the first Football League match in which the referee had taken the teams off the field for such reasons, some apportionment of the blame seems necessary.'

In Crowther's opinion, the referee was at fault as despite sending off Sandy Brown in the fourth minute, his control of the game was 'not firm enough'. The players then proceeded to take advantage of the leniency of the official, who 'decided to walk off' while Willie Bell and Derek Temple were being treated for injuries.

Linesman J.D. Williams appeared to be struck by an object as he left the field and the crowd was 'left to stew in its own juice' before an announcement stated that the referee would restart the game provided any missile-throwing ceased.

Crowther continued: 'The players returned and there was more throwing but yet the game went on. Rough play continued little abated. The refereeing was permissive, presumably in the cause of finishing the game.' Only Norman Hunter had his name taken during the game, albeit the correspondent felt he was 'unlucky to be singled out' as both teams were 'out of hand'. Crowther also expressed some sympathy for Stokes, however, having been 'tried so sorely' by not only the players but also the crowd, whose behaviour he labelled 'disgusting'.

He also noted that Everton did well to 'hold the major share of possession' with only ten men for 86 minutes following Brown's dismissal for punching Johnny Giles hard in the pit of his belly when they fell to the ground together.

Crowther concluded his report on a happier note: 'Leeds' goal, however, was a fine one. A foul by Vernon on Bremner in the 13th minute resulted in a free kick which Collins took from nearly 30 yards out. Bell raced in from the left wing, met the ball directly and headed it past Andy Rankin in goal. Everton failed to score for the first time this season. There were near misses galore by both sides, but no continuity except in the consistently good play of Collins and Charlton for Leeds and Stevens for Everton which transcended even this ill-tempered game.'

Ken Barker was in the Bullens Road Stand that afternoon, quietly reading his matchday programme. He was there with his friend, Rob Grimes. It was Ken's third away game with Leeds, and Rob's first. Ken said, 'I was in the lower stand in the corner towards the opposite end to the Gwladys Street End and half an hour or so before the game there was a threatening atmosphere, it didn't feel right. There was a lot of hate. I looked into the end to my right and I could see Leeds fans dotted about all over. The ones closer to us looked uneasy. Rob, on the other hand, seemed to relish it.

'But I think he changed his mindset once the game kicked off. I have never seen anything like it before or since. It was evil. We'd gone in my dad's Cortina and I just hoped it would be OK where we left it. I couldn't wait to get out of there. It was into the 1970s the next time I felt OK to go to Goodison Park; it was slightly better but to be honest, not by much.'

In the early 1960s Goodison Park was fast gaining a reputation for being a very intimidating place. A purpose-built semi-circular crescent-shaped barrier wall had been created and built behind one goal in an attempt to put more distance between the opposition goalkeeper and the home crowd. This came about after several complaints from visiting keepers that they were being constantly pelted with a whole range of missiles and objects by Everton supporters. During a league game against Tottenham, their keeper Bill Brown complained that darts had been thrown at him. This became big news, with the *News of the World* carrying the headline 'Everton supporters have got to be the roughest, rowdiest rabble who watches British football'.

London journalist John Moynihan was even less sympathetic, saying, 'Everton fans like to break things in the same way that a child likes to break toys. Evertonians are intensely loyal, but they are liable to go off the rails and if they don't get success they simply go mad! There is beer coming out of their navels.'

Philip Dobreen, The Minstrel, was at Goodison Park that day, 'The Battle of Goodison was a bit scary and as Leeds supporters we thought it best to stay quiet and not stir up more trouble especially when the teams were taken off. Willie Bell's goal made it worthwhile and Leeds were cleared of any wrongdoing anyway and it all fell on Everton's head.'

The notes in that days match programme had given no hint of the events that were about to unfurl:

'This afternoon we extend a warm welcome to the officials, players and supporters of Leeds United to Goodison Park. As this is the first visit of the Yorkshire club to this ground since they came back to the First Division at the end of last season we offer them our congratulations on their becoming the champions of the Second Division and gaining promotion. Good wishes for their success in the First Division must be qualified to the extent that we cannot hope to see them take any points back to Leeds from the game this afternoon.

'Leeds United have wasted no time in getting among the clubs who are making the running in the First Division this season and, among other things, have shown they are far from incapable of winning on opponents' grounds. Their last away fixture for instance was at Burnley where United collected both the points – and Turf Moor has never been a happy hunting ground for visiting teams. When Leeds United visited us last season, Everton won the encounter 2-0. This game was, of course, an FA Cup replay. The draw for the fourth round paired us with Leeds United at Elland Road. This match finished all square at 1-1. In the replay back at Goodison Park Jimmy Gabriel took the place of the injured Alex Young at centre-forward and it was Jimmy who put us in the lead, our other goal came from Roy Vernon and so we went through to the next round of the Cup.

'Leeds United were still still in the Second Division last season but even when they came to play us, the ultimate outcome of the Second Division table was beginning to take shape. Leeds, Sunderland and Preston North End were leading the field and this was, in fact, the order in which they finished. Leeds proved to be the season's champions in the section finishing with 63 points in all. This was the highest points total achieved in the Second Division since Tottenham Hotspur gained a record of 70 points back in 1920. The Leeds total was one point better than that of Liverpool in their championship-winning season a few years ago. Sunderland and Preston North End finished as runners-up in two different spheres; Sunderland came right behind Leeds in the League table with 61 points. This ensured the return of the Wearsiders to First Division football. Preston, on the other hand, reached the FA Cup Final only to come second best to West Ham United.

'The Second Division record of Leeds United last season is very impressive indeed. They didn't lose a single game at home – one of only three clubs in the country to achieve this; Gillingham and Mansfield Town being the others. However, United had the highest number of draws in the Second Division. They split the points on no fewer than nine occasions. The remaining 12 games at Elland Road were won, so that the goals aggregate for the games at Leeds was 35 for and 12 against. Away games, they won no fewer than 12 – without doubt the best performance throughout the entire Football League last season. A further six games away were drawn and Leeds suffered only three defeats all season.

'Finally, we would like to make all Leeds United supporters especially welcome this afternoon at the Everton Supporters' Club situated 100 yards from the ground on City Road.'

Johnny Giles said, 'Everton were clearly waiting for us that day. To teach us a lesson. They were an experienced side with a number of good, hard players, who were aware of our tough reputation and they seemed determined to do unto us, what they thought we were going to do unto them.'

Norman Hunter, speaking as a guest at Elland Road in 2003, said, 'There was no doubt that Everton had decided to rough us up that day. The whole 90 minutes turned into a game of frightening violence and Willie's goal, although great for us, totally exasperated the whole situation. It got very tasty.'

Going into the game, the Everton players and the management were under pressure. They had failed to defend their league title successfully in 1963/64 and even worse, their arch rivals Liverpool had taken it from them. Now Everton – a traditional giant of league football – were not even the best team in their own city. They had started well but by the time of the Leeds game, they had won only one of their last six league matches and were now lying off the pace somewhat in eighth position. The patience of the supporters was being tested and crowds had dropped from 55,000 in August to 40,000 for the previous home game against Blackburn Rovers. Leeds was a match that Everton could not afford to lose. Some 43,605 people were present at Goodison Park to witness Everton test themselves against the newcomers.

Players from several clubs had expressed their apprehension at playing in front of the hostile Everton crowd, and, conscious that further incidents of this nature could prevent Goodison Park from hosting games in the forthcoming World Cup in 1966, the directors of Everton took action and installed barriers. When Everton met Tottenham Hotspur the following season, a group of home supporters presented Spurs' keeper Bill Brown with a specially designed mock imitation of a dart. This must have frightened poor old

Bill as he let four goals in that afternoon. And so it came to pass that into this cauldron of hate, newly promoted Leeds arrived at Goodison Park on 7 November 1964.

Bobby Collins was playing his former club for the first time in a league game and described the encounter as 'nasty and brutal', adding, 'But you can't turn the other cheek, or the other team will kill you.'

A key factor that loomed ominously over this fixture was Collins's return to Goodison Park. He had been Everton's record signing in September 1958 when they paid Celtic £24,000 for his services, and he became a massive fans' favourite. 'The Little General', as he was known, was a diminutive figure but was the ultimate leader on the pitch. Playing at inside-right, Collins had an eye for goal. In 147 Everton appearances he scored 48 goals. Everton had been through a tough spell before the arrival of the Scot, but his move proved to kickstart the side as they went from relegation candidates to title challengers in his first couple of seasons. However, to the surprise of most, he was allowed to leave in March 1962 for Leeds and there was an overwhelming feeling among supporters and journalists that it was a premature ending. Frank McGhee wrote at the time, 'It's beyond belief that Everton have sold their most inspirational player. Leeds United have signed a real gem.'

And Everton supporter Mick Watson was absolutely incensed, 'What on earth is Catterick doing? Bobby Collins is our best player by far. I am not happy and am considering not going ever again!'

There is no doubting that Collins had played a vital role in helping Everton avoid relegation, but Harry Catterick had taken over as manager for the 1961/62 season and he harboured some doubts about his effectiveness. The new boss felt that at 31 years of age Collins's best days were behind him.

After a game at Fulham, in which Collins had scored two goals, Catterick told the player that he 'was not the player that he used to be' and also that he felt that he 'wasn't giving his all'.

Collins was livid. He told a journalist, 'Nobody criticises my work rate. Winning is all to me.'

Revie was looking for an experienced captain to take charge of his young team, struggling near the foot of the Second Division, and saw Collins as just the man he needed to drill winning habits into his impressionable young players. So Collins arrived at Goodison in the white shirt of Leeds determined to show the man who had deemed him surplus to his requirements just what a poor error of judgement he had made.

A fascinating account of that day is presented by author Jim Keoghan in his 2017 book *Everton Greatest Games*, 'To many modern fans, reared on a game where crowds are often dispassionate tourists, players overly protected and referees the agents of the authorities' aims to make football as bloodless as possible, the past must look like a foreign country. The days of the swaying crowd seething with a palpable sense of malign fury, defenders who would soften forwards up with a vicious tackle to "let them know they're there" and officials who seemed to be more generous in their definition of what constituted "contact" in the term "contact sport" are long gone (at least in the higher reaches of the game). For all the club's School of Science aspirations, back when football was a more aggressive affair, Everton could give as good as they got. It was an attitude that in the mid-1960s produced a match that is one of the most memorable to have ever taken place at Goodison.

'At that time, the opponents that day were Leeds United who were on the rise. Under the management of Don Revie the Yorkshiremen had just climbed out of the Second

Division and were on their way to becoming one of the dominant football forces of the decade.

'Although undoubtedly blessed with talented players such as Bobby Collins, Jack Charlton and Billy Bremner they were also a side that was developing a reputation for aggression. The Football Association had labelled Leeds "the dirtiest side in the country", and in their official journal, pointed to the evidence that cited them as having the worst record for players cautioned, censured, fined or suspended in the Football League. The former Leeds centre-half Jack Charlton provided a revealing insight into the Elland Road mentality in his eponymously titled 1996 autobiography. In a telling account, he related a story in which the young Leeds midfielder Jimmy Lumsden, while receiving physio treatment, had told Charlton and Don Revie how in a recent reserve match he had gone in over the top of the ball during a challenge, injuring his opponent in the process. Despite United's refutation that they were a dirty side, there remained a perception that the Football Association had got it right, and whenever Leeds played there was a sense that opposition teams took to the pitch expecting and preparing for a fight.'

One hot summer afternoon I was sat in the office of Duncan Revie in Dubai, chatting about Leeds United. The son of Don was the founder and chief executive officer of Soccerex, an organisation that Sepp Blatter once described as, 'When football meets the economy and football meets media. Then it is Soccerex.'

It was 2007 and Duncan had agreed to an interview for a book I was writing at the time. From then on we became good friends. That afternoon he told me how he considered taking ownership of Leeds, who were in dire straits and had just been relegated to League One, 'In order for me to take over, I insisted that all the existing board and the chairman

Ken Bates leave the club. This never happened and I took it no further.'

We discussed his dad and how Don had wrestled for years with the 'Dirty Leeds' tag. Duncan then produced a magazine from his files. It was the *FA News* from August 1964. 'This is where it started,' said Duncan. 'This article is what everyone took as read and what everyone perceived to be written in stone and the gospel truth.'

The report scalded Leeds, labelling them 'dirty' as a result of figures regarding disciplinary records of all league clubs for the previous campaign, 1963/64. While they had Leeds at the bottom, or top, of the table, they portrayed Ipswich Town and Sheffield United as having the best record. The figures showed the number of times a club had a player sent off, claiming that Leeds were the biggest culprits. But in fact the report was totally misleading. It transpired that the report didn't just take into account first-team matches – it also included reserve matches, including the aforementioned Jimmy Lumsden, and also junior matches. Leeds hadn't had one first-team player sent off, whereas Johnny Giles's former club, Manchester United, had had no fewer than five players dismissed in the same period.

And astonishingly, up to Gary Sprake getting sent off in a pre-season friendly against Scunthorpe in August 1965, Leeds had only had one player sent off since the early 1920s. *The Sun*'s chief sports writer, Frank McGhee, was there and reported, 'Gary Sprake, Leeds United's Welsh international keeper, smashed a magnificent club record on Saturday when he was ordered off in their too-tough friendly against Scunthorpe United at Elland Road. Until he was sent packing, Leeds had had only one man sent off in the last 43 years and well over 1,600 league matches. He was Archie Gibson, United's right-half who was sent off on Boxing Day

1958 against West Bromwich Albion at Elland Road. It was the most striking club record in the history of the game.'

Now, that's probably not what United's critics wanted to hear about.

In his autobiography, *A Football Man*, Giles wrote, 'The FA report was so unfair – it was totally misleading and inaccurate. But the damage was done. The dog now had a bad name. I am not for one minute suggesting that we weren't able to look after ourselves, as they say, but everywhere you went in that league, there were players who were well able to look after themselves. And to suggest that Leeds United were somehow the exception, that we were uniquely aggressive, is not just obviously wrong as a matter of fact, in many cases it is bordering on the hilarious.

'I was playing on the right wing that day, close to the Everton fans, and I received an education that day. They called me names I had never been called before, well beyond the regular "pig" or "bastard" and always with the word "Irish" attached – and this was in Liverpool, the most Irish of cities.'

The game at Goodison Park was barely four minutes in when the trouble started.

Stan Osborne, a one-time apprentice with Everton and the author of *Making the Grade*, a memoir about his time with the club and his life as an Evertonian, said, 'There was certainly a tense atmosphere that day. You got the feeling that it wouldn't take much to get the crowd riled up. The game had barely begun before the tackles started flying in.

'Pickering was clattered by Bremner. Seconds later, Charlton suffered a similar fate at the hands of Gabriel. Battle lines had been drawn. But the "Battle of Goodison", as the game subsequently became known, really burst into flames on the four-minute mark when Giles, notorious amongst opponents for going over the top of the ball, left his stud marks on the chest of Brown, tearing his shirt in the process.

'I was stood in the Boys' Pen and watched as Sandy Brown took his revenge, catching Giles with a good left hook that floored him. I remember watching the tackles raining in and with half an hour gone it was almost a surprise that Brown was the only player to be sent off for an early bath.'

Giles holds a different view, 'I wasn't always innocent but, on this occasion I was. Sandy tackled me from behind as I was dribbling towards goal. The two of us fell to the ground and with the referee in close attendance Sandy punched me. He had to go. The Everton fans weren't happy of course and their mood didn't improve when we scored about ten minutes after the Brown incident. Then it boiled over just before half-time when Willie Bell and Derek Temple challenged for a ball in the air. There was a clash of heads and the two of them ended up on the ground. It was definitely an accidental collision but the crowd saw Willie as the villain – again we were perceived as the bad lads from Leeds. It was the only time in my career that I actually thought the Everton supporters would invade the pitch. It was really scary.'

When it came to the rough and tumble on the pitch, Everton might have been missing their very own 'hardman' in Tony Kay, but he said, 'The Blues still had enough about them to meet Leeds, kick-for-kick. We had players such as Jimmy Gabriel, Johnny Morrissey and Dennis Stevens to give the likes of Norman Hunter, Jack Charlton and Billy Bremner a run for their money.'

Jim Keoghan continued in *Everton Greatest Games*, 'Brown received his marching orders, and the Goodison crowd roared in protest. It was a decision that coloured all that followed. The temperature rose as blood boiled. Any Leeds player who ventured too close to the crowd ran the risk of being pelted with coins. Life was particularly tough for Leeds keeper Gary Sprake, who was probably pelted with enough spare change to buy himself a good few drinks.

'Harry Catterick wasn't the kind of manager afraid to mix it up. The addition of more bite to the squad was one thing that set him apart from his predecessor, Johnny Carey. Amongst all the kicking, some football was actually played, and after 15 minutes Leeds capitalised on their numerical advantage to take the lead. From a free kick far out on the right wing, Collins swung the ball high into the heart of the Everton area. Rushing in at great speed, Leeds full-back Willie Bell met the ball perfectly, his header flashing into the net. It was a great finish from a player always willing to supplement the attack.'

From the start, the atmosphere was at fever pitch and Bell's goal was more than the home support could take. It only served to add to the fertile brew of crowd hostility. Meanwhile, it continued to be business as usual on the pitch as players from both sides went flying into a series of reckless challenges all over the field.

Jim Keoghan wrote, 'As good a footballer as Bell could be, he also possessed a mean streak, and, ten minutes before the break, revealed it at its worst when a chest-high tackle on Temple provided the moment that ensured the game would pass into infamy.'

But Bell offered a different take on the situation, 'We clashed and we were both high with our tackles. I had stud marks on my chest through my shirt. Photographs show that we were both too high with our tackles.'

This was in the 39th minute and was reported in the *Sunday Mirror*, 'Willie Bell and Derek Temple went flying into each other and both players were injured as a result.

Temple was stretchered off and Willie Bell was also taken off. It was yet another flashpoint.'

As Temple was being taken off, Les Cocker ran on to tend to Bell. He immediately found himself under a barrage of objects along with the referee, Mr Stokes, as the home fans vented their anger. Cocker quickly decided Bell had to go off too and called to the touchline for assistance. But the ambulanceman's terse reply was that Cocker should 'fetch his own fucking stretcher!' showing just how much everybody seemed to be getting caught up with the emotions of the match. With missiles still raining down on them, Cocker and Johnny Giles carried Bell off, with the ambulanceman and Norman Hunter on either side.

Leeds fan Alan Hewitt, from Batley, was close to where Bell left the field and felt the force of a full can of pop to the back of his head that was meant for the Leeds entourage, 'It hit me so hard that I felt blood trickling down my neck. Everton fans around me, presuming I was an Everton fan myself, began mopping my head with tissues or cloths or something. I thought it best to let them go on thinking I was a home fan and I just acted dazed and never said anything, I just nodded my thanks to the people around me.'

Then minutes later one irate supporter ran on to the pitch and headed for Bremner, and as Hunter moved to intervene, Everton hardman Johnny Morrissey helped restrain and reason with the fan, preventing him from committing a potentially serious assault.

As well as Sprake being constantly pelted with coins, any Leeds player who ventured too near to the touchline was met with a volley of missiles, making wingers Johanneson and Giles easy targets. Giles said, 'There were no barriers and at first, very few police, and the fans were so close to coming on to the pitch, with me first in the firing line because I was on the right wing.'

Everton's Colin Harvey recalled that 'an air of menace pervaded the ground'. Jack Charlton had already said that he never looked forward to playing at Goodison Park, viewing supporters there as 'the worst before which I have ever played. There always seemed to be a threatening atmosphere.'

Players from both sides could not fail to sense the tension in the air as the tempo continued to rise. After Collins had clashed with Temple and then Fred Pickering was fouled by Bremner, the Everton crowd screamed their displeasure. Then Charlton was the victim of a cynical challenge by Morrissey, who was allegedly one of the names that Jack kept in his infamous little black book for future retribution. There was no respite for either side as Giles upended Brian Labone. The crowd seethed in response. Further missiles were hurled down on to the pitch, the Leeds players were spat at, and intermittent fights broke out. And such was the level of hostility, the referee marched both teams off the pitch so that the players and fans could cool down. It was the first time this had ever happened in an English league game.

The players left the field with the frenzied chants of 'Dirty Leeds!' ringing in their ears. Managers Catterick and Revie used this unexpected opportunity to tell their players to calm down. Johanneson complained that an Everton player had called him a 'black bastard'. In these less-enlightened times, Revie advised Johanneson to simply call his opponent a 'white bastard'. Incredibly, this appeared to relieve the tension in the dressing room.

Temple recalled, 'I had been stretchered off and was lying in the dressing room when all the players came in after the referee had told them to go off. I heard him talking to the two managers saying that he was going to call the game off as there looks like there could be a riot out there. But both managers told him that there would be a riot out there if he didn't get those players back out on the pitch!'

During the halt in proceedings the referee entered both dressing rooms, lecturing the players and telling them that if their behaviour didn't improve, they would all be reported to the Football Association. The crowd had no way of knowing whether the game had been suspended or abandoned. But after five minutes, it was announced on the tannoy system that play would soon restart, although the fans were told that the police had warned that the match would be abandoned if any more missiles were thrown. Ten minutes after they had trooped off, the players returned. Temple and Bell came back too.

But despite the referee's warnings, little changed on the pitch. Some of the tackling, specifically by Hunter and Vernon, remained exceptionally aggressive and the game seemed to be powered by an undercurrent of venom and animosity. Hunter was booked, and Bremner, Collins and Vernon were warned for dangerous play. Astonishingly, no further players were sent off. Perhaps the referee didn't want to risk antagonising the crowd any further, so close to the precipice of further violence did those on the terraces appear. Despite being a man down and unable to play their natural game, Everton refused to submit throughout and were constantly on the hunt for an equaliser. But, although they chucked everything they had at Leeds, Revie's men hung grimly to the end.

Throughout the entire game the kicks and fouls barely relented, ending with 19 transgressions inflicted by Everton and 12 by Leeds.

Johnny Morrissey was on the left wing for Everton that day. He was a small but stocky player and not one you would instantly say was a hardman, but he could handle himself, of that there was no doubt. He and Charlton had a thing going between them. Morrissey went over the top of the ball and took his studs all the way down Jack's shin, drawing much blood and thus ending his part in the game. Afterwards, as Charlton hobbled out of the dressing room to get back to the team bus, leg in plaster and using a walking stick, Morrissey saw him and shouted from the Everton dressing-room doorway, 'Is the leg OK, big fella?' Jack swung around, almost falling over, and shouted back, 'I'll fucking have you! If it takes me ten years, I'll fucking have you.' And Charlton did. Then Morrissey got him back and it continued like that until both players had finished playing. It is widely accepted that Morrissey's name was in Charlton's infamous little black book, which contained the names of the players who had 'done' him. Charlton swore to have his revenge on every name in the book. He was severely reprimanded by the FA for this.

Everton fan Robert Zatz was there that day, 'Memorable, to say the least. I remember Willie Bell's flying studs tackle on Sandy Brown was the worst of many.'

Supporter Peter Tibke said, 'The tackle on Temple was somewhere round the chest area as Derek was running towards the Gwladys Street goal. I think the tackle was by Norman Hunter. Derek was carried off on a stretcher but returned after the cooling-off period. Willie Bell did kick Sandy Brown up in the air before Sandy retaliated.'

William Butterworth said, 'I was in the Boys' Pen that day, we were all screaming "we want our money back" when the referee took the players off. It was a really hostile atmosphere that could have easily spilled over into violence.'

'I was at the game in the Upper Bullens,' remembers Peter Mills. 'I was eight. I still remember the venom coming from the crowd as the teams came back on after the enforced break, "Dirty Leeds" being bellowed around Goodison. All I could think was "Wow!"'

Stan Osborne added, 'The hostility continued throughout the crowd, and it was so bad that it continued after the game and outside mounted police had to disperse us. It was the first time I had ever seen that at Goodison.'

Michael Pye had relatives there, 'My late dad and his brother Eric, sadly no longer with us, used to tell the tale of that game as they were season ticket holders throughout the 1960s. They said they had never seen anything like it. It was a bad atmosphere at a full Goodison Park, they said that after Sandy Brown had been sent off, a fan ran on to the pitch to confront Billy Bremner. Brown ale bottles littered the pitch and the ref decided to take off the players.'

Rob Rankin got in touch, 'My dad was in goal for Everton in that game. Some very interesting challenges in that one. I remember my dad saying about Harry Catterick going mad at Sandy Brown for getting sent off when they'd all been sent back to the dressing room by the ref. Sandy didn't say anything but lifted his shirt to show stud marks down his chest and on to his thigh and said something along the lines of "fair enough".'

Gerry Bryan, from Lofthouse, near Wakefield, was in the Park End that afternoon with a few mates. He remembers it getting a little bit too aggressive among the crowd, 'We didn't have our Leeds colours on, but those around us seemed to know that we were Leeds fans. At first we felt threatened by them, but eventually we were OK with them, but the mood of the crowd definitely shifted when the referee took the players off the field. We decided it was best to make our way to an exit and we did leave early, sometime during the second half.'

Horace Yates, reporting for the *Liverpool Echo*, said, 'For a time nobody knew whether the game had been suspended or abandoned and despite the break the crowd remained agitated to say the least. Fights were breaking out in the crowd while they waited for the game to resume and this incident was the most sensational I have seen in my years of watching football.'

Mike Turner was one of the unlucky Leeds fans making their way back to their coaches after the game, 'When I left my home in Stourton and went to get a coach to Everton, I had no idea of the scenes that were to unfold. There were five of us travelling together and before the game we had a drink with some Everton fans and everything was fine. But once inside the ground things changed quickly for the worse. The atmosphere was toxic from very early on and remained so throughout the whole afternoon. I could not wait for the game to finish and to just get on our bus and get back to Leeds.

'But on our way back to the coaches things turned very ugly. We lost our mate Kevin who came back to the bus almost glued to a policeman. But not before I was hit on the head by something – I still don't know what it was but I presume it was a small brick or a rock of some kind. I didn't look back, I just hurried to our bus. My head was split open and the policeman stood near our bus said it was a bad cut and I needed stitches and he wanted me to go to hospital, but I'd seen enough and I just kept a towel I'd been given close to the wound all the way home to Leeds. I am now in my early 80s and my four-inch scar is still very prevalent on my bald head.'

Even before the dust had settled on this whole sorry affair, the press were all over it. The occasion was 'spine-chilling' according to Jack Archer for *The People*. *The Observer*'s John Arlott described it as 'an unhappy day for English football'. Others called it 'disgusting' and 'vicious'.

The FA's Disciplinary Committee met the following month. Sandy Brown was suspended for two weeks and because of the behaviour of their fans, Everton were fined £250. Leeds were not punished in any way whatsoever. The FA went on to threaten harsher penalties for players and officials who misbehaved, and swifter closures at grounds where clubs had failed to stop 'rowdyism' among spectators.

In a report headed 'Disciplinary Measures', the FA pointed out that the home club was fully responsible for the spectators even if the rowdyism came from visiting supporters. Clubs were advised to gain maximum assistance from the police; the FA felt that anyone throwing toilet rolls and other articles, or invading the pitch, should be made to leave and, where necessary, prosecuted.

Commenting on this report, Denis Follows, the secretary of the FA, said that several clubs had employed plain-clothed policemen to mingle with the crowd and keep order. This measure had a good effect on behaviour. Warning notices, he said, had little effect on some grounds, and in future a first offence might mean a fine or even immediate closure.

The report went on to warn players to respect the referee at all times, unless it was proven that there had been a clear error, such as mistaken identity. Although things did improve slightly, the situation up and down the country soon reverted back to what it had been, but events at Goodison Park that November day in 1964 remain pretty unique and cemented in the memory of anyone who witnessed them.

David France of the Everton Collection said, 'The events of that day cemented the reputation of Don Revie's United in the mind for years to come – they would stop at nothing to win a game.'

Jim Keoghan was slightly more philosophical and then highlighted a surprising turn of events involving Everton and Leeds, 'Irrespective of their darker side, Revie's men could play and over the following decade were never out of the top four (an achievement unachievable by brute force alone). But certainly, John Moores, the Everton chairman, wasn't put off by the "Battle of Goodison". Don Revie had been offered a record-breaking annual salary plus a massive signing on bonus in an attempt to lure him to Goodison. The deal never came off. Revie opted to turn down Everton's offer and stayed at Leeds, citing "personal reasons" for his decision. For a time though, the move had been on. There was a moment, however brief, when the School of Science was close to metamorphosing into the School of Hard Knocks.'

Other Leeds fans had their say on the matter. R. Anderson of Harrogate wrote a letter to the local press, 'A strong tackling side, a relentless side, yes, but a dirty side – no chance. I write with a little authority as was a referee on the local scene for many years, and there I assure you, local fervour was of a very high order. The day has now surely arrived when United must take steps to check the image by which they are being presented to the football world by some reporters, who fail in their profession by yielding to undisguised bias. I should hate to see this young and very promising side victimised so as to prevent their playing the football we who watch them regularly know they are capable of.'

M.R., of Moortown, Leeds, was at the Battle of Goodison, 'May I congratulate United on their superb self-discipline in the Goodison ring. For Leeds fans lucky enough not to have witnessed this disgusting exhibition of play and partisanship, it was not the case of six of one and half a dozen of the other, as most newspapers would have you believe. The first half made the news, but in the second half Everton got away with a lot of fouls, especially against United's "least placid" player. He never retaliated and if had would doubtless have been dismissed, but even that would not have satisfied this lunatic crowd. I don't think anything short of Leeds having 11 badly injured men would have satisfied them. I write for the benefit of Leeds people who have read only reports condemning United.'

J. Shaw, of Amberton Crescent, Leeds, said, 'Dirty Leeds? What rubbish! I have supported them for 37 years and I have never known them branded as dirty until last season. Then they became Second Division champions – by playing as a team, producing good, hard football. What's dirty about that? Now that they are back in the First Division they are still playing good, hard football, and are in third place. But because United are giving the top clubs a football lesson, and refusing to be underdogs, the press and the FA are throwing everything at United. The FA should hold its head in shame for creating this bad feeling, and should be censored in future in what it writes.'

Just four days after the game, Leeds, without seemingly missing a beat, prepared to entertain Arsenal at Elland Road. The matchday programme, however, inevitably included recent events in its notes:

A BIG CHEERS FOR OUR BOYS – PLEASE!
HELP THEM FORGET GOODISON PARK
LAST SATURDAY

The programme continued, 'Our men will come out tonight with five consecutive victories behind them, and sitting in third place in the First Division. Knowing our crowd to be one of the most enthusiastic in the whole league we can, we feel, rely on you to give them the cheers they deserve. Which means EXTRA big ones, of course. The biggest of the season. For a good welcome will do much, we assure you, to remove the sad memories of that unfortunate match at Goodison Park last Saturday when large sections of the crowd quite lost their heads, and started throwing things on to the pitch at our players. It was a grisly experience for all our team and fans when the referee Mr Stokes of Newark stopped the game to let order be restored. On top of the throwing of sundry missiles (which could quite easily have hit a player in the eye and possibly blinded him), various "scraps" and incidents had started all over on and off the field.

'We admired Mr Stokes's firm, prompt and responsible action especially as it was done as a reproach to Everton's well-known fanatical army of supporters on their own ground. There was some risk to it, but the dignified demeanour backed his action, and vigilant work by the police plus the common sense of the great majority of those present, including our own supporters, restored order.

'But as we have said it was a grisly experience for our team, especially the younger element in it. Not even in nightmares had they experienced anything like this – and it was of course the first time in history of the league in peacetime that such a stand had to be taken by the referee of one of their matches. We hope not to have anything like the Goodison scenes happen at Elland Road no matter what the provocation. Such disgraceful behaviour is totally unacceptable – even if a championship or a relegation depended on the incident or incidents which caused it. We are prouder than ever of the general behaviour of our fans, at home and away, or in transit, and we earnestly ask them to maintain that average – which is much appreciated, as we have said before, all over the country. Heaven knows, our followers have had more than enough to excite them these last few years (at both ends of the table!) and we hope to give them even more at the top end of the First Division to keep them happy as well as excited.

'We do not want anything approaching the mass misconduct that came out of Goodison. It does no good to anyone. The usual sequel is that the poor old home club gets an FA warning, has to display notices, and so on – through no fault of their own, or indeed its board, its players or its officials – or even the police.

'Finally, we apologise to our distinguished and welcome visitors this evening, Arsenal, for having taken so long to mention them here. But we can only plead that we felt very keenly about this whole sorry occurrence.'

11

Double Vision

THE ARSENAL game gave Leeds United the welcome chance to get back to 'normality' after the dreaded Goodison affair. Almost 39,000 crammed into Elland Road to see how their team measured up to the mighty Gunners from Highbury. Leeds fans were soon looking worried as the players seemed to have an inferiority complex against a highly competent Arsenal team. Had it not been for Bobby Collins, United may well have gone under.

When Don Revie stole Collins from Everton, the critics rounded on Revie and Leeds claiming that the 5ft 4in midfielder was too old and was a crock due to a nagging leg injury. On top of that, they also said he was a 'thug' and 'cynical' and all those types of comments in general. Of course Leeds had very recently been called, however, unjustly the 'dirtiest team in the country'. This understandably infuriated Revie, 'I was very sore at the public attack in the FA bulletin last summer over the number of cautions my players have received. It makes me sick to even discuss it. I thought it was most unfair. Leeds were the only club to be publicly mentioned. As a result of all this publicity, managers of other clubs are saying, "You've got to go in harder against Leeds," whereas we've only to make one hard tackle and everyone says, "There they go again." In reality we have had one player sent off in 44 years. One club alone last season had five players sent off. Bobby Collins has of course been labelled dirty. Collins is a dedicated fitness fanatic, a terrific player and he is doing an absolute tremendous job for us. You cannot buy players like him these days.'

Arsenal must have wished that Revie hadn't signed Collins two years previously. After going in front on 20 minutes, the Gunners witnessed first-hand the ability of this pocket general. Collins grabbed his players by the scruff of the neck and thrust them back into the game. He shook his fist at his team-mates urging them to fight back. Collins assumed control of both defence and attack, playing deep when necessary but always around when the forwards needed his assistance. Rarely has one player assumed so much responsibility in any situation with complete authority.

Within two minutes of Arsenal scoring, Leeds were level. Collins sent in a long free kick which Jack Charlton latched on to and headed home. In the second half Rod Belfitt fired one in off the post, and just two minutes later Jim Storrie hit a beauty from 20 yards out to put the game beyond the visitors.

Les Smythe, who had been an Arsenal fan for three years, travelled up to Leeds with five of his friends, 'We came up in my old Commer van intending to sleep in it overnight. We had some cushions and blankets, all sorted. We called in at a pub called The Peacock, and as I got some drinks, I asked the landlord, I've forgot his name, if we could leave our van in the car park overnight, as we'd be sleeping in it. I don't think he was too keen at first but said as we would be drinking in there it would be OK. He showed me a corner where I could park around the back. After the game, which we lost, we went back into the pub to drown our sorrows. It was full of Leeds fans and we had a good night. When everyone had gone, the landlord gave us a nightcap and we retired to the van. It was November and it was freezing, we needed those nightcaps. We'd just nodded off, then someone decided he wanted a piss outside and that went on all night, the van never really got chance to warm with people in and out all night.

'Next morning I was going to thank the landlord when I noticed all these yellowish marks on the wall. All the pub walls were painted white and these marks stood out like a sore thumb. Closer inspection revealed it was our piss! I told the landlord of course and even offered to paint over the marks before we left. He just laughed and said, "Don't worry about it mate, not used to northern beer eh, and your lot lost last night, you've suffered enough!" He gave us all tea and toast and we headed home.'

Birmingham City arrived at Elland Road on the back of a spirited performance against Arsenal at St Andrew's the previous Saturday. However, the game against Leeds went off without serious incident, prompting *Daily Express* reporter Les Noad, not noted for his affection towards United, to proclaim, 'Leeds and Birmingham wore their Sunday suits. Not a tackle out of place, not a temper revealed. Collisions were sometimes hard, but I saw nothing done behind anyone's back, except when Charlton pushed a defender before Storrie scored the first Leeds goal in the third minute. Having accused City of back-alley football against Arsenal last week and Leeds of "dirty" football in the past, I must now raise my pen to the pair of them. This Leeds performance was vigorous, direct and short of devastating only in the firing line, where they lacked the deadliness of a great team.'

Revie responded immediately. 'Wait two years,' he said, 'then they will be great. Today we were 100 times better than when we beat Arsenal on Wednesday.'

Thompson cancelled out Storrie's goal before Leeds went back in front with two quick goals in succession, but according to Noad, the two headed goals by Charlton and Collins came about because a first-half back injury meant City goalkeeper Schofield struggled to move from his line. Schofield, however, was able enough to pull down the in-flight Albert Johanneson for a penalty, which Johnny Giles converted to wrap things up.

After eight games undefeated, Leeds slipped up at West Ham United. Young reserve forward Belfitt pulled a goal back but a three-goal deficit proved too much on the day. Robert Deane, from Harrogate, travelled alone by train that day to follow Leeds. It was his first away game and the furthest he had ever travelled before was on a family trip to Bridlington, 'I had just turned 19, and made a decision to go to an away game. It took quite a lot of planning but I thoroughly enjoyed it. After the defeat I was on the train home and I got to thinking that I was a bad omen. Leeds hadn't been beaten for ages and on my first game away we had lost 3-1.' Robert had little to worry about; after that defeat in the capital, it would be over four and a half months before United were beaten again.

Revie said, 'People underrated us before the start of the season. Both on TV and in the papers they said we'd either have a job on to stay up or else go straight back into the Second Division. But we've got three things working for us here. Team spirit: every player in our setup, irrespective of whether he's on form or not, has to work for 90 minutes. The off-form player must make up for it by worrying, chasing and doing twice the amount of work. In this way the opposing player has to beat two men all the time. Family spirit: this is a family club, from the chairman, the padre, the chief scout, the doctor, the coaches, the players and the supporters. Every footballer here is given talks on how to become a first class citizen as well as a first class player. There is no "Mod" or "Rocker" mentality here. Team psychology: above all we have encouraged the right frame of mind. Our players are honest and open. They accept constructive criticism from each other. They don't go into dressing room sulks or form small groups to pull pieces from some other player behind his back.'

Journalist Alan Hoby echoed this statement by saying, 'This then is Leeds United – unglamorous outsiders in the honours hunt. Don't underestimate them, despite that 3-1 defeat at West Ham yesterday. These championship chasers may be hard but they are intensely ambitious. They'll take a hell of a lot of stopping.'

First, Leeds bounced back with a 1-0 home victory over West Bromwich Albion. In a humorous match report, one journalist wrote, 'Dear old Aunty FA, who so primly branded Leeds as last season's dirtiest team, should have been at Elland Road on Saturday when Leeds were as pure as their all-white strip. They accepted referee Cattlin's interpretation of the advantage rule, even when play had been waved on with a Leeds man still measured on the grass. Not that it was a dirty game, far from it. But some of Albion's tackling might have been more harshly treated. The referee was certainly no homer and the Leeds players accepted one or two doubtful decisions like Little Lord Fauntleroys.'

Rod Johnson was enjoying a decent run in the side, and he scored the only goal of the game. It came in the 16th minute when Charlton, Bremner, Collins and Giles spreadeagled Albion's defence to allow Johnson to move forward and side-foot the ball into the net. Leeds were then denied a clear penalty when Graham Williams brought down Bremner. With Brian Williamson making his only appearance of the season in goal, for the injured Sprake, Leeds put in a hard-fought performance to secure the points. The game was won on tactics. Revie studied six pages of notes on Albion provided by coach Syd Owen.

A sterner test, a trip to Old Trafford and to what many in the game were calling a yardstick, was next on United's busy agenda. People were eagerly awaiting how they would measure up against a team who over the coming years would become one of their fiercest rivals, if not *the* fiercest rival. Leeds were almost at full strength with a settled defence in Sprake, Reaney, Bell, Bremner, Charlton and Hunter. Storrie, Collins and Johnson led the attack, with Giles and young Terry Cooper on the wings. They faced a team boasting Denis Law, Bobby Charlton and an 18-year-old genius named George Best.

On 5 December, as Leeds headed across to the 'dark side' escorted by thousands of supporters, Revie was still pondering over his line-up. Would it be Johanneson or Cooper on the left wing? Would Bremner be deployed to mark Law, or would that fall to Hunter? Would Reaney be able to handle Best? Similarly, would Nobby Stiles stop the triangle of Collins, Bremner and Giles from which so many Leeds moves stemmed? Whatever United's team would be, the hosts would be at full strength.

In the 55th minute, Collins, the star performer up to that point, put Leeds into a deserved lead. Winning every individual battle, they controlled the game and then Bremner slid a pass through to Cooper whose shot wasn't held by keeper Pat Dunne and Collins made no mistake in burying the loose ball into the bottom corner of the net. Almost 15,000 United fans, massed on the open scoreboard end, went wild. Deep into the second half, however, thick fog descended upon Old Trafford, and threatened the game, so much so that referee Finney took the teams off in the hope that it cleared sufficient enough for the play to continue. Thankfully for Leeds and their fans, the fog turned into a mist seven minutes later, and Finney deemed it well enough to continue with the final 12 minutes.

But when he blew the whistle everyone thought it was to abandon the game, and many fans left the ground. Leeds supporter Timothy was one of them, 'We were near the back and a Leeds fan near us swore and said something like, "Fuckin' typical, just when we were winning an' all," and me and my dad Brian got out before the rush. We were in our car when we heard through the crackly car radio the match commentary still going on.'

Then at 4.48pm the familiar throbbing roar of 'Leeds Leeds Leeds' rose from the mist-shrouded Old Trafford signalling two precious points for United, as the white shirts disappeared into the mist at the far corner with 'On Ilkla Moor 'at' ringing in their happy ears.

It was while on the way back across the Pennines from this memorable game that the Leeds team called in on a pub full of their supporters. Graham Wagstaffe was there and so too was The Minstrel, Philip Dobreen, who retrieved his guitar from the coach and the team and the fans together enjoyed a sing-song.

United carried on their form throughout December and after a 2-0 win at Blackburn on the 28th, once again 'Ilkla Moor' could be heard and a slightly modified version of Revie's favourite song, 'Bye, Bye, Blackburn'. Leeds would continue unbeaten in the league until mid-April, but in January they began their FA Cup campaign with a home tie with Southport.

'My dad was at that game,' says Southport fan Neil James. 'He told me about going to that cup game at Elland Road in 1964. He talked of a lad walking round the pitch playing a guitar and getting the crowd clapping and singing Leeds songs. We used to think he was making it up and we would humour him.' He certainly wasn't making it up – that lad with the guitar was The Minstrel himself, Philip Dobreen.

Rod Johnson celebrated his 20th birthday by leading the attack against Southport, and scored the third goal in a hard-fought 3-0 victory, which paired them with their old enemy, Everton, in the fourth round, at Elland Road.

Fans and players wearing black armbands stood silent before the kick-off in memory of Sir Winston Churchill, who had died six days earlier, aged 90.

As with the previous season's cup clash between the two, it finished 1-1, setting up another replay at Goodison. Leeds were two up with ten minutes to go thanks to Charlton and Weston, and even though Pickering pulled one back, the visitors went into the fifth round for another home tie, against Shrewsbury Town.

Goals by Johanneson and Giles saw them eventually overcome a plucky Shrewsbury side as Leeds looked ahead to a tricky-looking sixth-round tie at Crystal Palace.

United arrived in south London with Alan Peacock back following a cartilage operation that didn't quite go to plan the first time, resulting in a lengthy lay-off. But he bounced back at Selhurst Park with two goals and, with one from Storrie, Leeds were, unbelievably for their fans, into the FA Cup semi-final for the first time, where they would once again lock horns with their league rivals from Old Trafford.

A crowd of 65,000 packed into Hillsborough on 27 March for what was an explosive match from start to finish. On the hour Jack Charlton and Denis Law clashed with sickening intensity while in midfield, Billy Bremner and

Pat Crerand engaged in a furious wrestling match that lasted for over a minute, despite the strenuous intervention of half a dozen other players. Yet referee Dick Windle, from Chesterfield, seemed to do little more than peer uncertainly at the action, like a man peering over a hedge watching a dogfight.

After the game, a dour goalless affair, managers Revie and Matt Busby offered no comment over Windle's lack of authority throughout, so it looked likely that he would take charge of the replay four days later at the City Ground, Nottingham.

Before the game, Leeds chairman Harry Reynolds deemed it necessary to issue this statement on behalf of the board of directors, 'Whatever the outcome may be this season, we have one of the best managers in the game in Don Revie, who is backed by Maurice Lindley, one of the best chief scouts in the business, and dedicated workers in Syd Owen, Les Cocker, Bob English, Cyril Partridge and general manager and secretary, Cyril Williamson. We are looking forward to the future.'

Reynolds also thanked the supporters, 'We have had wonderful vocal support and their splendid behaviour has been noted outside of Leeds. We are proud of our supporters and their "Yelland Roar" which has a marvellous effect and gives our players a lot of encouragement.'

That support made themselves heard in no uncertain terms as the replay kicked off. It was an end-to-end, thrill-packed game that could so easily have gone to a second replay but ultimately it was settled with just two minutes remaining. Once more Revie's tactics were followed meticulously. After sustaining some heavy pressure, United sent Bremner forward and pulled Giles slightly back. Minutes later, Giles floated a free kick into the box and the tall Jack Charlton, Willie Bell and Alan Peacock raced forward, but as decoys pulled slightly wide and the defence went with them, leaving Bremner alone in the six-yard box. Facing away from goal he flicked the ball with the side of his head to guide the ball past the despairing Dunne, sparking scenes of sheer pandemonium as Bremner raced towards the massive Leeds contingent, where he was smothered by his jubilant team-mates. One irate hooligan from the opposite end ran on to the pitch and attacked referee Windle. Hundreds of Leeds fans then piled on to the pitch, but the 'sneak assailant' did not escape and he was marched off the field, much to the delight of the celebrating supporters in white.

Bremner didn't think the ball had gone in at first and had to look twice for confirmation, and he burst into tears. Afterwards, as the United dressing room bellowed out a deafening chorus of their 'Ilkla Moor' battle cry, a bemused Bremner said, 'I couldn't help myself with the celebration, I was dancing about waving my arms about like an idiot – and the tears were streaming down my face. But I don't care – this is the most wonderful moment of my career.' Revie, white-faced and almost choked with emotion, said huskily, 'This is the greatest moment of my career. Yes, greater even than when I went to Wembley as a player.' Close to tears, chairman Harry Reynolds, 64 the day before, croaked, 'I couldn't have asked for a greater gift. I am so choked up I don't know what to say.'

The Minstral, Philip Dobreen, was invited to the Main Stand by Don Revie, 'Don was jubilant and introduced me to the Liverpool manager [Liverpool would play United in the final], Bill Shankly, who shook my hand warmly and wished us all the luck in the final.'

As things settled down, both Bremner and Revie gave lengthy interviews to Frank Clough of *The Sun*. Bremner, who the season before had been suspended for 14 days and was now set to appear again in front of the FA Disciplinary Committee following several warnings this season, said, 'Just lately I have felt like a marked man. I have been afraid of going hard into the tackle at all. It's not getting kicked myself that I mind so much. I just see red when my mates get fouled. We are a team here in every sense of the word and if one of the lads gets hurt I blow my top.'

Revie, 'We have taken a lot of stick from the public and the press this season – a lot of it totally undeserved – but we have taken it on the chin. Now I feel we have proved ourselves, I must emphasise, we are not a dirty team.'

In the replay, Leeds conceded seven free kicks as opposed to 19 by the other side. However, it was a great game for the 46,300 crowd and wasn't blighted by fouls much like the first encounter had been.

Incidentally, at the disciplinary meeting Bremner was fined £100 and suspended for seven days, as a result of his fourth booking of the season. Bremner asked for a personal hearing and was then ordered to pay the costs of the commission, which made no difference to the outcome. It therefore meant that he would miss important First Division games, but would be available for the FA Cup Final against Liverpool, whose manager Bill Shankly said, 'I'm pleased for the lad's sake he can play. It's every player's dream to appear at Wembley, and it would have been tragic if he had missed it under those circumstances.'

Meanwhile, United were still at the business end of the league. Their triumph in the semi-final coincided perfectly with five wins on the trot. Peacock was back to full fitness and scoring for fun, although a 2-1 win at West Brom was too tight for comfort. Albion scored after 15 minutes through Ken Foggo and looked set to take the two points. Missing Bremner through suspension, and Revie who had been ordered by his doctor to take a rest from football, Leeds struggled. The boss's wife Elsie said, 'My husband had been in bed all day. He had sent the players a long telegram before the game and had been kept in touch with the game by telephone. He never lost heart even when they were still down with ten minutes to go. He was bathed in sweat, and kept saying to me, "They will do it ... they must do it ... I know they'll do it."'

Then almost immediately, Collins floated a ball out to Weston who sent in the perfect cross for Peacock to volley in the equaliser, and then at the death Peacock latched on to a Giles cross to head home the winner.

Collins, whose tremendous performances since his arrival in March 1962 had been nothing short of remarkable, was named Football Writers' Association Footballer of the Year for 1965, the first Scottish player to win the award, and he had also been recalled to the Scottish team after six years. His Leeds team-mate Jack Charlton was the runner-up for the FWA prize, but he would go on to win it in 1967. Billy Bremner would win it in 1970.

Leeds were only defeated twice in eight games in April and had gone into their final match, at Birmingham City, still with a chance of winning the First Division title. They had beaten the two Sheffield clubs, Wednesday 2-0 at Elland Road and United 3-0 at Bramall Lane, which left them leading the table by one point on 60, but having played one game more than Manchester United.

Leeds misfired at Birmingham, coming back from behind late on to draw 3-3, but Busby's men beat Arsenal 3-1, and despite losing their game in hand at Villa a couple of days later, the title went to Old Trafford on goal average.

Leeds still had the FA Cup to play for, but from the outset the final was a disappointing day. Don had an argument with Brian Williamson and Ian Lawson in connection with match tickets, a distraction he could well have done without. Charlton and Collins were having a dispute at the Selsdon Hotel where the team were staying, but Revie was used to that by now. Manchester City had made what could certainly be called 'an ungentlemanly' attempt to get Revie to be their manager less than a week before the final – a move that was muted after talks with Harry Reynolds and Don's friend and colleague at City, Johnny Williamson. But all this was a nagging distraction from the little matter of an FA Cup Final at Wembley. Leeds fans were upset too as Liverpool had received more tickets than them. This was denied at first by the football authorities, but was indisputable as it turned out.

Keith James said, 'I worked in the Leeds ticket office at the time and I know for a fact that Liverpool fans received more tickets than Leeds. I seem to remember that it was supposed to be because Leeds had just been promoted the season before and it was assumed that they wouldn't sell all their tickets. This despite the fact that Liverpool were only promoted themselves three seasons earlier. I'm not sure how many more tickets Liverpool received but it was definitely in the region of six or seven thousand more than Leeds. I asked the United secretary at the time, Cyril Williamson, about it and he said it was something to do with one end holding more supporters than the other. He just shrugged his shoulders.'

Liverpool fan Roy McAdams was in the Leeds end at Wembley, 'My dad was a Liverpool fan and was born in Stanley in Wakefield, which is where I was born. Dad's boss said he knew someone who could get cup final tickets. Then this man came to our house one night with two tickets, he said that they would be in the Leeds end, but there would be other Liverpool fans in there anyway, as a lot of Leeds tickets had gone to Liverpool for some reason.

'We actually went in a car with two Leeds fans, Jimmy and Mick, who lived near us. It was Jimmy's car, a green Hillman. We went down the A1 and saw loads of Leeds coaches who kept looking at our car that had a red scarf out of one window. It seemed to take ages to get there.

'When we did get to walk up to Wembley Stadium, I remember seeing Ken Dodd who had one of his red tickling stick things. We all sat together and to be honest the half an hour extra time was the only part worth watching. We won 2-1 – I say "we" but I became a Leeds fan in the 1970s. My dad died in 1974 and I know that he knew that I had started to favour the white shirt. I still have my dad's treasured 1966 Liverpool shirt framed hanging on my dining room wall. I'm 69 now and still get to the odd game at Elland Road.'

Leeds fan Pete Bullough, a long-time friend of mine, told me, 'I went down to Wembley with my future brother-in-law, Barry. I was 12. I remember wandering off while Barry was in the pub, and it was a good job I had the match tickets in my bag because I couldn't find him anywhere. The game was just the first of my many disappointments over the years. Barry missed the game and missed our coach home and then, unbelievably, I bumped into him at Watford Gap services. He was absolutely stewed, he had no idea where he'd been or how he got there. Worse still, he'd forgotten that he'd even taken me. It cost him a fiver to bribe me into not telling my sister. It was a disappointing final, Leeds never got going and looked a bit nervous I thought. They were much better in extra time and for a time I actually thought we'd win the cup. Bremner's goal was a stunner, but it wasn't to be our day.'

Leeds had come so remarkably close to winning the famed Double on their return to the First Division. They had gained 61 points but lost out on the title on goal average by the smallest of fractions. Their points total was the highest ever recorded by a side in second place, and four more than the 1963/64 season when Liverpool won the championship with just 57 points. They had then lost the FA Cup Final by one goal in extra time. It was heartbreaking, but it would make Don Revie even stronger.

12

The Forgotten Forward

ROD JOHNSON was on the Leeds United bench for the 1965 FA Cup Final with Liverpool. He sat in his white tracksuit, but underneath he was fully clothed. Substitutes would not be allowed until the following season and not until 1967 in the FA Cup. Johnson's appearance on the bench therefore was merely a token gesture.

After scoring on his league debut at Swansea in September 1962, Johnson spent much of his Leeds career on the sidelines. However, his time as a youth at Elland Road had been nothing short of exceptional, and he can consider himself extremely unlucky that Don Revie brought additional forwards to the club.

He excelled in all sports at Cow Close Secondary Modern School, and accumulated a huge array of metal badges over the years proclaiming 'SPORTS 1st Prize West Leeds Schools AA'.

Young Rod grew up with his parents at Penrith Grove, Wortley. He was picked for the school football team making an immediate impact and rising quickly to captain. In the team's first season, 1958, they shone in the Leeds Schools Shield, reaching the quarter-final where they beat Foxwood 3-2, with Johnson firing home two goals. That same season, three teams were vying for the Leeds Schools Senior Division Two title: Green Lane Juniors, Ingram Road and Cow Close. Unbeaten Green Lane had reached the semi-final of the Wynne Cup with a 2-0 win over also unbeaten Becketts Park. Cow Close, meanwhile, were also unbeaten and were having a remarkable first season in schools football. So far in the league, Cow Close had played seven, won six and drawn one, scoring 52 goals and conceding only 14. They sat at the top of Division Two. Captain Johnson set a great example by scoring 27 of those goals from the inside-left berth.

Next up for Close were Ingram Road, who were soundly trounced 15-0, then Belle Isle were put to the sword on their own ground in a 10-0 thrashing, Johnson scoring five and four goals respectively. Johnson bagged four more a week later in a 7-0 win over Brownhill.

A 'Schoolboy Portrait' published by the local press in 1959 proclaimed, 'Rodney Johnson played his junior and intermediate football at Upper Wortley before moving to Cow Close in September. He has played in every single City Shield game this season thus qualifying for this award.

'A natural worker and accurate kicker, Rodney is developing into a top-class inside-forward, with a nice bag of goals to his credit. A failing which Rodney is gradually mastering is his tendency to attempt too much. Rodney is captain of Cow Close who are so far unbeaten this season.'

Rod soon progressed to the Leeds FA team and then on to the elite Leeds City Boys, gaining representative honours, which also had youngsters Paul Reaney (Cross Green before moving to Middleton Parkside) and Paul Madeley (South Leeds before moving to Middleton Parkside) among its ranks. Initially Rod played with the City Boys in friendlies, getting a brace in a 5-2 win over Harrogate Boys at Oldfield Lane and then he played against the North East Derbyshire

Boys in the first round of the English Shield. On leaving school Rod had played for Middleton Parkside where he had been spotted by Leeds' scouts and was soon playing for the club's junior team. It wasn't long before a crop of Leeds juniors were picked to represent the West Riding FA team. Winger Dave Schofield, Clive Middlemass and Rod all lined up against Hallamshire in the second round of the FA County Youth Challenge Cup at the Swillington Miners Welfare ground. Madeley, who was now with Farsley Celtic, also lined up alongside the Leeds United trio. West Riding won it 3-0, in front of a good crowd.

Johnson continued to be outstanding in United's juniors, which included a youthful Norman Hunter in attack. Johnson was sometimes at centre-forward and at other times he was an inside-right with Hunter at inside-left. In 1960, in a 6-1 win for the juniors over Wolves at Fullerton Park, Hunter scored two goals, leaving the *Yorkshire Post* to enthuse, 'Leeds United juniors tamed the young Wolves in no uncertain fashion. The home goal tally in fact might have been doubled if all the scoring opportunities had been snapped up. Revelling in the heavy going, inside-forwards Hugh Ryden and Norman Hunter continually bamboozled the visiting defenders by their elusiveness and superb ball control. Hunter, in top form, rounded off much clever work with two goals and speedy right-winger Dave Schofield and roving Rod Johnson were also menacing raiders. Schofield blending excellently with Ryden to net a couple himself.

'A thrustful leader Johnson was always ready to have a go and deserved more than his one goal. Right-half Terry Casey slammed in a terrific "goal of the match".

'Behind the United lines, a solid defence nearly always had the measure of the Wolves attack, centre-half Paul Reaney playing resolutely to gradually subdue Swinburn, the Wolves centre-forward and an outstanding player, who managed to grab a consolation for the visitors near the end.'

Another report, on a 5-0 victory over Rotherham, was remarkably similar in its description of the United youngsters, 'Showing a splendid understanding are the middle trio in attack – 17-year-old Norman Hunter from the north-east, 17-year-old Scot Hugh Ryden, and 15-year-old groundstaff boy Rodney Johnson. Behind them there is a half-back line that has developed into a potent force. Its members are Welsh youth Terry Casey, Leeds-born Paul Reaney and Michael Addy from Ferrybridge.'

Meanwhile, the papers were awash with reports of Johnson, 'In a 3-0 win over Wolves by the Leeds United juniors Johnson rattled the bar from fully 30 yards before "the live wire in the United attack" scored with a 25-yard drive on the hour.'

A report of a 2-0 win over Sheffield United's juniors said, 'In the 50th minute another left-wing raid led to a second Leeds goal. A half clearance was snapped up by Johnson and the young centre-forward gave the Sheffield keeper no chance with a strong rising drive.'

Johnson was then invited to take part in an England youth trial at Peterborough on 6 January, with one newspaper reporting after his successful venture, 'Rodney, a centre-forward or inside-forward, will be 17 in a fortnight when United manager Don Revie intends to sign him as a full-time professional. Rod came through the trials and into the England team to meet Scotland in the amateur youth international at Peterborough where he'd had his successful trial. Alongside Rod on the right wing was a young David Pleat of Nottingham Forest. Paul Madeley was picked to play at left-half but had to pull out because of after effects of a smallpox vaccination. With the score standing at 1-1 at half-time England tore into the Scots in the second half and three goals in six minutes fired England into a 4-1 lead, Rod Johnson scoring after 50 minutes. Hulme pulled one back for Scotland near the end.'

Leeds and Johnson had agreed to hold back his signing so that he could get an England amateur cap, and with that now done, he signed professional terms just days after the win over Scotland, and United had captured an international for just £20.

Johnson even had his own fan club – his mum and dad. 'Violet and Ron are there whether it is raining or snowing, for a Northern Intermediate League game they are there on the touchline,' said Revie. 'If he continues to develop as he has done over the last six months he can be a very good player indeed. His heart and soul is in football, and of course, now he is a professional he has to work twice as hard!'

There was even an occasion where Rod played alongside Revie in the reserves. Revie, who had decided against cancelling his registration as a player, chose himself for a reserve fixture at Blackburn Rovers. It gave him the ideal opportunity to get out among his players and draw upon his experience to give them a guiding hand. To mark their appreciation of Revie's efforts, all the players gave the manager a leather golf bag. Revie, who had a single-figure handicap, would use it for a set of clubs given to him by Manchester City players after he left Maine Road to join Sunderland. Golf was a big part of the Leeds United family, and competition was always intense. Unsurprisingly for an all-round sportsman, Rod actually won the Leeds United Golf Cup one year beating off joint runners-up Gary Sprake and Jimmy Greenhoff. He proudly showed me a photograph of him holding the trophy while we had a cuppa in his kitchen on Epsom Road in Kippax.

He also showed me some letters that he had written to his family in 1961 while away attending the Football Association's School of Excellence at the famous Lilleshall site. One started with the address, 'National Recreation Centre, Lilleshall Hall, Nr Newport, Shropshire.' It continued:

> Dear Mam, Dad and Twins, We arrived safely at about 4pm. The car we set off in, the Consul, was broken so we went down to Brown Lane and changed it for a brand new Humber Super Snipe. There is a juke box here and the place looks just like a castle. We had dinner at 7-30 and then Walter Winterbottom said there was a change in the programme, instead of the FA film we had a game of attack and defence. All of us have been put into teams with 8 teams altogether. In my team I am inside-right and on the right wing is Norman Ash who has played for Aston Villa first team. On the way in from training Billy Wright said to me, 'Sweating son?' so I said, 'Aye' and then he said what have you been doing and I told him, attack and defence, He then said, 'That's the way' – Well love I'll have to finish now as it's 11-30. I will write again before the week's out.
>
> Lots of Love, Rod, XXX to Mam, Dad, Marilyn and Fay XXX.'

He then showed me one from a club youth trip to Tuscany in Italy,

> Dear Mam, Dad, Twins, We have arrived safe at Montecatini and we are going to the coast

tomorrow. Hoping to get a bit of a tan. The weather is still as bad as ever, it's raining more than it does in Leeds. We have the last game on Thursday and I am playing inside-forward. They have changed the arrangements for travelling home on Friday, they can't get seats on the plane to Ringway so they have to wait five hours in London for a plane to Yeadon. I have wrote and told Margaret that you will come and meet me. I told her to ring you on Friday so you can arrange what time to see her. The plane arrives at Yeadon at 9pm on Friday so I hope you come and meet me. I have bought nearly everybody a present but still have a few to get. I have still not broke into my £10 yet but I will probably do so tomorrow. I bet the weather in Leeds is better than it is here. I must go now as it's very late, I will send a card later.

Lots of Love Rod XX

ps Give my love to all at 17

pps Don't forget to arrange with Margaret what time you will meet her on Friday so you can be at Yeadon by 9pm.

These letters emphasise just how close to his family Johnson was. He said, 'I went on a tour of Italy with Leeds first team in June 1963. Although I'd made my debut almost a year earlier, I was still considered one of the young ones. Jack Charlton and Bobby Collins were definitely the seniors of the club, so you can imagine my delight and also nervousness when they invited me to come along for drink with them in a bar near our hotel. The boss didn't like to encourage drinking but always trusted his players to do the right thing. Billy Bremner and Jim Storrie came along. We had only sat at an outside table for about an hour when Jack and Bobby started arguing with each other. It wasn't a quiet argument either and soon escalated to loud shouting at each other and pushing and shoving. The next thing they were involved in what is best described as an altercation with each other, while the few locals in the bar were looking on – although I don't think they knew who Jack and Bobby were. Even though there was about seven or eight inches difference in height between them it got a little intense. Billy and Jim separated them and less than five minutes later the two of them were sat at the bar chatting away as if nothing had happened. Obviously nothing was ever said to the boss. But it turned out that this little feud was not an isolated incident. Bobby was a very small man, but nobody messed with him, he was a hard little bastard. And I think Jack was a little fearful of him too.

'That first game in Italy was against Roma on 5 June at the Olympic Stadium. It was part of the John Charles deal between Roma and Leeds. Charles was in the Roma team. Unfortunately I wasn't selected for Leeds but it featured a half-back line that Don Revie had been working on; the line-up was: Sprake, Reaney, Hair, Bremner, Charlton, Hunter, Weston, Lawson, Storrie, Collins and Johanneson. Leeds lost 2-1 but an incident at half-time saw Jack and wee Bobby at it again. Jack had made a mistake in the first half and Bobby wouldn't let it go and tore into Jack, verbally. Jack ignored him and went to get a shower but Bobby followed him. We sat in the dressing room looking at each other and we could hear them at it, hammer and tongs. Nobody moved except Don Revie who raced into the shower.

'The two players came back, Bobby in his shorts and Jack with a towel round him. Then the gaffer walked in and his suit was absolutely drenched. How nobody started laughing I'll never know, we stared at the floor, so as not to look at them.'

Eddie Gray recalled another incident with Charlton and Collins, 'It was in a hotel in Harrogate before a game with Burnley in 1965. Jack knocked on Bobby's room door and when he opened it, Jack threw a jug of water over him. Bobby immediately chased Jack down the corridor and then he accidentally put his arm through a glass door. Bobby was taken to the hospital and had 16 stitches put in his arm. Don was not in the hotel and when he found out, which wasn't until the next morning, matchday, Bobby said he was OK and begged Don to let him play. Don relented, possibly knowing how much of an asset to the team he was, and Les Cocker put a massive bandage on his arm. It was so big that Bobby couldn't bend his arm; they wouldn't allow that these days, but anyway, Bobby had a tremendous game in a 5-1 win that took Leeds to the top of the First Division.'

Weirdly, Charlton and Collins got two goals each that day – Albert Johanneson getting the other.

Just after I had retired from playing in goal for my Sunday local team in 1994, our manager retired too and the club was left without a keeper and a manager. We soon had someone to replace me between the sticks and we approached Rod Johnson to become our manager. I took over the role of secretary and Rod, who had considerable experience in managership in top-level amateur football once he had retired from playing, was cajoled into becoming our team boss. He had turned us down a couple of times, but eventually accepted our offer. I knew Rod very well by this point and he had told me that he was sceptical about running what in effect was a Sunday league pub team. This was not because it was beneath him, far from it, it was that he had certain standards of discipline that would probably be difficult to enforce in such an environment. I must admit I didn't really understand what he meant at the time, but our form on the pitch had dipped slightly and we needed some proper leadership to steer us back on track.

Rod made an immediate impact and we chalked up back-to-back victories over the top two teams. In such a short space of time, Rod had got our players playing at a level even they didn't know was possible. I remember one of our players, Dave Rawnsley, walking off after one game saying, 'I thought we were Barcelona out there.'

But then I discovered why Rod had reservations about taking over as manager. We were in our pub, the Royal Oak in Kippax, after a game when a little fracas broke about between a couple of lads. It quickly spilled over into where we were all sat and one or two of our lads became involved. It escalated and the next thing, Rod leapt over a table and tried to reason with one of the offenders who took a swing at Rod, who in turn ducked and executed one of the best right hooks I've ever seen, leaving this lad flat out. Order was soon restored and we all dismissed it as one of those things and returned to our drinks.

But Rod was upset. His philosophy was that if he couldn't control himself, how could he expect his players to do the same? He hadn't acted aggressively, he was merely backing his own lads up. He immediately resigned and left the pub. I spoke with him a couple of times during the week and eventually he agreed to resume his role. All was well for the next couple of games and we got a win that put us back on top of the league. Then we played a cup match against a high-flying side, Hambleton, from the division above us. They were a well-drilled outfit and were aloof, and for the want of a better word, a bit posh. They had a reputation for being a bit smart and well equipped. Within the first quarter of an hour we were one up. And just before half-time it was 2-0.

After a team talk from Rod our lads stormed into the second half and were soon three up. Our opponents were fuming. Then our full-back Chris was coming up the wing close to us with the ball when he was clattered almost waist high by one of their players. Fisticuffs ensued and one of the first involved was Rod. To put it simply, he proved that his previous right hook was no fluke. Rod was annoyed with himself even though it was not his fault, but there was no return for him. He was such a lovely bloke, an amazing family man, but he was the ultimate professional and the ultimate team man. All for one and one for all.

Paul Madeley was brought up at 14 Dalton Grove in Beeston. He became possibly one of the best players Leeds United ever produced. And like Rod, he featured in the coveted 'Schoolboy Portrait' – it said, 'Paul was captain of Cross Flatts Juniors and his lucky thought is that he has yet another season of schoolboy soccer and a bright chance of highest honours.'

13

The First Venture into
European Competition

LEEDS UNITED began their first European campaign on 29 September against Torino at Elland Road, in front of an eager 34,000 crowd. Leeds had almost qualified for the European Cup at the very first attempt, finishing second in their first season back in the First Division. Back then only the national champions would qualify for the European Cup, so Leeds were competing in the Inter-Cities Fairs Cup, which was later replaced by the UEFA Cup and then the Europa League.

James Foster was stood in the Lowfields Road that evening with his dad, Victor. James said, 'It was so exciting. I had been to a few night matches and it always added that extra sparkle playing under floodlights, but this was Europe, it was new, it was special. The atmosphere was electric. There were a handful of Italian supporters in the corner of the West Stand, but the night belonged to Leeds.

'Stood with us was my uncle Stan, dad's brother, and I was a little bit jealous to be honest – he was going to the second leg in Italy. But all that was put aside as the white shirts tore into the Italians with real vigour and passion. And we should have won by more than 2-1.'

Billy Bremner and Alan Peacock scored for Leeds that night, and although they really should have won by more, Don Revie knew that as long as they kept a clean sheet in the return leg they would go through to the second round. Leeds had become experts at defending an advantage but this was Europe – a whole new ball game.

Rod Johnson was on the plane that carried Leeds to their first competitive game in Europe. He said, 'We had a bit of a panic at the airport when Big Jack couldn't find his passport, you could tell that the boss wasn't pleased but as always he tried not to show it and just said, "Did you have it when you left home, Jack? Check your pockets and your bag." Then a crackly message came over the airport tannoy saying that they had a passport belonging to Mr Charlton from Leeds. He'd left it on the table in the lounge. We knew our lead was slender, and that they'd scored a vital away goal at Elland Road, but Don Revie held an informal team talk. I was sat near the window and Bobby Collins was sat beside me. The boss stood hunched up in the aisle talking to the players behind him and in front of him. After his talk, we felt we could win the away leg too. He always had a cautious attitude but also a positive one, if that makes sense.

'When we got to passport control in Turin, Bobby Collins started laughing at Big Jack, who was patting each of his pockets furiously. "Lost your passport again, Jack?" said Bobby. "Yes," said Jack.

'Just then one of the stewardesses came running through to us. He'd left it in the leather pocket in the back of the seat in front of him. I think it was Alan Peacock who said something like, "You're going to need that, Jack, if we have a good run at this European lark," to much merriment from the lads, including the boss who smiled.'

Soon it was down to the serious business of eliminating Torino from the competition. The first 45 minutes went according to plan, as United snuffed out any challenge that the Italians threw at them, and then the strategy in the second half was to add to their tally from the first leg and get the job done. The crowd of 26,000 had become agitated and that was playing right into United's hands. Then after 55 minutes, Collins was racing towards goal when the Torino right-back, Poletti, went racing into the tackle. Collins fell to the ground, and that was the end of him in Turin.

Jack Charlton said, 'As I watched Poletti go into the challenge I winced as I saw Bobby hit the ground. I knew he had broken his leg. Our trainer, Les Cocker, tended to him for five minutes assessing the damage; he had broken his thigh bone.' Revie reacted furiously at first claiming, 'It was a terrible foul. Collins was kicked deliberately.' Collins, muffled in Don Revie's coat, was slowly carried off the field and taken by ambulance straight to the Maria Victoria Hospital. Poletti said later, 'He was going so fast. It has been such a shock to me and I am sincerely sorry.' Poletti went to hospital to see Collins the following day to apologise in person. Collins, a combative warrior himself, readily accepted the apology. His wife Betty was flown out by the club to be with her husband.

While Collins lay in his hospital bed, it was a backs-to-the-wall fight with a vengeance. Revie reshuffled the team, leaving only Alan Peacock and Peter Lorimer up front as Torino, now with a man advantage, pressed forward constantly. During this hectic spell, Billy Bremner, Jack Charlton and Norman Hunter held the line magnificently and Gary Sprake performed heroics between the sticks. Then, with the Italians becoming more and more frustrated, United began to probe the Torino defence. All of a sudden the hosts were on the run, and Bremner came agonisingly close to snatching victory when he raced through the home defence to unleash a powerful shot that scraped the post. The game finished 0-0 and Revie was delighted, saying, 'This was one of the greatest performances I have ever seen, it proves what great professionals my players are. But I would sooner have lost the match than have Bobby injured like this.'

Bremner said, 'Bobby's injury sickened us all. This wee man is the greatest player in the world, so far as we are concerned.'

Collins must have been chuffed to bits when he returned a couple of days later. Walking with crutches, following an hour-long operation, aided by Betty, his arrival at Yeadon Airport was greeted by Revie and Harry Reynolds, teammates and hundreds of Leeds fans.

The second round paired Leeds with the East German team SC Leipzig, and it was a complete reversal of the first round. Leeds travelled behind the Iron Curtain for the first leg, which would become a regular occurrence during their early European years. The Iron Curtain was the political barrier that divided Europe into two separate areas following the end of the Second World War. Instigated by the Soviet Union, to cut itself off from 'the West', it stretched for almost 4,500 miles. The barrier that divided the east from the west divided Germany, and also incorporated the Berlin Wall, the iconic concrete structure between east Berlin and west Berlin. Travelling from the west to the east meant that you had to travel through Checkpoint Charlie.

Peter Lorimer remembered those early ventures into eastern countries, 'We were always playing East German teams and Hungarian teams. So we had to go through Checkpoint Charlie in Berlin. Our coach would be stopped for an hour at least, police guards would board the bus and search it thoroughly. It was annoying. Our hotels were always first-class, and we couldn't wait to get to them, it was like a sanctuary. And Don would arrange, with difficulty at times, to bring our own type of food with us. We always seemed to play well in east Europe.'

Lorimer scored the opener in Leipzig with ten minutes to go, and Bremner made it two within a couple of minutes, although the home side quickly got one back and Leeds took a 2-1 advantage back to Elland Road. After playing Willie Bell up front in East Germany, Revie reinstalled him at left-back to great effect at home and another efficient 0-0 display sent the crowd of 32,000 home eagerly awaiting their next European opponents. And it was an outcome worth waiting for, as Valencia rolled into town.

Mike O'Grady, a Leeds lad, had unusually slipped through the net of the club's scouting system. He went to Corpus Christi School in Halton Moor but was recruited by Yorkshire neighbours Huddersfield Town, who were managed by Bill Shankly, in 1959. Leeds eventually got their man in 1965, and he was on the left wing against Valencia. 'It was quite an eye-opener, to say the least,' said O'Grady.

Valencia had scored first in the first leg and Lorimer levelled in the second half, but then with a quarter of an hour remaining and with Leeds pressing hard for the winner, all hell broke loose. Charlton challenged a Valencia defender for a high ball in the Spaniards' penalty area, and was kicked. Charlton shrugged it off, and then it happened again as he was kicked from behind. Once more he remained fairly calm, although he was restrained by Paul Madeley. It was as if the Valencia defence was testing him, then one of them threw a right hook at Charlton and he went berserk.

Then all at once, the players were going at each other as tempers flared, with arms and legs swinging in all directions.

Charlton was chasing Valencia's left-back, Francisco Vidagañy, all over the pitch. Charlton had completely flipped and nothing was going to stop him. Police came on to the pitch and it was mayhem. Then, the Dutch referee Leo Horn summoned his linesmen and walked off the pitch signalling both teams to do the same. Charlton had already left the pitch as he chased Vidagañy down the tunnel, but luckily for the Spaniard, the Leeds man was restrained by two burly policemen. Charlton reflected afterwards, 'I admit I lost my temper. Suddenly I was conscious that I had been singled out for some diabolical treatment. And I wasn't going to take any more of this, without giving some of it back. Even my own team-mates could not restrain me, I was so angry. I chased around the pitch intent upon one thing only, to get my own back. And nothing was going to stop my pursuit for vengeance.'

Lorimer recalled, 'I thought the referee, Mr Horn, lost control that night. Foreign players seemed to be very highly strung and it was very confusing in those days playing in different countries, with different interpretations of the laws by different referees.'

Horn said, 'I have always regarded Charlton as a fine man. He was the cleanest player on the field, until he lost control. I saw a Spanish defender kick him, and if Charlton had given a reprisal kick, I could have understood it and let it pass, because it happened so often. But, as captain of Leeds and an international, Charlton should have been the first player to exercise complete control.'

Then Horn blamed something else for the trouble, 'There was something in the air, something unpleasant. Money was the cause of the trouble; you could see it in the nervousness and excitement of the players. Leeds were on £1,500 bonus to win. When Leeds lost a goal this nervousness spread among them. Valencia had nine men in front of their goal. They too were gripped with this terrible feeling. These games have become too important for the players.'

When both teams returned to the field, both Charlton and Vidagañy had been sent off. Revie pleaded with the referee, saying to him, 'Do you know what you're doing? This is an international,' to which Horn replied, 'Do you think this is the first time I have refereed a game? I don't care if Charlton is an emperor, he is not coming back on the field tonight.' Revie also took issue with Horn's comments on money. 'It's untrue,' he said. 'My players were on no special bonus. Mr Horn is guessing, or he has been misinformed. I resent these allegations, but I am saying no more now. It's time to let the whole thing simmer down.' When play resumed, a third player, Valencia's inside-forward, José Sánchez Lage, was sent off for kicking Jim Storrie. But the game did eventually settle down as the teams played out a 1-1 draw. Charlton was later fined £80 by the FA Disciplinary Committee.

In the return leg in Spain, the anticipated trouble between the teams did not happen and both sets of players put on an excellent display of football. Mike O'Grady was very impressed with the Mestalla Stadium, 'When we walked out earlier on to the pitch in our suits I remember thinking, "How high are those stands?" It was immense.'

The game was settled by O'Grady. Paul Madeley sent a magnificent 30-yard ball over the full-back's head perfectly into the path of O'Grady, who drew the keeper and sent his shot skimming past him into the net.

The Leeds fans who had made the trip were delirious, even though one of them got the goalscorer wrong. O'Grady said, 'We were having a drink in the hotel bar afterwards, a few Leeds fans were in, and one of them, who'd had a glass or two of San Miguel, came over to congratulate Jim Storrie for scoring the winner. Billy Bremner pointed to me and said, "This fella here got the goal, pal," and the fan then shook my hand a little apologetically.

'Don Revie trusted the players to have a drink and trusted them implicitly to behave and not exceed their quota. Unlike Bill McGarry when I was at Wolves – he wouldn't allow any players a drink at all. Even Bill Shankly, when he managed Huddersfield, encouraged us, if we were staying in London, to go to the cinema as opposed to a quiet bar. Don Revie treated you as an adult.'

United ventured into central Europe next round to play Hungary's Újpesti Dózsa. In the home leg they crushed Dózsa 4-1 with Cooper, Bell, Storrie and Bremner chipping in. But Revie was cautious about the second leg. Leeds had beaten the Hungarians on a heavy Elland Road pitch and Revie knew they would be a very different proposition on their home soil. And so it proved.

The manager said, 'Dózsa could have had at least six goals, they were brilliant in playing those little one-twos around the box, and had countless shots cleared off the line, or hitting the woodwork. But in the second half we got lucky and Peter Lorimer suddenly scored against the run of play, and fortunately this seemed to knock the stuffing out of them.' The match ended 1-1.

Jason Thomas wrote in *The Leeds United Story*, 'Leeds' luck ran out in the semi-final, however, when they were outclassed by Real Zaragoza. The Spaniards possessed one of the world's most feared attacks and, although Leeds managed to hold them to a 2-2 draw over the two legs, they were well beaten 3-1 in the play-off at Elland Road.'

Leeds went one better in the following season's competition. After disposing of Amsterdam side DWS with an aggregate victory of 8-2 in the second round, they came up against, unbelievably, Valencia. Fortunately there was no repeat of the drama that had engulfed their meeting the previous season, and nobody was sent off, although Les Cocker had to be stopped by Don Revie from getting kicked out of Valencia's ground. Cocker, incensed over a foul on Rod Belfitt, jumped up out of his seat and on to the running track on the edge of the pitch. He was shouting at the referee when two policemen grabbed him and were pushing him down the tunnel. They had mistaken him for a spectator and Revie had to run after them to explain who he was. Leeds won 2-0 on the night and went through 3-1 on aggregate.

Next, a trip to Italy took them to play Bologna in the first leg of the fourth round. Leeds lost 1-0 but then won by the same score at Elland Road thanks to a Johnny Giles penalty, to make it 1-1 over two legs. Back in the day there was no extra time or penalties; it was settled by the primitive method of tossing a disc. The practice was called 'ludicrous' by Spurs manager Bill Nicholson, 'a pathetic way to settle a tie' by Joe Mercer of Manchester City, and Liverpool's Bill Shankly said, 'Flipping a disc is farcical, in a competition of such importance.' The visionary Revie agreed 100 per cent with these sentiments, 'It would be much fairer to play extra time or even some form of a penalty shoot-out.'

But for now a round red and blue disc the size of a coaster would be used to settle the tie. The 42,000 Elland Road crowd were silent as the disc spun in the air. Charlton was now the team captain as Bobby Collins, although fully recovered from his injury in Turin, only played a handful more games before moving on to Bury. As the disc descended, Charlton shouted 'blue'. And blue it was.

The semi-final draw paired United with Scottish opponents in the shape of Kilmarnock. A brilliant hat-trick from Belfitt and another Giles penalty helped them to a 4-2 victory at Elland Road and the aggregate score remained the same after a 0-0 draw in Scotland. So Leeds were on the way to their first European final, in only their second continental season, where the crack Yugoslav (now Croatia) side Dinamo Zagreb awaited them.

Henry Stogdale of the Black Horse was one of the Leeds fans present along with a few of his locals, making their first trip abroad. Terry Cooper had established himself in the first team by then and said, 'The travelling was still quite tiring in those days, especially into eastern Europe. We'd fly to Warsaw and then venture over the Berlin Wall, but we were all feeling confident about our first European final.' Zagreb would prove too powerful, winning 2-0 over the two-legged final, and United would have to wait a little longer for European success.

But one thing had emerged from these first couple of years on the continent – Don Revie was an expert at playing European teams at their own game, and then some.

He had the right people around him. His right-hand man, Les Cocker, often had to run on to the pitch while the game was going on and drag a player off to receive treatment because the referee refused to stop the game. Leeds had their own doctor, Ian Duthie Adams, who would travel abroad with them. 'Doc Adams' ran his surgery on the corner of Trentham Street in Beeston. In 1957 'Doc' started two years of airborne service and became a captain in Two Para, serving in Jordan and Cyprus. He was the chairman of the British Association of Sport and Exercise Medicine as well as an executive of the European Federation of Sports Medicines Association. Many a time on their travels on the continent, 'Doc' would tend to a player retrieved by Cocker, who took no abuse from the opposition. Once, in Budapest, Les did kick a bucket while an opponent was receiving 'treatment', making a diving simulation and telling the 'injured' player to get up.

14

A Kick in the Goalies

WHEN I started watching Leeds United as a ten-year-old kid, Gary Sprake was definitely my hero. He certainly inspired me to become a goalkeeper, albeit at a much lower level. I would watch him taking crosses with ease and his saves were unbelievable at times. He lived near our school and would visit Garforth Comprehensive on a fairly regular basis along with other Leeds stars who lived in the area. It was usually on a Saturday morning when Leeds were at home.

There was a spiral staircase in the main entrance building that leads up to the staffroom which had a couple of sofas placed around the bottom of it. When Gary had finished his talk, which was always in the music room, he left. On one occasion I was walking back to the main entrance with a friend, 'Tab', when we saw Sprake sat on one of the sofas, and going upstairs was a young teacher with a short dress on. He was wearing a round-necked red sweater, and when we went and sat on the sofa next to him, his face was as red as his sweater, or as red as his face when he let an easy goal in. 'We get into trouble for doing that,' I said to him.

He was about to make an excuse and then thought better of it and just laughed. We had a chat about Leeds

United and he was great. When we were leaving, he gave us a complimentary ticket each for that afternoon's game at Elland Road.

We saw Sprake on several more occasions when he visited the school along with the likes of Norman Hunter, Nigel Davey, Paul Reaney and Terry Cooper, who all lived nearby. Jack Charlton, who had a sports and fashion shop in the main street, would often be asked to hand out medals and certificates on sports day. Me and Tab, my partner in crime, would see him in the nearby pub, the Gaping Goose, a haunt for some of the older generation of the teachers. They didn't seem to mind us being in there as long as we didn't show ourselves up. We were on our lunchtime break, but we were also only 16.

Me and Tab would sometimes 'copper up' and buy Big Jack a pint, but I never knew him to buy us one. In fact, over the years I spent a lot of time in his company and always bought him his favourite pint of bitter, be it Tetley's or John Smith's, but not once can I recall him ever buying me, or anybody for that matter, one back.

It was worth it, however, to hear some of the really funny tales he would tell of his days at Leeds. He used to call me 'his mate' – that'll do for me. Even though he seemed to have 'other mates'. We would often share a pint right up until his illness later in his life. My neighbours Sue and Paul were once at an 'Evening with Jack Charlton' event and they brought me back a book personally signed to me from him. He never put mate, though!

Gary Sprake went on to play for Leeds for 11 great years, but things turned a little sore after 1977. The issues stemmed from allegations by Sprake that Don Revie and Billy Bremner attempted to bribe the opposition. The case ended up in court.

Sprake, by now retired and not doing particularly well financially or health-wise, accepted an offer of £7,500 by the *Daily Mirror* to give evidence for a dossier alleging bribery claims against the club. The main journalist behind the dossier was Richard Stott, who was never a Leeds admirer, shall we say, a fact that he told me in no uncertain terms, many times during our heated exchanges of phone calls, emails and letters in the early 2000s. He wasn't well received within the club, to the point where many felt he had an agenda.

Sprake's actions would result in a massive reaction from his former team-mates.

About five years ago, I received a phone call from a friend of mine, Andy Wigglesworth, who told me that Sprake's daughter Julia had reluctantly decided to sell off some of her dad's private collection. Items such as photographs, letters and telegrams were all to be sold, and if I was interested he had everything at his house. I think Andy was still talking to me on the phone when I hung up and quickly arrived at his place, knocking loudly on his door. 'Bloody hell,' he said, 'What kept yer?' As I drove home with the collection on the back seat, my mind was full of all sorts of different emotions. Julia had found the collection in a case under the bed after Gary had died in 2016. She'd had no idea it was there.

Gary had been a hero of mine right from me being a kid, teenager and then into my 20s, then, fuelled by a self-confessed Leeds-hating journalist, hard-up Sprake, who had long since left Leeds and was no longer playing football, agreed to the deal put before him. He was to accuse the club, and in particular Revie and Bremner of bribery. From that day I began to hate Sprake, much like most Leeds fan and players. Then as I drove home with his private collection I began to really feel very sorry for him. Here was a man, playing for one of the best sides in Europe, and very popular, despite the odd mistake, among his team-mates. Then there was what he would call the 'Revie incident'. And that was the end of his relationship with Leeds United and his old playing colleagues.

Sprake had thrown all that away for what really amounted to a pittance. He was instantly shunned by the club and by his former team-mates who in every sense of the word were his mates. Together, they had all been through so much together for over a decade. It seemed that everybody in football was united against Leeds, but they stuck together with a fierce determination. They looked out for one another. Now, he would never be invited to players' events or get-togethers again. The players – his mates – would never speak to him again. And here I was, driving home with all of his possessions in a cardboard box.

Neil Jeffries was the editor of the official club magazine *Leeds Leeds Leeds* (*LLL*) and in 2006 he was granted a telephone interview with Gary Sprake, which was never published. Jeffries, a journalist and author, has written for several publications, including *Kerrang!*, *Mojo*, *Empire* and *Classic Rock*, meeting and interviewing countless rock stars along the way. He also plays a pivotal role in the production of the club's official matchday programme. He has kindly allowed permission to publish the interview here in almost its entirety for the first time.

Sprake began with his feelings about Leeds United at the time.

Sprake, 'I've got the book *The Essential History of Leeds United*, and I'm number nine in it, I'm very proud of that. I've followed them all the time since I left the club. It's the first result I look for. I last saw Leeds play a few years ago against Birmingham City with a few friends, and I also went to see them play at Villa as well.

'I worked for Birmingham council for 23 years. I was a tutor in the Youth Training Department, interviewing and tutoring the National Vocational Qualification. I finished this in 1997 though because I had two massive heart attacks in 1995 and went back to work. Then in 1997 I had a quadruple bypass operation and took early retirement in 1998.'

Jeffries, 'How did the book *Careless Hands: The Truth About Gary Sprake* by Tim Johnson and Stuart Sprake come about?'

Sprake, 'I went to my brother-in-law's funeral about three years ago and I saw my nephew, Stuart. He has always been upset about the way that I was treated. However, I don't think anything of it at all now. It used to upset me but it's been ages now. Tim and Stuart decided to write the book, I had no intention of writing one myself.'

In my first book, *Paint it White*, I said that in the 1968 Inter-Cities Fairs Cup Final against Ferencváros in 1968 Gary Sprake produced the best goalkeeping that I've ever seen. One save in particular from a free kick was out of this world.

'That final made your reputation didn't it?' asks Jeffries.

Sprake, 'Yes, but I'm getting old now, I'm 61, I can't remember much about it! I remember one save in particular. It was from a free kick and I dived to my left and the ball hit my hand and went miles over the bar. Some say that was my best game for Leeds.'

Jeffries, ' You were given cortisone injections to help you play through the pain barrier sometimes?' Sprake sounds weary at this point.

Sprake, 'Yes, my back is terrible. I had cortisone injections in it since I was about 20. It wasn't only me, Allan Clarke had it too for his knees. But for me it was my back and I've had several operations for it. But these days I just go to the pain clinic ... I've just got to live with it really. The Professional Footballers' Association have been looking into it for years. I had a letter about it around six years ago – all the players who have suffered after cortisone did. Tommy Smith of Liverpool was another. I met him at a memorabilia fair at the NEC a few years ago and he's virtually crippled, so I'm not too bad compared to him.'

Jeffries reminds Sprake of the bizarre mistake at Anfield in 1967 when he threw the ball into his own net.

Sprake, 'It was just a one in a million chance. I went to throw the ball to Terry Cooper and I just got it wrong. I've done it right thousands and thousands of times but it happened in front of the Kop, and the match announcer as we were walking off at half-time said, "I'm going to dedicate this one to Gary," and he played "Careless Hands" [by Des O'Connor].'

Jeffries, ' Were you able to laugh about it?'

Sprake, 'Well, I didn't laugh at the time! But a few matches later ... But Revie never gave me a rollocking. It was just one of those things. I had a good game apart from that. And when we went back there the following season, we won the league title and the same crowd gave us a standing ovation.'

Jeffries, 'The mistakes, it must bother you that people remember them all so vividly – but you say that wasn't the reason for the book?'

Sprake, 'No, the main thing I was upset with about was what happened when I left. Paul Reaney was my best friend ... and before I left Leeds I was one of the best keepers ever. As it says in the book, I've got letters, telegrams and loads of citations from players and managers. But after the Revie episode, that all changed. Suddenly I was the worst keeper in the world. That can't be right, can it? Unfortunately the

"Revie incident" did happen and there is a chapter in there about it.'

In those days the Leeds players would frequent the city centre on a regular basis, and would rub shoulders with international stars such as Frankie Vaughan, Ronnie Hilton and the like. In the eyes of Mike O'Grady, with Sprake around there was no such thing as a quiet pint.

Sprake, 'We would go in Rockerfellas, Cinderellas, a nightclub [part of the Merrion Centre] in Leeds to have a drink after the game and a lot of stars would go there. Near Leeds was Batley Variety Club where a lot of them would perform. We would go there to watch and then go back to Leeds for a drink and sometimes they would come with us. I wouldn't say we got to know any of the stars personally, but we did get to meet them.'

Jeffries, 'Were you a hell-raiser?'

Sprake, 'No, I wasn't a hell-raiser, haha. But every time we went out, the players would say I was smart and good-looking and I did get a lot of attention from the ladies. But lots of them were out with their boyfriends and some of them would get a bit needled – so there were a few arguments. But I don't think I ever had a real fight with anybody over it. It was a standing joke with me though.'

Jeffries, 'Did any other teams try to buy you?'

Sprake, 'When I was at Leeds in '69 Lazio made a bid for me. But the boss, Revie, just said no – I wasn't going, full stop. That was it. I didn't get any say. But I hadn't said I wanted to go, this was just something that appeared in the papers. I never asked for a transfer and I was happy to stay at Leeds.'

Jeffries, 'You had a special relationship with Don?'

Sprake, 'Well, yes, he went to my wedding – but he didn't stay. He just had a drink and left! But it wasn't only me that he had a special relationship with, he treated all of us like we were his family. Treated us all the same. It was a great side, we all got brought up together. Grew up together. Myself, Paul, Norman – Billy Bremner was only a couple of years older than me – all that team, there were about 19 of us who were there all together for about 19 years. It was a great team and there was nothing Revie wouldn't do for us – for all of us.'

Jeffries, 'It must make what happened all the worse for you?'

Sprake, 'Yes. But I haven't fallen out with everyone. When Terry Cooper was manager at Birmingham we used to go out for meals together. Terry's got no axe to grind. Mick Bates is OK with me. I've spoken to him and Mick O'Grady. I've spoken to Peter Lorimer. Really, I asked Paul Reaney to do an interview for the book and he told Stuart he didn't agree with me writing the book. But why should he say that? Paul was my best mate. But after this Revie episode, Paul, Mick Jones and Allan Clarke have just cut me off. It's just one of those things, I was upset about it at first but I don't lose sleep over it now.'

Jeffries, 'David Harvey's monkey?'

Sprake, 'He loved his animals, did Dave. But I never met it. I think it was a monkey, not a chimpanzee. I haven't spoken to him for ages – he's up in Scotland I think, in the Hebrides, doing his farm. We were at Leeds for ages and there were no problems between us at all. In fact I had no problems with any of the players while I was at Leeds. We were all best of mates, great mates. I had a lovely farewell party and they bought me a lovely farewell gift when I left. They kept in touch with me until the "Revie incident" happened later on. Some of them just changed their attitude to me. I've since picked up books by Mick Jones, Allan Clarke and Eddie Gray and they've all just slagged me off.'

Jeffries, 'They're not accusing you of lying are they? But it's a story they didn't want told.'

Sprake, 'It happened and that's it. And they know it happened. The story was done by the *Daily Mirror* and nobody's sued me. It was the truth. If I'd told lies I would have been sued. But I never got sued by Revie or any of the players. I was with Big Jack at the NEC and we had a couple of drinks together. He was fine, we had a laugh and a joke. It happened and that was it. I doubt if Leeds were the only side – but I have no proof of that.

'[Former Leicester, Arsenal and QPR defender] Frank McLintock mentioned Revie in his book. He said he and his wife were offered a holiday anywhere in the world – and I didn't know about that. Francis Munro of Wolves says things in his book that happened in that game [the 2-1 defeat 48 hours after the 1972 FA Cup Final which cost Leeds the title and the Double] that I didn't know about either [Sprake wasn't playing]. But it only happened four or five games toward the end of the season. It didn't happen all the time. We were a great side and if this thing hadn't come up maybe we would have been an even better side and won more games. It's just one of those things. As I've said in the book, Revie promised me a testimonial. I'd been at Leeds 13 years but never had one. I wasn't the only Leeds player involved in the *Daily Mirror* story – Terry Hibbitt, who's dead now bless his soul, Mike O'Grady. Jimmy Greenhoff.

'But I seemed to be the only one who's been singled out. I don't know if they had a go at the other guys. But I've nothing to worry about. I never got sued. It was the truth. And that's it. Paul took the attitude that he didn't want my book coming out. Maybe he was frightened of something. I don't know. But who is he to say I shouldn't write a book?

I was a bit disappointed that he wouldn't contribute but if that's the way that Paul feels that's fine.

'I'm really a shy lad. I've always been shy – I know my temper suggested a bit different now and again – but I've really enjoyed these question and answer sessions that I've done in Wales. And I'm looking forward to others lined up for the book. Tim and Stuart went to see Peter Lorimer at his pub and they said he softened up after a while and said we should invite Gary back into the fold. Peter Ridsdale invited me to Leeds a few years ago, but I declined. I've been back in the crowd but I've never met any of the Leeds lads. I met Norman at St Andrew's when I was doing corporate hospitality and Norman Hunter was there, he shook my hand and said, "How are you?" Eddie Gray has done the same. I don't think there'll be a problem, Everything I've said I'm quite pleased with. We're all part of the family – a family of about 20 people – even if we don't see each other. I still know how much I enjoyed it and as long as I live I'll follow their results.'

Jeffries reflected on his stunning interview with Sprake: 'The facts are clear but the opinions are divided. Facts: Leeds United won more silverware with Gary Sprake between the posts than any other goalkeeper. Sprake is currently ninth on the all-time appearance list. Opinions: in *LLL*'s Greatest 100 Leeds players of all time poll [of 2002], Sprake was ranked 38th. He was only third among the goalkeepers, behind both his immediate successor David Harvey, and Nigel Martyn.

'There are two reasons for the apparent discrepancy. One: a commonly held perception that Sprake was error prone; and two: another that he was disloyal to both Don Revie and his former team-mates. There are facts in both of these opinions. First, his mistakes are documented in old press reports and on film. Second, in 1977 Gary did speak to *Daily Mirror* journalists seeking evidence for a 315-page dossier alleging Don Revie's attempts to fix matches by offering financial incentives to opponents.'

Sprake has never lived either charge down, but it is the second one that has proved most damaging to his reputation and standing among the Leeds legends he would otherwise stand alongside. In 1973, after 11 years in the first team, he was sold to Birmingham, but he was 'sent to Coventry' by several of his team-mates after the *Mirror* published its article. It was a bitter wall of silence towards Sprake that suggested anyone who broke the unwritten rule of dressing rooms, that what happens behind closed doors remains behind closed doors, should be prepared for many years of bitter silence or hostility from men who were formerly his best friends.

I have known Mike O'Grady for many years, both professionally – as a decorator – and over the odd pint or two in his local, the Arabian Horse in Aberford, a charming village on the outskirts of Leeds. 'Shady', as he was called by his team-mates, joined Wolves after leaving Leeds, and was with them during the 'incident' in 1972 that Sprake mentioned. He didn't play that evening but was on the sidelines of a packed crowd of 53,379 at Molineux. He had told me previously that he turned down a more substantial offer from the *Daily Mirror* as well as other publications to contribute to Richard Stott's dossier. It's also interesting to note that Wolves striker Derek Dougan, who played on that Monday night at Molineux, gave evidence on Leeds United's behalf that he never heard any mention of alleged bribery anywhere that evening or leading up to it, and if that had been the case then surely he would have been one for the papers to contact. Also intriguing is the fact that Sprake refused to repeat any of his allegations under oath.

Several years prior to Sprake's claims, Revie had said on many occasions that one of the biggest regrets he had at Leeds was not replacing Sprake with David Harvey much sooner than he did.

On 5 April 1972 Sprake was injured in a 3-1 home win against Huddersfield Town. He had regained his fitness by 1 May but Revie opted to let Harvey, who had taken Sprake's position for the previous three games, keep the keeper's jersey, which included the FA Cup Final win over Arsenal. Sprake only played one more game for Leeds, a West Riding Cup Final against Halifax Town at Elland Road on 12 May. In front of a crowd of 6,256, Leeds won 4-3 with the crucial goal coming from Lorimer, spectacularly scored from the halfway line. Harvey retained his place the following season and after putting in a transfer request, Sprake was sold to Birmingham City, for whom he made 22 appearances before retiring.

When I arrived home with Gary Sprake's collection that evening I started looking through it. A couple of things struck me straight away: there were telegrams wishing him all the very best from Leeds on his debut for Birmingham at Arsenal in 1973. I began to wonder what Sprake himself thought looking through those telegrams of best wishes, four years later, from the directors and staff and others, telegrams of good luck from his mate Paul Reaney and Johnny Giles and Don Revie, after he had betrayed all at the club.

That said, and God knows why, I began to lose some of that hostility towards Sprake and I began feeling sympathy for him.

It had taken seven years for Harvey to break into the first team. In competing with Sprake for that number one jersey, he had shown remarkable patience and loyalty to wait for his chance to come along, and once it had he was determined to keep hold of the shirt.

Born in Leeds on 7 February 1948, Harvey went to Foxwood School and then Seacroft Grange School where he had first been taken note of by Leeds' scouting system. He was employed in a shoe factory when he represented Leeds City Boys and it wasn't long before he was picked up by United's scouts and drafted into the club's under-18s where he joined a crop of other promising young teenagers such as Peter Lorimer, Mick Bates, Jimmy Greenhoff and Eddie Gray. He made his first-team debut against West Bromwich Albion in the third round of the League Cup in October 1965 in a team consisting of mainly reserves, waiting for their chance to stake a claim on a regular spot, including Lorimer, Rod Johnson and Nigel Davey. Sprake's brilliance in goal would block Harvey's route and Revie's man-management skills were of paramount importance because a goalkeeper of Harvey's calibre could easily have walked into other first teams elsewhere, and that also went for several of Revie's other fringe players too. But United's boss knew he needed two first-class goalkeepers with the team battling on all fronts.

Revie would admit in later years that he should have put Harvey into the first team sooner than he did. 'I think Leeds might have won even more trophies had I done so,' Revie said. It was a great testimony to a loyal keeper who was always composed and courageous, and one hell of a hard, hard trainer, throughout his career.'

Harvey played in goal when United won the 1972 FA Cup Final and from that he received recognition from Scotland. Although he was born in Leeds, Harvey's dad was Scottish, enabling him to represent Scotland should he wish to do so. Harvey was named the best goalkeeper at the 1974 World Cup in West Germany, after Scotland's elimination despite completing their group matches without defeat, and he went on to win 16 international caps. Remarkably, considering how long he played in the reserves, Harvey made 445 appearances for Leeds.

Richard Petty was once at a reserve game at Elland Road, 'I was sat on the wall in the corner of the West Stand and the Scratching Shed. Harvey took a goal kick and while the ball was in the other half of the field, he came over to me and gave me a piece of his chewing gum.'

Gary Senior recalled, 'I was an 11-year-old budding goalkeeper when I went to the David Harvey Goalkeeping School which took place on Fullerton Park at the back of the West Stand. He was a tough master, but once he called me brave, that is something that has stayed with me ever since that day. He was one of my favourite players and definitely not one that I'd want to argue with.'

David Besser went to Foxwood School with Harvey, 'I played in the same school team as him. You knew straight away he was going to be a professional goalkeeper, he was a natural.'

Harvey loves Scotland and since retiring from football he has always lived there. He moved from his Stamford Bridge home in North Yorkshire to Sanday, one of the few inhabited islands of Orkney, where he restored a 150-year-old stone cottage with his wife June, five children, pigs, sheep and a variety of poultry, all close to the sea. 'It was bliss,' he told me. 'I just loved it.'

Sanday is the third-largest island and Harvey was a postman there for many years. He is somewhat of a recluse, which he admits himself. And he doesn't like public appearances.

Harvey was recognised as the bravest keeper that Leeds United ever had, and he had to be brave to live on Orkney. He laughed when he told me, 'The weather is extreme there and people have to constantly lean in into the heavy wind as they walk; it is often said that when the strong winds drop, people fall to the ground.'

Years ago, I was at an evening event with Lesley (aka Wub) to celebrate the 1972 FA Cup-winning team. The compere interviewed each player separately for their recollections. First up, having been the number one on the day, was Harvey. As he sat down in the leather chair opposite, the compere said to him, 'I understand you're a man of few words, David?' To which he replied, 'Aye.' The compere then said, 'We're not going to get very far here are we?' To which Harvey replied, 'Nah.'

As Harvey left the stage to much amusement in the audience, the compere said, 'I don't think I'll have any trouble getting my next guest to talk. Ladies and gentlemen, Paul Reaney.'

I was at a very recent evening event featuring Johnny Giles, Allan Clarke, Paul Reaney, Eddie Gray, and most surprisingly, David Harvey. It was short-lived, however, as on the stage there were five chairs, but just four guests. After about half an hour I went for another pint and got talking to one of the stewards there, George, a lovely fella. 'Hello George,' I said. 'Where's Harvey?'

'He's in there Gary', said George pointing to a door, 'he won't come out. Do you want to go in and have a chat with him?'

The first thing that hits you when talking to David Harvey is his very strong Scottish accent. There is no trace of his Yorkshire accent left. It transpired that he didn't mind one-on-one chats, he just wasn't one for large audiences. Strange, when you consider the considerable crowds he played in front of during his career.

He told me that his favourite Leeds game was at Arsenal in 1966. 'I was in for Gary, who was injured, and I couldn't put a foot, or hand, wrong that day. I saved everything that was thrown at me. Big Jack scored the only goal of the game for us, so I was delighted. This was in November and Gary returned to the team for the next game. I didn't play again until the final game of the season, at home to Sheffield Wednesday,' he told me without the slightest hint of bitterness.

I mentioned that Lesley and I go to Oban on the west coast of Scotland every year for our holidays. His face lit up, 'Och, that's brilliant, you'll go right past my house, I live in Lockerbie now.'

I asked Don Revie's daughter, Kim, to contribute a few words about the man, her father, who had planned this Leeds United journey from the very beginning.

She said, 'I went to most games from being a tiny tot – we had the rosettes, scarves, the lot, we lived and died with every result. But Dad was very superstitious, as were the whole family, we all had things on matchdays that we did or didn't do; none of us wore the colour green to matches for instance. And Dad considered birds unlucky too.

'We lived in Southlands Avenue growing up and then we later moved to Sandmoor Drive. I went to Leeds Girls High School and Duncan went to Leeds Grammar School. Dad dropped us both at school every morning on his way to the ground and we had to be there very early, as he wanted to be at Elland Road first thing every day.'

Duncan Revie told me in 2012 that his dad lived and breathed Leeds United Football Club, but that he never forgot his family or indeed his friends, 'When we moved to Sandmoor Drive, the whole of Mum's family and our family had our own little headquarters. And Dad had a small house we called "Offside" built on to it to accommodate everyone within the family.'

Kim said, 'Offside was built for my mum's family: my gran, two great aunts and a great uncle – they were collectively known as the old folk. The house was connected to our house by a corridor. Dad brought them down to live with us from Scotland when they retired – they used to run a corner shop in Fife and they were wonderful people, real characters and they loved Dad and he loved them. We had great Hogmanay parties at new year when everyone had to do a turn, a real sing-song, and Dad was the master of ceremonies at each party. Great memories.'

Kim was always fond of music and singing. She is still in the music industry today. She remembers, 'I was about eight or nine years of age when I was first allowed on to the Leeds United team bus and my memory is of such a happy family. Jack and Billy in particular were so friendly, they would encourage me to start the community singing on the bus journey home – if we'd won. It was always the same three songs … "Glory, Glory, Leeds United", "It's a Grand Old Team to Play For", and "Bye Bye Blackbird". Jack would always give his rendition of "Blaydon Races".'

The "Blackbird" song was a favourite of Don's. Kim confirmed, 'Dad loved his music; Frank Sinatra, Nat King Cole and Flanagan and Allen. Mum and Dad loved a sing-song and Dad would sing "Bye Bye Blackbird" and "Underneath the Arches" regularly.'

Jim Lister was the coach driver in those days, 'Some away games, the children weren't allowed on the bus, such as Everton and sometimes even Liverpool. It was always on the East Lancs Road and as we were leaving, the windows were smashed by bricks if Leeds had won.

'Don Revie was unperturbed though, he would tell the players to get down on the floor and he would lead the lads singing "It's a Grand Old Team to Play For" and other such songs. I can still see the players laughing as they were singing. Don was really funny as he crouched down, laughing and chuckling like a schoolboy. He had a really infectious laugh, which you didn't hear that often.'

I asked Kim about Don's conversations with Bill Shankly of Liverpool every Sunday, 'Dad would lie in with all the Sunday papers spread out over the bed and he'd be talking to Bill Shankly on the telephone. We used to go for a carvery on a Sunday for Sunday lunch but they liked family dinners at home mostly. I do remember we would go to Bryans of Headingley to get fish and chips to take home. Dad loved their fish and chips. Also enjoying those fish and chips on occasion would be our guests, Johnny Williamson and his wife Lorraine.'

The Queen's cousin, the Earl of Harewood, and his wife Patricia would regularly visit Don and his family and vice versa. 'They were lovely people and very good friends with Mum and Dad,' said Kim.

It was a fascinating insight into the Revie family, and finally I asked Kim what were her fondest memories of her father. 'I loved and adored him,' she said. 'He was a fantastic dad, he made everyone he cared about feel special. I particularly remember New Year's Eve parties and family get-togethers in general, which Dad loved, surrounded by family and friends, the songs, the laughter; great times. We were very fortunate to have a very close family and I miss Dad, Mum and Dunc so very much, but they left us with such amazing memories, so their spirits live on for sure.'

Shortly after retiring from a consultancy job at Elland Road in 1986, Don and his wife Elsie moved into a lovely bungalow, 17 Broom Road in Kinross, 20 miles north-west of Edinburgh.

Sadly, he was soon to be diagnosed with motor neurone disease and died on 26 May 1989 in Spire Murrayfield Hospital. He was cremated at Warriston Crematorium and

I was among the many fans who attended. Also there were Kevin Keegan, Graeme Souness, Brian Moore, Ray Wilkins, Paul Gascoigne and many more. The Football Association sent no representative to the funeral.

Sadly Elsie Revie, who had become president of the Leeds United Supporters Club, died of cancer on 28 March 2005. Then their son Duncan died after a short illness in 2016.

Soccerex chairman Tony Martin, who chaired the first Soccerex convention along with Duncan Revie in 1996, said at the news, 'This has come as a tremendous shock to us all. Duncan was revered throughout the global football industry, it was his passion, his vision, drive and determination that established the Soccerex brand in 1995.'

In 1967 I left Kippax Mixed Infant School and headed two miles away, nearer to Elland Road, to 'Big School' – the newly built Garforth Comprehensive School. I had discarded my old pump bag and replaced it with a shiny new briefcase.

Leeds United, meanwhile, had still to win a major trophy. That was, though, about to change in dramatic fashion. During Don Revie's final seven years at Elland Road, United appeared at Wembley four times, in three European finals, and won the League Cup, the FA Cup, two European trophies, two league championships and one Charity Shield.